Professional Approaches
with Parents of
Handicapped Children

Professional Approaches With Parents Of Handicapped Children

Edited by

ELIZABETH J. WEBSTER, Ph.D.

*Professor, Department of Audiology
    and Speech Pathology
Memphis State University
Memphis, Tennessee*

With a Foreword by

Alan J. Weston, Ph. D.

*Professor, Department of Audiology
    and Speech Pathology
Memphis State University
Memphis, Tennessee*

CHARLES C THOMAS • **PUBLISHER**
Springfield • Illinois • U.S.A.

Published and Distributed Throughout the World by
CHARLES C THOMAS ● PUBLISHER
Bannerstone House
301-327 East Lawrence Avenue, Springfield, Illinois, U.S.A.

© *1976, by* **CHARLES C THOMAS ● PUBLISHER**

ISBN 0-398-03521-0

Library of Congress Catalog Card Number: 75-33988

With THOMAS BOOKS *careful attention is given to all details of
manufacturing and design. It is the Publisher's desire to present books that are
satisfactory as to their physical qualities and artistic possibilities and
appropriate for their particular use.* THOMAS BOOKS *will be true to those
laws of quality that assure a good name and good will.*

Printed in the United States of America
R-1

Library of Congress Cataloging in Publication Data

Professional approaches with parents of handicapped
  children.

  Bibliography: p.
  Includes index.
  1. Handicapped children--Family relationships--Ad-
dresses, essays, lectures.   2. Handicapped children--Ad-
dresses, essays, lectures.   I. Webster, Elizabeth J.
[DNLM: 1. Handicapped. 2. Child care. 3. Parent-
Child relations. 4. Rehabilitation. WS113 P964]
HV888.P76   362.7′8′4   75-33988
ISBN 0-398-03521-0

For Charlotte

CONTRIBUTORS

Mary B. Bernard, M.A.
Associate in Pediatrics
Albert Einstein College of Medicine
Early Childhood Center of the Children's Evaluation and Re-
    habilitation Clinic
Rose F. Kennedy Center for Research in Mental Retardation
    and Human Development
Bronx, New York

Norman E. Bissell, Ed.D.
Assistant Head
Department of Special Education
University of Cincinnati
Cincinnati, Ohio

Nanette L. Doernberg, Ph.D.
Assistant Professor of Pediatrics
Albert Einstein College of Medicine
Director, Early Childhood Center of the Children's Evaluation
    and Rehabilitation Clinic
Rose F. Kennedy Center for Research in Mental Retardation
    and Human Development
Senior Psychoeducational Consultant
Bronx Developmental Services
Bronx, New York

Vilma T. Falck, Ph.D.
Associate Professor, Division of Continuing Education
The University of Texas Health Science Center at Houston
Houston, Texas

Marvin I. Gottlieb, M.D., Ph.D.
Professor of Pediatrics
Director, Leigh Buring Clinic for Exceptional Children
The University of Tennessee Center for the Health Sciences
Memphis, Tennessee

Carol F. Lenz, M.A.
Associate in Pediatrics, Albert Einstein
College of Medicine
Early Childhood Center of the Children's Evaluation and Re-
    habilitation Clinic
Rose F. Kennedy Center for Research in Mental Retardation
    and Human Development
Bronx, New York

Betty Jane McWilliams, Ph.D.
Professor of Speech Pathology
Director, Cleft Palate Center
University of Pittsburgh
Pittsburgh, Pennsylvania

Albert T. Murphy, Ph.D.
Professor of Language Pathology and Special Education
Schools of Education and Medicine and College of Allied
    Health Professions
Boston University
Boston, Massachusetts

Audrey Simmons-Martin, Ed.D.
Director, Early Education
Central Institute for the Deaf
St. Louis, Missouri

Flonnia C. Taylor, M.S.
Director, The United Cerebral Palsy of the Blue Grass
Lexington, Kentucky

Mary Todd, A.C.S.W.
Section Head: Social Worker
Leigh Buring Clinic for Exceptional Children
University of Tennessee Center for the Health Sciences
Memphis, Tennessee

Gertrud L. Wyatt, Ph.D.
Psychologist, Speech Therapist
Consultant, Wellesley Public Schools
Coordinator, Federal Early Childhood Programs
Wellesley, Massachusetts

FOREWORD

DURING the last few years, increasing emphasis has been placed on the participation of parents in habilitation, rehabilitation and education programs for their children with handicapping conditions. This emphasis has resulted in new parent training programs as well as in a variety of parent training procedures. Much of the attention given to parental training is the result of the federal government's emphasis on parental involvement in all federally-funded programs for exceptional children. Other factors promoting the upsurge in parental training endeavors are the continued concern expressed by teachers and clinicians regarding carry-over of gains children make in their educational or therapy programs and the development of behavior modification techniques that may be easily taught to parents.

The current emphasis on parent training raises many potential problems. This is not to question the appropriateness of involving parents in their children's training program; however, an overemphasis by professionals on assisting children through the medium of their parents may produce potentially damaging consequences for the parents, their children and the family itself.

Parents desire to be good parents. Within their capabilities, they wish to do the best job of child-rearing that they can visualize. While their ideas and values may not be the same as those of the professionals with whom they deal, parents attempt to make their behavior consistent with their own ideas and values. In my opinion, parents have primary responsibility for child-rearing, and the role of professionals should be to support parents' attempts to be good parents. I think, further, that clinicians and/or teachers have the primary responsibility for therapy or formal education procedures with the child, and these professionals should not shirk their responsibility by asking parents to function as clinicians or educators.

Parents who seek professional help for a child with a handicapping condition also need help in understanding their child. Parents of children with handicapping conditions encounter many
problems just by virtue of having to cope with such a child. Parents want to deal consistently with their children, and I think that
it is here that professionals should focus their greatest effort with
parents. Many parents seek professionals' suggestions about ways
in which they can behave more consistently. Teachers and clinicians may think that when parents express such concerns as what
to do for their child, they want to serve as the child's educator or
therapist. However, this is often an erroneous notion. Most parents are not educators nor therapists, and the teacher or clinician
who asks them to acquire the skills of the professional may be
asking for a disgruntled parent. Even parents who have professional skills often express confusion or pressure because of their
standards for their child's performance; they feel that they cannot
work as effectively with their own child as they can with others'
children. Thus, even when we have professionally-trained parents, we are asking them to do an impossible task when we ask
them to participate objectively in training their child.

It is known that we can train parents to do a good job of utilizing behavior modification procedures. However, what we do not
know is what effect parents' use of these procedures has on the
long-term interaction between parent and child, or what effect it
has on the parents, their perceptions of their roles, their self-
concepts, etc. Another potential problem when asking parents to
be trainers of their children is an economic one — when parents
are asked to pay for services for their children, do they not have a
legitimate right to question why they paid for services when they
can do them themselves?

At this stage of our knowledge we know that there are children
with problems and we know that there are parents with problems.
However, we know very little about how to alleviate parental
problems. It seems crucial that we attend to this matter, particularly because we also know that parent-child interactions have
been assumed to bear some relationship to children's problems. If
we focus too much attention on producing parents who are trainers of children, we will obscure or overlook some very real

questions that we should be asking about the effects of parent training procedures, not only on changes in the child's target behaviors, but on other childhood behaviors, and on the parents who apply the training procedures. To the extent that this text focuses on more than parent training, it is felt that it will help answer some of these questions and will suggest other questions.

Alan J. Weston

INTRODUCTION

THIS book is the product of collaboration between two groups of people, one group highly visible, one less so. The obvious collaborators are the authors, practicing professional specialists, who have shared their experience, stated the rationales on which they base their work, suggested procedures they have found useful, and pointed out some issues inherent in working with parents of handicapped children. The less obvious collaborators are the many professional persons and students in various fields who have doggedly, and often frantically, raised such questions as, "How can I help parents of handicapped children?" "What can I do for them?" "Where can I start?" It was the frequency and persistence of such questions that prompted us to share in this form the ideas and experience of a number of those who have been actively engaged in work with such parents.

While it is now accepted practice to include parents and often entire families in the treatment programs of handicapped children, this was not always the case. There was a time within the memory of these authors when professionals viewed their roles more narrowly than most do now. In that time, professionals seemed to rivet their attention almost exclusively on the needs of handicapped children; professional concern was focused on habilitating or rehabilitating a child while largely ignoring that child's family milieu.

Most professionals could not visualize themselves as helpers of parents or families; their assumption seemed to be that if, through treatment, the handicapped child improved, parents and other family members would also automatically improve. In some cases this assumption was correct; in some cases it was not. Satir has pointed out some possible reasons that a child's family might not progress as the child progresses in therapy.[1]

---

[1]V. Satir, *Conjoint Family Therapy* (Palo Alto, Science and Behavior Books, 1967).

In the time that professional persons seemed unconcerned about parents, one problem was that many of those who worked with handicapped children could not see that parents and other family members were central partners in a child's treatment team. Parents often were viewed as analogous to a football team's *taxi squad* — they were permitted to *dress-out*, they were informed of all the plays, and they could view the action, but parents seldom were full-fledged participants in the team's decisions and planning; they just learned to carry out the plays. Others were always in the forefront. Parents were standbys; and often other family members were not even accorded standby status. In their desire to help handicapped children, at their best professionals were aware of the continuing crises experienced by parents but unable to visualize ways to help alleviate such crises. At their worst, well-meaning professionals helped to create some of these family crises while zealously attempting to accomplish what they thought needful for the handicapped child.

Then, as many professionals enlarged their field of vision, they came to see what others had known all along — that parents are the core of a child's team[2]; professionals are helpers.

Fortunately, times change and people change. The former myopic view of the professional role with the handicapped child has changed dramatically in the past few years. Parents and other family members have been promoted from the taxi squad; more and more they are being considered in planning the action; and more and more they are being brought into it. Parents are more often considered as being central to successful treatment for handicapped children. Professionals no longer argue the question of whether or not to involve parents of a handicapped child in that child's treatment program. Professionals know that parents are involved and are participants in all programming. In recent years the viable question has become, "How best can we assist these involved individuals to cope with their situations and to participate productively?" To put this another way, part of the professional's task is now seen as that of working out ways of interacting with parents that are productive and satisfying to both parents

---

[2]H. V. Bice, *Group Counseling With Mothers of the Cerebral Palsied* (Chicago, Nat. Soc. Crippled Children and Adults, 1952).

and professional.

Thus, one reads and hears increasing numbers of references to techniques for intervention with parents. Certainly it is no news to readers that there has been a proliferation of programs in which parents are involved in treatment for their children and in which many such parents and families are themselves recipients of professional services. There seems to be at least the following two reasons for this increased activity with parents and families.

First, there has been increasing recognition of the centrality of the family milieu in relation to children's development, no less to the development of a handicapped child. Professionals have seen the necessity for intervening in one way or another in this milieu if they are both to help parents cope with the fact of rearing a handicapped child and to provide continuing assistance for a child. Parents also have recognized their centrality and have verbalized their needs to be a part of the professional team, to plan with the various professionals involved with their child, and to receive help for themselves. Thus, various formal and informal parents groups have evolved around parental needs (1) to participate in planning for children and (2) to receive help for themselves. Such formal and informal parents groups are discussed in later chapters. Further, federal programs have recognized the centrality of parents to any education or treatment program for handicapped children. Federal agencies have not only mandated the inclusion of parents in programs for the handicapped but have also provided funding for parent training and counseling.

The second factor prompting increased services for parents seems to be the compassion of professional persons. As professional workers listened to the parents of handicapped children and came to understand more about them, they became increasingly aware of the human needs of these people. More professional persons grew to understand parents as human beings who need more than information about, and prescriptions for, their children. Professionals now recognize that these parents are like other people. People, including those who are parents, feel hurt, anger, guilt, discouragement; they also feel success, satisfaction and happiness. Perhaps the feelings of parents of handicapped children are magnified; at least we know these parents experience periods

of confusion, questioning, discouragement. Their lives as individuals and their lives within families consist of periods of relative equilibrium punctuated by ever new challenges and periods
of frustration. It is a hurtful thing to have a handicapped child; it
is also confusing. There can also be joys and satisfactions in the
experiences with that child. I think that professionals have always
been aware of the human needs of these parents, and in recent
years have tried to implement their concern with more systematic
intervention procedures.

While more professionals are making their work with parents
less exclusively child-centered and more parent-child-centered,
and the scene appears better, it is not altogether rosy. There is still
some abuse of parents. Some professionals still are quick to re-
buke or blame parents if all does not go well with a child. Some
openly or subtly side with children against their parents.

Further, the provision of more parent programs means that
increasing numbers of professionals are called upon to interact
with parents; and while thrust into this work, many have received
little training for it. These persons recognize their need for additional assistance. While they can turn to a growing body of literature *about* parents,[3,4,5,6] there is still a paucity of literature with
specific suggestions to help them improve their practice *with*
parents.

This book came about in an attempt to help fill this void. It is
the result of numerous requests from practicing professionals as
well as from students in training for help in the areas of (1) building a rationale for work with parents and (2) planning procedures
to use in parents counseling and training.

In anticipation of the ideas that will be found in the following
chapters, it should be remembered that there is no one *best* model
for parent-professional interaction. Various models are currently
in use and seem to promote productive and meaningful relationships and to yield satisfying encounters between parents and

---

[3]R. H. Barsch, *The Parent of the Handicapped Child* (Springfield, Thomas, 1968).
[4]L. Goldstein and W. Dahlstrom, "MMPI differences between parents of stuttering and
non-stuttering children." *Journal of Consulting Psychology, 20*:365-370, (1956).
[5]E. T. McDonald, *Understand Those Feelings* (Pittsburgh, Stanwix House, 1962).
[6]L. K. Wing, *Autistic Children: A Guide For Parents and Professionals* (New York,
Brunner/Mazel, 1972).

professionals. The authors of this book attest to the fact that many models of parent-professional interaction work well, that there are valuable similarities and differences in all approaches, and that there are valid reasons for variety in approaches.

One reason for variety in approaches to parent-professional interaction is that each professional group instituting and maintaining programs of service for parents will approach the task from the perspective of that profession. For example, the task of persons in social work differs in major ways from the task of the physician; just so, the teacher's task with parents differs in a number of respects from that of the speech and hearing clinician.

Within any given professional group, variety is also introduced by virtue of the fact that each professional is a unique personality. Each worker has uniquely individual values and commitments, ideas and forms of creativity. Each is engaged in his own way in the process of being and becoming. The way in which each professional will approach parents, then, is determined by such factors as (1) his assumptions about parents and about parental needs at that time; (2) background, training and experience from which the professional has built a rationale for work with parents; and (3) the goals the professional sets for parents and for himself in his interactions with them.

Professional work with parents varies as to length and frequency of contact. For example, the neurologist may see a child and a parent for a relatively short visit every month for several months in order to check on the child's status and to give parents information and instructions; the family's later contacts with the neurologist may be as infrequent as one visit per year. Another example is that of the special education teacher who sees a child's mother quite regularly for short periods of time before or after school, and then holds longer conferences at the end of a school semester.

The following chapters are designed to provide an in-depth look at several models of interaction with parents. Contributors are professionals in a variety of fields, and all have had continued direct experience with parents of handicapped children as part of their professional practices. Each was asked to state his/her assumptions about parents, to discuss the rationale upon which work with them is based, to indicate procedures found useful in practice, and to suggest crucial issues in such work with parents. Even as the approaches used with parents vary widely, so also do the terms used to refer to this work. The reader will note that some professionals speak of *parent education* while others refer to it as *training*, and yet others call it *guidance* or *counseling*. As stated previously,[7] the terms used only refer to the many functions professionals can serve for parents. The terms are the least of the professional's problems; the crucial task is to make operational the wish to be *helpers*, as the construct is used by Benjamin.[8]

It is recognized that these contributors represent a very small sample of those giving high-quality service to parents. These particular authors were selected because each has developed, over time and through practice, a point of view about the needs of parents of handicapped children, about the dimensions of the professional role with the parents, and about counseling practices with them. Each author has engaged actively and directly in providing services to parents. Thus, each is not giving an *ivory tower* view; each has experienced the vicissitudes and satisfactions of day-by-day encounters with parents.

Each author has been most generous in sharing ideas, and each hopes to stimulate readers to think further. Some readers will find many of their own points of view reflected in these pages. It is hoped that these practitioners will assist others to develop a point of view. In either case, it is our hope that readers will find herein some new and worthwhile ideas.

Elizabeth J. Webster

---

[7]E. J. Webster, "Parents of Children with Communication Disorders" In A. J. Weston (Ed.): *Communicative Disorders: An Appraisal* (Springfield, Thomas, 1972).
[8]A. Benjamin, *The Helping Interview* (Boston, Houghton Mifflin, 1974).

ACKNOWLEDGMENTS

I AM of course most deeply grateful to each author who has so generously shared information and thoughts in manuscript form. I am grateful also for all the assistance I have received in the preparation of this manuscript and the support and encouragement of colleagues at Memphis State University. A special thanks is due Marilyn Newhoff who proofed the manuscript and prepared the indices and to Donna Douglas, Kathy Simpson and Shirley Rias who typed the manuscript.

E.J.W.

CONTENTS

Professional Approaches
with Parents of
Handicapped Children

Chapter 1

PARENT COUNSELING AND EXCEPTIONALITY: FROM CREATIVE INSECURITY TOWARD INCREASED HUMANNESS

Albert T. Murphy

COUNSELING AS A PROCESS OF CREATING SELF IN HELPING RELATIONSHIP WITH OTHERS

A S the late Abraham Maslow used to say, a first-rate soup is more creative than a second-rate painting. Cooking or parenthood can be creative while poetry need not be. Because the word *creative* can be applied not only to the conventionally-accepted novels, paintings, experiments or poems, but to such activities as teaching, housekeeping, cabinet-making or gardening, Maslow, in his extensive studies of creativity in self-actualizing people, distinguished "special talent creativeness" from "self-actualizing creativeness" (8), the latter springing more directly from the personality and showing itself widely in a broad range of ordinary life affairs.

In counseling parents of impaired children, the two kinds of creativity may be revealed by both counselor and parents. However, it is primarily the self-actualizing type which is most applicable. As a counselor, the writer envisions his work at its best as a process of creating self through a helping relationship with others. This may sound *selfish* in the worst sense, but it is intended as growth-oriented *self-interest* in the best sense, an interest in self-improvement which can lead to more productive functioning with others. To help another person to grow, to help him to accept himself more fully, and to help him to care for something or someone apart from himself, involves encouraging him; it involves aiding him in locating and creating parts of himself and

3

his valued life zones so that he is more capable of knowing, feeling, relating, sharing and caring. All of this applies to the parents of an impaired child, it applies to the child himself, and again, it is applicable to the counselor. Finally, the premise is appropriate for all parties concerned as they work together in a relationship geared to the enhancement of an individual's or a family's existence. As a counselor, instead of trying to dominate others, one wants and expects them to grow in their own right. One senses others' growth as tied up with one's own sense of well-being.

While Maslow's studies of creativity in self-actualizing people are too extensive to be adequately described here, the writer purposes to cite some characteristics found in such individuals. Most have a special kind of perceptiveness, an ability to see not only the general, the factual, the abstract and the categorized, but the fresh, the new, the idiographic as well. They are relatively more spontaneous and expressive, more *natural* and less self-controlled, and inhibited with less self-criticism. They are more spontaneous and open to life in the larger sense. They are less upset by the unknown, the strange, the puzzling, and indeed may enjoy becoming absorbed in them. Their security is less bound to the measurably certain, the knowable, the safe. There is a lack of fear of their inner impulses, and more acceptance of the range of emotions expressed by others.

The parent-counseling process is regarded by the author as one in which improvement in functioning of the child occurs primarily via improvements which occur in the parent-child relationship as prototypical, and in more peripheral relationships with others such as teachers. In counseling, one has the opportunity not only to find and accept oneself but to invent oneself, to continue to grow afresh. At the root of mature living is the creativity which faces insecurity as the growing point of life. Any flight from insecurity is antagonistic to any desired human growth.

Parents of impaired children, especially those of severely handicapped children, have more chances than most to feel insecure, but such a moment can contain growth potential if it can be regarded as a "creative insecurity" (2). The insecurity of one mother concerned her not knowing what the effect would be on her six-year-old, homebound, cerebral-palsied daughter of not having playmates. She had said that she did not know what to do, but as soon as this mother thought about and discussed the problem freely, having finally assumed that a good answer was possible, she came up with the idea of inviting neighborhood children to her home from time to time. She prepared ahead, with the help of recreation therapist, games which would be fun but could allow the inclusion of her daughter who was soon being invited to the other children's homes.

CREATIVE COUNSELING AS LEARNING TO MOVE TOWARD MORE COMPLETE HUMANNESS

As counselor one is not a teacher in any traditional sense. One regards oneself as co-learner in the process. There are phases, of course, in which parents may be assisted in ways of observing, noting or recording the behavior of the child or periods of training in the application of educational procedures; for example, parents can be helped to use certain reinforcement techniques applied to specific behaviors. But these activities, in the writer's own primary work setting, the Boston University Psycho-educational Clinic, are usually conducted by the clinical teachers or other staff members. While they are related, this writer does not regard them as specific to the core of the *counseling* aspect of the program though they may be of utmost importance in the total program. Such activities will be further discussed a bit later.

For now we want only to stress that counseling is primarily focused on interpersonal relationships — attitudes, feelings and reaction patterns as they relate to the impaired child's behavior and development. Where the truly important matters of relationship between parent and child are concerned, one cannot *tell* parents how to act as parents, but can discuss varieties of ways of parenting, share one's own personal experiences or those of others (such as other parents), but one cannot directly tell them how to behave.

Once again, behavioristically-oriented practitioners might disagree on this point. They might, and often do, maintain that parents can be taught, for instance, how to execute operant conditioning at home. While the writer believes such techniques have utility in relation to more specific motor deviations such as psychogenic tics, a certain small range of emotional phenomena such as specific phobias or biologically basic need functions such as eating and dressing (in general, that is, the more specific or primitive functions such as the production of vocalization as compared to complex verbalization), we believe their utility wanes as individual behavior and interpersonal processes become more complex. In fact, they wane in value the more the processes and behaviors of concern resemble those found in most social situations such as small group or family interactions, much less large groups like classrooms. The writer gives more consideration to this view elsewhere (13).

Without overstating the point, this writer came to believe many years ago that the most productive and far-reaching moments in counseling are those in which the parents take the lead in thinking, feeling and relating their way to a happier, more productive relationship with their child. Self-discovered truths endure.

The writer recalls Mr. P., whose son, a second grader, was showing many of the characteristics typical of learning-impaired children — reading disability, writing and spelling errors, handedness and direction confusion. The father had resisted full participation in his counseling group, claiming that the responsibility for helping the child was mainly his wife's, and besides, he could not really get the boy to behave the way he wanted him to anyway. Mr. P's hobby was watercolor painting. One evening the writer asked him if he would comment on the well-known phrase, "The material creates the artist." Among other statements, he commented that "The artist lets the object of his study suggest to him how to appreciate and develop it." The writer asked him if a parent could be thought of as an artist in relation to his children. He allowed that it could be the case. He realized that much of the refinement of an artist's vision occurs as he works toward realizing his creation through *interaction* with his materials, and he was able to relate this to his role, responsibility and opportunities with his son. The analogy served also to clarify that the quality of an effort to be creative depends on the material, the tools and the artist's hand whose movements they subtly control. This led to a realization of how the boy was being much more effective in shaping the father's behavior than was the father in shaping the boy's. With increased awareness stemming from a perspective that was meaningful and interesting to him, Mr. P. went on to take a much more active and mutually-enhancing part in the life of his son.

Counseling has the most potential when it is somehow responsive to the deeper needs, curiosities, wishes or fantasies of those involved. The writer realizes that this view may be idiosyncratic for him.

KEY INGREDIENTS FOR LEARNING IN COUNSELING

What does it take for both child and parent to *learn?* Thousands of books have been written on the learning process and *laws of learning.* What is not discussed in these volumes turns out to be what is most crucial in the learning capability of parents and their children, especially when children have special needs, and what constitutes cruciality where handicapped children and their parents are concerned. The writer would suggest that the degrees and forms of *hope, faith, love, trust* and *courage* do, and while full consideration of these crucial life attributes is not feasible here, and though they are spoken of elsewhere (10, 15), we will at least try to point up something of their place in parent counseling.

Faith is future-oriented. To have faith at all implies a belief in the possibility that something desired can occur. Many of the problems experienced by parents of impaired children derive from past unpleasant experiences, the effects of which persist into, and affect their views of, the present. Other problems flow from what the writer terms overemphasis on present orientation, a parental inclination to do whatever is right or efficacious here and now, but there is an absence of an overarching perspective which includes past, present and future, and which denies the value of none of them. All have an important place in creative parental functioning and in creative counseling too. Not least important is the degree to which the impaired child has faith in his own capacity to become something more than he now is in terms of a specific skill or in terms of total life functioning. It is quite remarkable in a child who has failed perhaps a thousand times to successfully accomplish a task, be it to walk without falling, speak without stuttering or read without failure, to see him try yet again. The trying must be related to a faith in a possibility, just as a lack of trying may be related to a lack of faith in a possibility.

It is similarly remarkable to see parents who, in the face of a child's repeated problem inadequately coping with a particular challenge, continue to participate with and provide nurturances for their child after so many disappointments. Any counselor of experience has heard words similar to these spoken by the mother of a child diagnosed as autistic, "To realize that you have given everything and that it hasn't been enough; that you have done all you could and it wasn't enough. That you weren't enough. That is more than enough. That is too much." The faith to go on beyond such hurt must include a belief in one's own ability not only to care for oneself, but to care in a way which is responsive to one's need to care for a child. It includes, whether consciously recognized or unwitting, a faith in one's ability to learn from experience and to be attracted to the growth possibilities in the relationship. It includes the possibility, one could say, of creating self in relationship with others. It is a faith which abhors habitual conformity in which, for the approval of others, one shows an indifference to one's own special needs and the special needs of the child to evolute as a more fully-functioning individual. Faith's way of being and becoming in relationship is to move with increasing confidence into the risky known and the even more dangerous unknown. All of the above characteristics the writer regards as parts of the process or as a portion of the goal structure in parent counseling.

Trust is similarly conceptualized. Trust clearly is related to faith. It would include a trusting of the other by the counselor of the parent or by the parent of the child to grow in his own time and in his own way. It includes trusting the other to make mistakes and to learn from those. Mayeroff (9) has stated that trusting the other is to let go; it includes an element of risk and a leap into the unknown, both of which take *courage.* The parent *or* the counselor shows a lack of trust by trying to squeeze the *helped one* into a mold, or even, perhaps, by caring too much or over-protecting. Trust mistrusts indoctrination. Indoctrination serves most to satisfy the indoctrinator's needs, not the needs of the one to be helped. Faith and trust are the blood and bones of creative counseling.

And what of *hope?* It is amazing, given its importance in life, that such a paucity of concern has been demonstrated for this experience in the literature on handicapped individuals. Certainly, success with parents or children varies as hope varies within their individual and combined experiences. At the outset of therapy, with many families affected by exceptionality, the counselor realizes that one or more, perhaps all, members feel and act disorganized and unintegrated as though, in fact, no desirable future could exist. They have been reduced to the concreteness of the everyday, to emptiness, to hopelessness. The goal in counseling is to work together to come to see that hope is possible, that it can be made real through efficient planning and the tapping of previously unrealized potentials (12).

Hope is not achievable in isolation. The creative counselor works to have the participants leave their isolation by engaging them in dialogue, both verbal and nonverbal. Hope must be differentiated from fantasy. The writer has known two score cerebral-palsied adolescents whose severe speech impairments rendered them almost unintelligible to most people, yet whose deepest wishes were to become radio announcers. Seldom did the parents clearly declare to them the impossibility of their dreams. In their earlier and sometimes continuing *homeboundedness,* disc jockeys had been a prime source of enjoyment and comfort and also a rich source for unfulfillable fantasies. Hope must be differentiated from fantasy.

One needs to come to see that authentic hope imagines real things, things that have at least some possibility of coming true. Hope must be imagined, and this imagining succeeds best in dialogue. One imagines *with.* Counseling is often a process of imagining *with* the parents or the child, then going on together in the quest to achieve that which has been imagined. Thoreau of *Walden* made this point quite beautifully in this favorite quotation,

I learned this, at least, by my experiment; that if one advances confidently in the direction of his dreams, and endeavors to live the life he has imagined, he will meet with a success unexpected in common hours. He will put some things behind, will pass an invisible boundary; new, universal, and more liberal laws will begin to establish themselves around and within him; or the old laws be expanded, and interpreted in his favor in a more liberal sense, and he will live with the license of a higher order of beings. In proportion as he simplifies his life, the laws of the universe will appear less complex, and solitude will not be solitude, nor weakness weakness. If you have built castles in the air, your work need not be lost; that is where they should be. Now put the foundations under them.

Creative counseling tries to point up the strengths and possibilities of the present; it stresses assets more than pathologies in parents or child. It also tries to stir a sense of what is possible in a way that enlarges the goodness of the present in relation to an attainable future, for example, the setting up of realistic goals and the growth experience of working together to reach them. It will take deep support from others and courage from within oneself to try new ways, break fixed belief systems, and go beyond safety and nondevelopmental security to take the risks involved in creative insecurity. To hope is to come to believe that, as William James long ago said, "The pull of the future is as real as the push from behind."

THE BASIC URGE TO FULLER HUMANNESS AS A UNIVERSAL LIFE FORCE

The writer believes that each individual has a natural drive to be in mutually nurturant relationship with others. This is the case no matter how impaired the child, his parents or their relationship. Twenty-five years of counseling parents of children with a wide variety of disorders have done nothing to shake the writer's belief that parents want to become something more than they are, both as individuals and in relationship with their family members and others.

Yes, there have been times when this belief has been severely challenged, as in the case of a child-batterer, or a father who as punishment held his children's hands over the flames from a gas stove, or others who derogated their children in even more horrifying ways. It has been very difficult in such instances to avoid rejecting the person while abhoring the action. However, in every case in which the writer had the opportunity to learn of their frustrations and hurts, his appreciation grew for their particular ways of struggling to be human. Many a cry of anger has been but a disguised cry for love and the desire to feel oneself to be a person of some worth.

Ah, but this view of goodness as recessive is only an assumption some would say, certainly one which cannot be proven. Of course it cannot be, in any scientifically objective, measurable sense, but the writer concluded long ago that where critical human relationships are concerned, one's attitudes and assumptions are more important than facts, even scientifically-respectable ones. In addition, he realizes that while what he thinks about parents in counseling is important, what he *feels* about them is much more important.

IDENTIFICATION OF OUR COMMONALITIES AS MORE VITAL THAN IDENTIFICATION OF OUR DIFFERENCES

In a poem the writer was unable to locate, and therefore cannot properly identify for the reader, Walt Whitman stated in roughly these words

I walk with delinquents with passionate love.
I feel I am one of them.
I belong to those convicts myself
And henceforth I will not deny them —
    for how can I deny myself?

This tree grows tall, that one taller; this bends in one direction, that in another; but deep down in the earth, the roots touch. So it is with people together as in parent counseling or in family. The deeper we delve, the more we find ourselves in file with a great number of other persons.

This realization occurred to the writer resoundingly two decades ago. He had completed extensive analyses of protocols of stutterers and their parents who had been in either individual or group counseling. The protocols emanated from counseling processes he had been doing research on at the University of Southern California under the direction of Lee E. Travis and Joseph Johnston.

Clients were given Murray's Thematic Apperception Test. As many readers know, one card in the twenty administered is blank, the client being asked to make up his own pictured story to go with it. Clients were then requested simply to visualize the blank card in their mind's eye, and to project their own images into the imagined card, describing in a kind of running commentary what they were visualizing. Within a few hours, most individuals project such images and verbalize their description of them quite freely. The counselor in these instances did absolutely nothing — no commentary except "Would you like to continue?", no interpretation. In his own brand of clinical shorthand he recorded what the person was saying. It was amazing to observe after fifty or sixty hours of this *projective therapy* how similar the projected images and levels of language usage had become among groups of individuals, especially those having symptomatology in common, such as severe stuttering behavior (17).

He later came upon a statement by Havelock Ellis in his remarkable book, *The Dance of Life* (5), which described this reaching of commonality most appropriately,

> They had all gone to the depths of their own souls and thence brought to the surface and expressed — audaciously or beautifully, pungently or poignantly — intimate impulses and emotions which, shocking as they may have seemed at the time, are now seen to be those of an innumerable company of their fellow men and women.

As a further step in acknowledging commonalities, the creative counselor recognizes and accepts his own *limitations.* He realizes that he cannot be as factually knowledgeable about all areas of exceptionality as he can about some as their range is so enormous. He recognizes that he cannot be as helpfully sensitive and comfortable with some areas of human feelings, relationships and dysfunctions as with others. He also knows he can encourage freedom of expression and loving spontaneity only to the degree that he is capable himself of expressing it; he can show attitudes of trust and faith in the capacity of those he counsels to the extent that he genuinely *feels* that trust in himself. The showing of such realizations will further strengthen the freedom of commonality between parents and counselor, and will serve as a desirable model to the parents for their own behaviors with their child.

Creative counseling is a voyage of self-discovery, a journey to a wider horizon of conscious awareness of self and others. It is designed to uncover uniquenesses, what each one of us peculiarly is, what we prize, what we hope for and how we search for fuller humanness, but it is also geared to discovering that which we share, our specieshood. Vehicles and structures employed in this voyage are further suggested in a later section.

It is remarkable how great an impact can occur on parents when they realize that the counselor (to whom in their own need they had perhaps already attributed characteristics of perfection) is at least something like them, a person who, for example, knows what is to be problemmed. As one father commented, "When you said you were ready to give up on me, I felt for the first time that we had something in common. Before, I just couldn't get on your wave length, or at least I didn't think you could ever get on mine." As discussed elsewhere (10), it is remarkable how frequently counselors, although they might not wish to be so characterized, present to their clients the image of the flawless person.

Counselor authenticity means that the feelings one is experiencing are not only consciously available, but that one is able to live those feelings, truly be them and to share them when appropriate. The therapy relationship is unreal if, over a long period of time, the counselor never expresses annoyance, skepticism or similar feelings. There are limits to such expressions of authenticity, but to be rigidly consistent or unreally perfect will eventually erode the counseling relationship.

COUNSELING AS MOVEMENT
TOWARD DEEPER SUBJECTIVITY

Perhaps this view has already been overstated, but its importance deserves emphasis — counseling is most creative when feelings are given precedence over facts, when attitudes are given precedence over techniques, and when subjectivity is revered by professionals at least as much as is objectivity. The writer has tried to elucidate these points elsewhere, and, for brevity's sake, must refer the interested reader to those sources (14, 15, 16). Let us say here simply that there is an important difference clinically between describing, analyzing and explaining behavior on the one hand, and *experiencing* and *relating* to it on the other. The counselor the writer has in mind tries to bring these differences together in a creative merger in service to those in need of him. He tries to avoid excessive specialization, excessive attention to minor details and excessive emphasis in technical precision. The poet, E. E. Cummings, once said that when you *think,* you're somebody else, but when you *feel,* you're nobody but yourself, and being nobody but yourself can be the most wonderful thing on earth.

COUNSELING GOALS AS GUIDES
RATHER THAN FIXED POINTS

Certainly the counselor has goals in mind in working with parents. Goals vary greatly in their specifics if the counselor customarily interacts with many parents of children representing a great variety of disorders. The Boston University Psychoeducational Clinic serves children ages two to twenty years, persons with emotional, intellectual, speech, hearing, language and various learning disorders, and their parents. Under such circumstances, not only goals, but counseling structures, roles and procedures vary. Staff members themselves vary in training, experience, philosophy and methodological preferences. This is all to the good; a wide variety of views and approaches should be available when a wide variety of children and parents is being served, on the simple assumption that no one methodology represents the one truth for all. Obviously, however, there are counseling centers which focus on one theory or methodology; this is not inappropriate, of course, if clients are carefully selected who have need of that specific approach.

This discussion has been shaped by the view that certain basic ingredients of interpersonal behavior tend to manifest themselves and to be of worth across *categories* of exceptionality. For instance, the parent counseling developmental process common-ly reveals typical features. As Barsch (1) has pointed out, most parents start group processes at information-seeking levels. They ask direct questions and may be given direct answers. They want to know what to do, how to do it and when. From this level, movement is usually toward a *sharing stage* in which helpful suggestions are exchanged and discussed, emphasis being on technique. Gradually, a *feeling* stage develops; parents examine their own and others' feelings, attitudes and motivations and try to see how these are related to their children's behaviors. A gener-alization process follows; insights and behaviors are related to the larger family group, to neighbors and communities beyond. With counseling thus proceeding successfully, a state of maximal func-tioning is reached in which the impaired child has been brought into mutually nurturant relationship with all family members.

Quite commonly at the outset, whether in individual or group counseling, the following characteristics will often be observed. These characteristics are seen especially in those situations in which the family relationships, particularly in relation to the impaired child, are significantly disturbed.

1. Participants do not communicate clearly with one another; thoughts and feelings are sent in distorted fashion or are mis-perceived.

2. Participants are not in effective touch with their own feel-ings or in fact deny feelings they actually do have.

3. Participants treat exceptionality or differentness as guilt-connected, threatening or conflict-imbued.

4. Participants deal unrealistically with each other or situa-tions; things are wished for or fearfully expected, rather than dealt with in their context in the here-and-now, or in terms of hope which has some possibility for fulfillment.

5. Participants deny responsibility for what they feel or do, attributing what happens to circumstances or to others.

While extended treatment of details of such manifestation is not possible here, an excellent discussion of counseling ap-proaches found to be valuable in relation to such dysfunctions as these may be found in the writings of Satir (21).

COUNSELING AS A PROCESS OF
ENHANCING COMMUNICATION

From the perspective of special needs of individuals, how does one even begin to approximate what one wishes and indeed ought to say when discussing human communication? Let us consider at least a sampling of thoughts which have been meaningful in parent counseling, whether in working partnership with parents of autistic, retarded, hearing-impaired, speech-disordered, cerebral-palsied or children impaired in other ways.

Counseling with parents consists of dialogue, verbal and/or nonverbal. For our present purposes let us look at dialogue from the viewpoint of one of this century's most important representatives of the human spirit, Martin Buber. Buber's classic presentation of his philosophy of dialogue is his poetic book, *I and Thou* (4), wherein he distinguished between the I-Thou relationship which is direct, mutual openness between persons and the I-It or subject-object relationship in which one relates to the other only indirectly and nonmutually, perhaps using him. I-It dialogue occurs and is necessary in the world and is not evil in itself, but it should not predominate in movements toward the I-Thou. Here is a philosophy concerned with the difference between mere existence and authentic existence, between being human at all and being more fully human, between being fragmented and moving toward greater wholeness through greater awareness and fuller response in each new situation.

In *Between Man and Man* (3) Buber distinguished among three types of dialogue which he has adapted and found useful in counseling. *Technical dialogue* is prompted solely by the need of objective understanding; it makes no pretense of relating to the other as a Thou. Much of television advertising could serve as example; often very little concern is shown for the truth or accuracy that is communicated to the audience. There is an overconcern with the *techniques* of communication; there are persons who speak fluently and with proper enunciation and pronunciation but who say little of real content or feeling. Parents with perfectionistic strivings, who have learned to an extreme to attribute great value to *proper speaking habits* and perhaps have had dramatic training or interests, will sometimes seek aid for their child's speech problem when in fact the child's speech behavior is quite in keeping with speech norms for his chronological age.

In the second form, *monologue disguised as dialogue*, the counseling participants are together in space, but speak in strangely-convoluted and circuitous ways. The parent in the group who makes a point of memorizing everyone else's names and flattering them so that they not only think he cares about them personally, but will like him also, is representative. Such persons, as T. S. Eliot has stated, "put on a face to meet the faces that they meet." They are *seeming* persons rather than *being*, much less *becoming* persons. Discussions of this nature are suggestive of theatre of the absurd scripts applied to exceptionality, which has been written about elsewhere (11).

In *genuine dialogue* the participants open themselves to the otherness of their fellow participants. The others are kept in mind in their present and particular being and are attended to with the intention of establishing a living mutual relationship. Authentic dialogue may be verbal or silent. It does not always mean love; it may mean anger, but it is direct, honest and personal and *confirms* the humanness of the other even while opposing or differing from him. One can enter genuine dialogue to the extent that one is a real person.

This view of dialogue brings us to the question of what is required for parents *or* their impaired children to communicate, regardless of social or therapeutic structure or setting, especially in those parent-child relationships which are disordered by dysfunctional feelings or attitudes? Although techniques will vary with circumstances, the writer is convinced that the following conditions contribute to the development of genuine dialogue or communication:

1. Whatever helps the client feel freer, share himself and affect others in socially desirable ways
2. Whatever helps the client come closer to others, touch them and be touched in any humanizing sense
3. Whatever helps the client live with greater joyful spontaneity, nonverbally and verbally
4. Whatever increases his feelings of hope, faith and trust in

others and in himself

5. Whatever increases his willingness to risk complete living, the courage to be himself fully

6. Whatever increases his feelings of personal worth and his ability to live and be loved.

CREATIVE COUNSELING
AND NONVERBAL COMMUNICATION

Harry Stack Sullivan used to say that a great deal of what may be called "the way the wind blows" is conveyed tonally, that it has nothing in particular to do with content, but is instead a matter of how verbal content is expressed. Such nonverbal indicators have always constituted crucial information for counselors of psycho-dynamic orientation. In recent years there has appeared a veritable cascade of techniques, some excellent, dealing with non-verbal communication. We have always availed ourselves of a great number of such procedures in counseling parents (17). Only several shall be mentioned here as examples of procedures found productive. Again, the creativity of the counselor and partici-pants in developing appropriate methods and processes is given free rein.

Drawings. Talking is sometimes unsatisfactory in communi-cating what one wishes or in arriving at fresh perspectives on old relationships. Drawings are quick to produce and inexpen-sive. They are made during the sessions, usually with groups of parents or with a family group of parents and the handicapped child, and sometimes the siblings. Drawings are shared and discussed. A common suggestion is to have each member draw his own family; comparisons follow. The counselor needs to explain carefully the rationale for the inclusion of this tech-nique and should feel comfortable in its use. Of course, diag-nostic impressions occur. The writer has found drawings to be particularly helpful in relation to children who are physically impaired.

Still Pictures. Occasionally, in working with parents and their child in a group, one will ask them to bring in family snapshots, their favorite pictures of themselves or of each other perhaps, or ones they dislike most. Perhaps he will suggest that the family album be brought in; it is a helpful way to move quickly into the family inner circle. Many individuals find it easier to characterize others or themselves when looking at pictures. Some persons find motion pictures of counseling sessions helpful when fed back into the group process. However, technological requirements are often irksome.

Body sculpture. The counselor asks the parent or child to act as sculptor. The sculptor positions the other person or persons in a way which shows some important characteristic about the person. The participants thus form a tableau. Usually a group sculpture is suggested, each member taking a turn altering the sculpture or creating an original one. Facial expressions may be molded, too. The sculptor may work himself into the tableau. The counselor intermittently comments or interprets and may speak with the tableau members.

One of the great benefits of body sculpture is that it encourages touching. Also, statements are often made in this mode which have been difficult to express verbally. Another variation which has proven helpful is to have each member make a declaration in sculpture concerning what he would like to see the group or an individual become in the future.

At times the effect of body sculpture on parents is eye-opening. One deaf adolescent positioned his parents in erect standing positions, heads up and arms held straight down rigidly against their sides facing away from each other. He then sat down facing away from them, staring out the window. When asked how he would make the sculpture most beautiful, he positioned them all sitting in a circle, facing one another and holding hands. When asked once more to edit it, he changed only his own position, standing up as though about to walk away, blowing both parents a kiss with one hand and waving goodbye with the other.

Counseling becomes more creative when the participants are actively and totally involved in the process. Insight is valuable, but insight applied is better. Choosing one's own highways, structuring one's own plans, making one's own decisions and being willing to take the consequences are all characteristic of counseling which is open to alternative modes of trying to achieve authentic relationship.

OPENNESS TO CHANGE
AND LOVING PERCEPTION AS CRUCIAL

Change is a key element in counseling. It includes, as has been suggested, an openness on the part of the counselor to the possibilities of goodness across a wide continuum of procedures. It represents an openness on the parents' part to consider, if necessary, different ways of behaving, thinking and feeling as mates and as parents. Finally, it includes the idea of the openness on the part of the impaired child to express more freely with others his deeper feelings, thoughts and wishes, and also to be more receptive to the honestly-expressed feelings and thoughts of others. Degree of openness for anyone will vary with the type and degree of affect; in general, defensiveness closes, spontaneity opens; anxiety closes, confidence opens; humiliation closes, feelings of acceptance and personal worth open; mistrust closes, trust opens; anger closes, love opens.

Love opens. Perhaps this is the key of keys, the *Arcanum Arcanorum*. Thoreau said that the only way to speak the truth was to speak lovingly. Goethe held that one did not understand anything unless one loved it. And Jung said that with love anything was possible, that love put one in a mood to risk everything; this would include taking the risk that accompanies creative insecurity.

A therapist who works with cerebral-palsied children and who enjoys the work thoroughly, who genuinely likes children so impaired, has in a sense a certain perspicuity, a greater accuracy of perception of their behavior, in a sense augmenting the objectives, than if he disliked this particular behavior in children. "Loving perception," as Maslow (7) termed it, produces interest and even fascination, and therefore great patience with long hours of working with certain problems or under trying conditions. This way of perceiving and knowing another, a mother and her baby, or a clinician fascinated by the mystery and human misery and ways of improving stuttering, inclines them to release, open up, become less defensive, allowing themselves to be seen and known more fully.

The more loving the perception, the less likely we are to interfere, manipulate, control. Maslow once said that that which one loves one is prepared to leave alone. Of course, while love may allow a parent to stick to the task of trying to enhance the child's behavior, to remain resolved to do something and to learn more about a problem, one realizes that in extreme cases *love blinds.* This blindness sometimes becomes the focus of that needing to be worked through in the counseling session.

FIXED BELIEFS AND THE COURAGE OF ONE'S DOUBTS

Any learning-in-counseling which involves a fundamental change in self-organization in the way in which one regards and behaves toward himself and others tends to be threatening, and therefore may be resisted. This is as true for impaired children as it is for their parents. It is likely to be true for counselors as well. A creative counselor does not feel driven to espouse but one point of view, one technique, nor does he feel that he must strive always for agreement between parents and child; he respects and encourages the personal validity of each individual's view, even when they appear conflicting. It is difficult to see how this could be anything else but the case when he is working with children or parents representing a wide spectrum of dysfunctions. For example, the writer found himself working with a six-year-old referred to our clinic because of mounting behavior problems. The thirty-two-year-old father had suffered a stroke eighteen months before which has left him hemiplegic and almost speechless. There are two younger children and the mother, a mild-mannered person with serious health problems of her own, who had always left the major decisions up to her husband. Counseling, rehabilitation and therapy procedures must be varied to suit such a range of needs.

In any single situation with parents and child together, the counselor may find himself giving direct information; asking very specific questions; acting as arbitrator, interpreter, resource person for allied medical and welfare supportive services, language analyst, accepting supporter, utilizer of nonverbal techniques, and so on. Rigid adherence to set or pet methodology in such circumstances could, to say the least, cause wonderment. What one might at least hope for in such instances is the realization that fixed beliefs tend to be noncreative foundations; that it behooves us to tolerate, respect and try to see goodness in the views of others, however unintelligible they may seem to us; that neither all of truth nor all of goodness is given to any one individual, although each may derive value from his particular perspective; that perhaps we need but be faithful to our own situations and opportunities, making the most of them most humanly, without taking it upon ourselves to impress our own views overbearingly upon others.

COUNSELING DURING THE INITIAL DIAGNOSTIC PHASE

Even during initial evaluations of impaired children, a counseling component is usually developed which may be crucial in itself, that is for gaining perspective on a presented problem. Or it may be critical in terms of its implicit suggestion as a model of how some of the time will be spent with the counseling staff in the future. We are all familiar with the parent who has a *drive for closure,* who wants to know precisely what is wrong and, in fact, precisely what it is called, preferably in a single term. Or, we know the parent who offers two alternatives to the clinician for consideration ("Is Billy a brain-damaged child or is he not?" "Is he below average in intelligence or is he not?" "Will he be able to speak within a year or two or not?"), and with often remarkable pursuit tries to get the clinician to give a yes or no answer. That is a difficult time for the professional. If he is himself insecure, he may become trapped into premature diagnosis and labelling. On the other hand he may recognize the deeply-felt need of the parent to *know,* to resolve the nagging doubt. He may also consider it most vital to keep all options open as to the possibilities, especially, let us say, in cases of difficult differential diagnoses. He may also consider it vital to help the parents to increase their capacity to live in a state of doubt but with improved comfort.

On the other hand, there are times when labels or specific diagnostic terms must be used for administrative purposes (for example, when a severely language-impaired child is listed as *aphasic* in order for the family to receive necessary financial assistance under state laws). Such terminology will require careful consideration in the counseling sector. So, sometimes, will terms that turn out to be vague, like the term *emotional problem* if applied to developmental lag or deviation when there is no significant psychogenic component known; such terms are reacted to by some parents in self-blaming ways which may be therapeutically harmful.

The openness we have been discussing of the professional person is as applicable in the evaluation phase as in the therapy phase. Our inclination is to exercise a great variety of evaluation options as they seem appropriate to individual cases. For example, because so many of the youngsters seen are nonverbal, anxious and withdrawn, evaluation in a strange building, in a strange room, and perhaps a small room with white bare walls at that, may be of limited value. Frequently, therefore, one should conduct much of the evaluation in the natural home setting, in the neighborhood playground or in the child's school setting, or he might have a child's siblings join in the evaluation; they can be extremely helpful as interpreters and sources of helpful perspectives on the family life. While a discussion of the point must await a later publication, let us at least say that the differences between diagnostic impressions gained in a clinic as compared to those collected in the child's natural settings have sometimes been astounding.

VARIETY AS THE SPICE OF COUNSELING

Counseling can be tradition-bound and boring. It need not be. The writer has mentioned a few ways in which the usual verbal exchange format (which nevertheless remains the crucial one) may be varied. There are other variations on the theme which seem to be worth mentioning at this point.

Writing. Certain writing procedures have been in use for so long that they hardly need comment, such as autobiographies. Daily diaries can be quite helpful, including the recording of dreams and, occasionally, personal letters. Keeping written records of assignments or categories of events may be useful. In reply to requests to write responses to the question "Who am I?" the following statements have been among those given:

1. A thirteen-year-old girl with severe cleft lip and palate, "I am a princess disguised as a toad."
2. A twelve-year-old boy with muscular dystrophy, "I am a snowflake melting in your hand."
3. An emotionally-disturbed high school girl, "I am the guitar string you plucked too hard that screamed as I broke."
4. A mother of a deaf girl who had overcome a serious social problem, "I am a fallen leaf who waited for the wind to lift me again."
5. A father who chronically beat his wayward son, "I am the boss and nothing else."
6. A nine-year-old child with cerebral palsy who was becoming more independent, "I am my baby tooth under your pillow."

Role-playing, Sociodrama, Creative Dramatics and Music Therapy

These processes have been available for many years, but it is the writer's impression that they are insufficiently used in counseling parents or families having handicapped children. Readers who have not yet seriously considered or utilized these techniques are encouraged to explore their possibilities. One excellent source for all of these areas is the recent book on family therapy by Ferber *et al.* (6). Satir's book (21) is a basic source of novel ideas. The work of Murphy and FitzSimons (17) has particular relevance to the problem of stuttering.

The creative counselor is inclined to employ a variety of roles, techniques and materials rather than adhering to routinized formats. Again, this is more likely to be particularly true when one is working with a great variety of impairments in children. The clinics with which the writer is involved are not atypical, and deal with families with children having disorders of visual or auditory functioning, emotional or social maladjustments, speech, voice, reading and writing problems, and multiple disabilities. The gamut of etiologies, behaviors and needs manifested by such families is enormous, and necessitates a similarly-wide gamut of helping or counseling procedures.

COUNSELING AS THE CREATION OF SELF IN HELPING RELATIONSHIPS WITH OTHERS

Nowhere that the writer knows of has it ever been promised that life can be simple, easy, and free from pain or uncertainty. Parents of impaired children have a particular task, but also a particular opportunity to become more human persons through relationship with their children. Counselors have a similar opportunity. Many such parents and many professionals have concluded that the purpose of life is not to be forever happy. The purpose of life is to matter, to be productive in the deepest human sense. Happiness in the noblest sense means self-fulfillment, stretching our professional resources and the resources of the mind and heart.

A decade ago the writer was asked what significance there was to working with children with special problems; he tried to reply, not only as a professional, but for parents. To say what it means to work with handicapped children is to express a view toward all children, all people, and to express a personal philosophy, at least in capsule form. He believes that such work enhances the chances of discovering one's noblest nature, of continuing to evolute as a fully-functioning person. Indeed one may, in the clinical setting, find his religion. To work with handicapped children is to have said that, where human beings are concerned, the smallest number is two; I cannot exist fully except in relationship with another.

A broken body need not contain a broken mind. To see a child grow is to see the future in the making. It is awesome and gratifying to be able to partake of another's process of becoming something more than he is. It is somewhat selfish, too, for it nurtures one's own evolution; one must recognize how he seeks for the secrets of life. One does not seek to make others in his own image, but he cannot deny that he has in his mind an image of what they might become, and through such ways of what he may become.

REFERENCES

1. Barsch, R. H.: Counseling the parent of the brain-damaged child. Chapter XIII in Frierson, E. C., and Barbe, W. B. (Eds.): *Educating Children with Learning Disabilities.* New York, Appleton, 1967, pp. 145-151.

2. Bertocci, P. A.: *Religion as Creative Insecurity*. New York, Assn Pr, 1958.
3. Buber, M.: *Between Man and Man* (Smith, R. G., Translator). New York, MacMillan Paperbacks, 1965.
4. Buber, M.: *I and Thou* (Smith, R. G., Translator). New York, Scribner, 1958.
5. Ellis, H.: *The Dance of Life*. New York, G & D, 1923.
6. Ferber, A., Mendelsohn, M., and Napier, A.: *The Book of Family Therapy*. Boston, HM, 1973.
7. Maslow, A. H.: *The Farther Reaches Of Human Nature*. New York, Viking Pr, 1971.
8. Maslow, A. H.: *Toward A Psychology of Being*. Second Edition. New York, D. Van Nostrand, 1968.
9. Mayeroff, M.: *On Caring*. New York, Har-Row, 1972.
10. Murphy, A. T.: Feelings and attitudes. In *Stuttering: Treatment of the Adult Stutterer*. Memphis, Speech Foundation of America, 1974.
11. Murphy, A. T.: The quiet hyena: Two monologues in search of a dialogue. Chapter II in Emerick, L. L., and Hood, S. B. (Eds.): *The Client-Clinician Relationship*. Springfield, Thomas, 1974.
12. Murphy, A. T.: Hope, hopelessness and exceptionality. *Except. Parent, 2:*23-29, 1972.
13. Murphy, A. T.: Stuttering, behavior modification, and the person. In *Conditioning in Stuttering Therapy: Applications and Limitations*. Memphis, Speech Foundation of America, 1970, pp. 99-110.
14. Murphy, A. T.: Educational materials and individual psychology. *J Educ, 152:*1, 59-68, 1969.
15. Murphy, A. T.: Love may be enough: The passionate investments of clinicians. *Semin Psychiatry, 1:*3, 262-269, 1969.
16. Murphy, A. T.: Objectivity, subjectivity and research. *Except Child, 26:*400-405, 1960.
17. Murphy, A. T., and FitzSimons, R. M.: *Stuttering and Personality Dynamics: Play Therapy, Projective Therapy and Counseling*. New York, Ronald, 1960.
18. Murphy, A. T.: Personal relations in a profession. *Volta Rev, 56:*261-2, 1954.
19. Rogers, C. R.: *Freedom To Learn*. Columbus, Merrill, 1969.
20. Sapir, S. G., and Nitzburg, A. C.: *Children with Learning Problems: Readings In A Developmental-Interaction Approach*. New York, Brunner/Mazel, 1973.
21. Satir, V.: *Conjoint Family Therapy*. Revised Edition. Palo Alto, Science and Behavior Books, 1967.

Chapter 2

VARIOUS ASPECTS OF
PARENT COUNSELING

Betty Jane McWilliams

INTRODUCTION

T HE clinician suggesting parent counseling usually assumes that some aspect of the parents' interactional pattern with their child requires modification either for the welfare of the child or of the parents. On the other hand, parents for whom such counseling or guidance is recommended often assume that their need for such help means that they either *are* inadequate as parents or that professional people playing vital roles in their lives *believe* them to be. In actuality, the term *counseling* has a much broader meaning than current usage would suggest and may be accurately applied to many aspects of professional-parent interaction involving a wide variety of situations, needs and techniques.

In the strict sense, every professional person who interacts with parents and children becomes a counselor. The role may vary from parent to parent; and the methodology may be, indeed should be, based upon the clinician's assessment of the parents' requirements at a particular time. Thus, in every encounter the child's primary problem must be identified; the information with which the parents will handle it must be decided upon; a method for imparting the information must be selected and applied; the effectiveness of the approach must be assessed; and what may be required in addition must be determined. The basic task is always the same, but the way it is approached will depend ultimately upon the clinician's insights, the therapeutic goals and the collateral services available. In short, there is no blueprint to be followed in all cases, no foolproof system of counseling that can be adopted and used with equal success for all parents, and no known substitute for the concerned, involved clinician who

27

places a high priority on working with parents and who is persuaded that the time necessary to do so is well spent.

Starting with the assumption that some form of counseling is inherent in every clinical encounter, it is clear that there are necessarily many possible approaches. Clinicians will select a procedure with which they are comfortable and which meets the needs of the parents and child.

THE CLINICIAN

Since the clinician must be able to assess the parent's current status, there is the implication that the clinician is competent to make the assessment. Unfortunately, the exact nature of the clinical competencies essential to this kind of evaluation remains somewhat nebulous. Dorothy Baruch (4) once suggested that major assets for parents are "... the ear that listens, the eye that watches, the open mind, and a true, deep, and earnest wish to develop sympathy and accord." Clinicians must also have these unique and human capacities. Thus, as Travis stated (46), they must be fully in charge of themselves and must be able to cast off their own personal responses so that they will not project their own feelings into the lives of others. As Rogers (35) noted, they must be personally mature,

> ... the optimal helping relationship is the kind of relationship
> created by a person who is psychologically mature. Or to put it
> in another way, the degree to which I can create relationships
> which facilitate the growth of others as separate persons is a
> measure of the growth I have achieved in myself.

Clinicians must be able to understand and act upon the philosophy that what constitutes pain or uncertainty for the parents may not appear painful or uncertain to them. They are then in a position to deal with the parental conditions as they are rather than with what they think they are or should be. Clinicians who would do any kind of counseling must be capable of identifying with others. They must be able to respond accurately to parental messages sent through verbal expression with all of its intricacies, through behavioral clues, through body language and even through silence. Clinicians will not do well if their clinical eyes are turned inward rather than outward. They must recognize their own limitations and realize that they will not be appropriate sources of help for all parents for reasons that neither they nor the parents may be able to understand or resolve. Counseling involves communication and a relationship of the type described by Spock (42),

> The way to have an agreeable, meaty conversation ... is to put yourself in tune with them by listening attentively and sympathetically, with your eyes meeting theirs and your facial expression mirroring their mood, whether that mood is humorous, indignant, or awed. Then when it's your turn to speak you take off from their remarks, showing that you respond to them in thought and feeling. So a conversation is woven by two sympathetic souls working with the same threads.

It is clear that counseling must take place in a caring, supportive atmosphere conducive to the development of trust on the part of troubled, hurting parents.

Counseling, like parenthood, is often undertaken in one form or another by individuals who have had little or no formal training. Knowledge about philosophical and historical backgrounds of counseling and the various processes of counseling and supervised clinical practicum would be desirable credentials for all members of the helping professions. However, the ideal is seldom the reality, and compromises become necessary in order that people who require help may find it. Clinicians who lack academic and practical preparation but who must provide counseling may feel inadequate and somewhat threatened in this special relationship with parents who look to them for support and direction. Clinicians can sometimes find the support they require by informally broadening their own background through reading programs and by working with other, more experienced clinicians in ongoing parent programs. There is a vast body of literature available, and no one should be discouraged or overwhelmed by the size of the task. The beginner may wish to simplify early explorations by seeking materials that provide good overviews of many aspects of parent-counseling, such as those by Noland (30, 31, 32) and then expanding reading experiences to include materials on a variety of counseling processes ranging from psychoanalysis (21) through client-centered therapy (34) and behavior modification

(40, 50). There are, of course, many other variations on the counseling theme that the clinician may eventually wish to consider.

THE PARENTS

Anyone undertaking parent-counseling must recognize the in-
dividuality of parents, the variety of their personal strengths and
weaknesses, the influence in their lives of their cultural and ethnic
heritages, and the role of their total environment — home, occupational, social and community — in shaping and maintaining
their attitudes. Throughout this discussion, frequent reference
will be made to parents as people. If the counseling relationship is
to prosper, clinicians cannot afford to lose sight of this aspect of
their work. It is relevant to this consideration to recognize that the
social milieu of parents and clinician will undoubtedly influence
the direction and content of counseling. The counselor's goal
should be to help parents become more effective in their interactions with their children regardless of the life-style of either counselor or parents. The counselor must respect parents from a
variety of social heritages and recognize that all kinds of mothers
and fathers come out of both ghettos and palaces. This means that
the successful counselor must be attuned to many different patterns of living and must be capable of accepting variations in
people and ethnic groups without evaluating them as somehow
pathological. More than that, recognition must be given to the
fact that both counselor and parents are undoubtedly more comfortable with living patterns that are consistent with previous
experience and with those of their own larger social groups.
Thus, it may be dangerous to assume that the family without a
father is necessarily a bad family. It may only be different. It may
be erroneous to accept such statements as "Another phenomenon
in unstable families is the nonevolved grandmother. Here the
daughter relinquishes her own motherly role to the grandmother,
who takes over the maternal functions toward the children, thus
confusing generation lines" (16).

The "nonevolved" grandmother may be a real problem for
average white families living in suburbia. She may have positive
values for families from subcultures with strong matriarchal

structures. Clinicians must be aware of these varying life patterns and must assess them not in their own terms, but in the terms of the parents and their children with whom they counsel.

The counselor cannot allow unrecognized prejudices to influence clinical behavior. However, there is emerging evidence that clinicians are often less than objective (37) about families whose backgrounds are either greatly different from their own or so similar as to recall attitudes with which clinicians wish to disassociate themselves. In either event the clinician may work less intensely than would otherwise be the case, categorize the parents inaccurately, be unable to surmount the communication barriers imposed by the differing social backgrounds, or make inappropriate judgments about parental strengths and weaknesses. Thus, clinicians must be personally honest about their motivations, prejudices and blind spots. Only then will it be possible to work fairly and compassionately with parents from many different ways of life.

One additional word of caution involves the clinician's being personally threatened by an aggressive parent who demands too much too quickly and who pushes the clinician to bypass waiting lists, to help acquire special services, or to undertake the working of miracles. The clinician cannot afford to allow attempts of that kind to result in irresponsible or unreasonable behavior or to be occasions for distress. A part of the clinician's usefulness to parents depends upon the ability to withstand personal invasion and psychic threat. A counselor must be a caring human being capable of making the separation between involvement on a clinical level and involvement on a personal level.

PARENTS' NEEDS

Parents' needs change over time as they are subjected to different stresses in relationship to their handicapped child. Thus, the parents of a newborn are in a different position from that of parents of an older child with either a congenital or an acquired handicap, and these latter parents differ from each other. The nature of the handicap, its prognosis, the severity of required treatment, the influence of the problem in the family, and many other unique factors must also be taken into account in working with parents. It may be helpful to examine briefly certain parental needs as they relate to the age of the child.

The Birth of a Handicapped Baby

When a handicapped baby is born, as the author has previously discussed (28), the parents face a condition of stress with which they must cope. In order to do this, they call upon those psychological mechanisms that have served them in the past. Those mechanisms may be representative of strength at one end of the continuum or they may be devices that have emerged out of a deep psychic distress at the other. Parents come to this particular stressful experience with a variety of backgrounds and personality structures. Thus, no one can measure the degree of impact that a particular handicap will have or precisely what form the initial reaction will take.

Unfortunately, the parents' ability to receive and handle information about a baby with congenital abnormalities can almost never be a factor in determining whether they are to be informed of the condition or not. They must be told almost immediately if the anomaly is visible, if it has life implications, if they themselves ask, if required care involves aggressive procedures, if the parents cannot see the baby, or if the baby must be moved to another hospital. These are circumstances that will not permit the obstetrician or the pediatrician to delay informing the parents until they are able to receive the news in the most positive manner possible for them. They must be told.

How they are told is the crucial issue, and the quality of the support and guidance they are given may determine in part whether the parents are able to mobilize and use whatever strengths they have or whether they will be so devastated that they cannot call upon any but the most primitive and destructive of their coping powers.

Parents of handicapped children report a variety of experiences related to learning about the handicap (43). A few are splendid examples of the best in counseling provided by practitioners who are not primarily counselors but who recognize the need to fill this role as an integral part of their responsibilities. Parents remember the physician who sat quietly with them, told them of the baby's condition in terms they could understand, remained to help them with their first overwhelming feelings of grief (45) and confusion, answered their early questions patiently, and was ready with a plan of management, however temporary, to provide for the baby in his first weeks of life. Even more important, the physician was with them when they saw their child for the first time and helped them begin to establish initial positive relationships upon which future life satisfaction for parents and child depended. Parents remember even longer and more positively the physician who continued to be available to them in those early days and to understand their feelings as they mourned the loss of their dreamed-of, perfect baby and learned to accept and cope with the reality of a baby with differences (45). However, if the reports of mothers and fathers are to be believed, encounters of this type are all too rare (43).

There is a human tendency to avoid unpleasant confrontations, and professional people are not immune to this condition. When they do not understand this personal attribute, they may deal with parents in a less than ideal manner. The result is that they provide the bare information as quickly as possible to whichever parent is handiest and leave without rendering any emotional aid whatsoever. Even worse, they may abdicate the responsibility to someone else. Thus, when parents of handicapped babies are asked how they were told about their child's condition, their responses run the gamut from the best to the worst.

More often than not, their memory is a miserable one. "Your baby was born with a cleft lip and palate. Don't worry about it. It can be fixed." This is a frequently-reported experience. Often, the mother is told while she is still a bit groggy. Only later does she realize that she does not even know what her informer was talking about and that she must tell her husband. Perhaps she is not permitted to see her baby as the other mothers are, and she secretly believes that her child is dead. Not infrequently, her introduction to the handicap occurs at that precious moment when she sees her infant for the first time; and she is simply not prepared in advance. While this sounds like shocking, inhuman behavior on the part of professional people, these kinds of mismanagement continue to occur not because professionals are inhuman, but more often because they have not come to terms with their own feelings and are, therefore, not able to set themselves aside so that they can treat their patients with understanding and compassion.

Much professional training almost ignores feelings in its urgent attempt to include everything in the book about the physical aspects of people. This enormous lack in the training of professional people leads to disasters that could be avoided if supportive work were recognized as an urgent necessity, sometimes of greater value than any other treatment procedures that could be selected.

Special Needs of the Handicapped Neonate

Most handicapped infants have some special necessities dictated by the restrictive nature of the disorder. Parents must be informed about these needs rather than left to discover them for themselves. In addition, they will usually require instruction and support in cooperating in programs of special care. How this instruction is provided will depend upon the nature of the handicap as well as upon the skills of professionals, paraprofessionals and volunteers, including other parents, but it must be provided over time so that parents can modify their own behavior and gradually acquire new, more effective skills which they are helped to use easily and habitually. Professionals must realize the importance of this task in the parents' eyes and care enough about achieving appropriate goals to state them clearly, program experiences to achieve them, and then follow up after the baby leaves the hospital to be sure that intervening events have not served to extinguish the desired behavior on the part of the parents. In short, clinicians must learn to teach and to evaluate the effectiveness of their educational procedures.

Too little counseling at this level is presently going on with newborns and their parents. Mothers of infants with cleft palates still almost routinely report harrowing experiences with feeding their babies, and they seem to derive little training or support from hospital personnel. In fact, too often mothers report feelings that the nursing staff did not know how to feed their children and that there was a concerted effort to get the babies out of the hospital as fast as possible with no source of help in view, and the parents were left to struggle and seek help on their own. During the preparation of this material, the writer visited a neighborhood drug store and was asked by a concerned pharmacist where he could get "cleft palate" nipples for a young baby whose inexperienced parents had been trying unsuccessfully to feed him in the absence of any help from the hospital where the child was born, and in a city where assistance was a phone call away. She helped the pharmacist make up the type of feeder described earlier (33) from things available on his own shelves; but that was accidental, indirect aid. It should have been deliberate and planned.

Thus, these hungry, poorly-nourished babies and their tense, weary, frightened parents are asked to lay the foundations for future parent-child relationships.

It simply is not true, as one misguided hospital chief of staff recently suggested, that parents "cope because they have to." *Cope* means to struggle, of course, but it means to struggle in even terms with the hope of some degree of success. In order for most parents to do that, they will require instruction, emotional support and some benevolent surveillance.

After the Baby Goes Home

Under the best of circumstances, parents of handicapped children will go through the previously-mentioned period of mourning (45). Under the least desirable circumstances they will experience a variety of other emotions including guilt, anger, shame, fear, anxiety, depression and hostility. Indeed these feelings may interfere with the mourning process and may prevent the parent from coming to grips with the child as he is. This is not to say that *all* parents are crippled by all of these emotions, but some are, and they require assistance, support and counseling so that they can move with their child into society and into appropriate, well-conceived treatment programs designed to help the child reach his maximum potential. Until they have such help, they are likely to be immobilized, secretive, defensive and denying. These parents eventually become shoppers for a quick or quack cure, and the attempt to solve the problem becomes the major problem. In short, as Travis stated (46), "Hard work on problems *is* the problem and is used by the patient to deny the truth that sometimes he will just have to suffer and there is nothing at all he can do about it." The child never really gets what he needs because the parents move too rapidly from place to place in their frenetic effort to find someone who will either join them in their denial or offer some treatment that will guarantee a cure.

There will always be parents whose own psychological complexities, even with the best counseling, will direct their behavior into these fruitless endeavors. However, much of it can be prevented with judicious, caring support, guidance and programming.

The Older Child

As the baby who was discovered to be handicapped at birth matures and develops, the treatment requirements are likely to change. In addition, the social-emotional condition will alter as a function of age; and the parents must learn, as must all parents, to establish new goals, revise old ones and allow their child to establish independence from them to the fullest extent of his capabilities. This means that the parents must eventually become realistic about the impact of the handicap upon their *child* as well as upon themselves and must, while accepting limitations, permit and foster the emergence of strengths and autonomy where these are possible. They must help their child learn to handle the social implications of the handicap and realize that some handicaps carry with them minority stigma that cannot be successfully denied (3, 9, 8, 36, 28).

For the clinician, this concept of optimal development for the handicapped child demands personal investment, often over a number of years — certainly over a long enough period of time to be sure that the parents are able to function in this regard without continued support and guidance. Parents often cloak their child in nurture and protection long after the child's need for such nurture has passed into history. In doing this, they either deprive and frustrate the child or reinforce primitive, immature emotions and behavior which, in their turn, prevent the child's full participation in life at any level.

Every clinician can point to numerous cases where this condition exists. The etiology of such parental malfunctioning cannot be explained in simplistic terms. Hundreds of factors undoubtedly interact to create the attitudes that determine the parental behavior. However, parents play a major role in the shaping of their child's life patterns through reinforcement or lack of it. Because parents may reinforce, however subtly, those behaviors which they somehow wish to maintain and withhold reinforcement for other behavior which, on the surface, seems more desirable to the objective observer, it is clear that they may require assistance before they can be expected to handle their child rationally.

Full consideration of these issues suggests that ongoing concern for such parents may help them move comfortably from one stage to the next, and that problem-oriented solutions achieved in response to one developmental level may not be effective as the child encounters new hurdles at later stages in his quest for maturity. Thus, clinician recognition of parents' specific dilemmas versus the generalized one becomes crucial.

Perhaps an example will serve to illustrate this point. The mother of a five-year-old boy with skeletal defects was concerned about his general lethargy and disinterest in his environment. The pediatrician commented that the child appeared to be a little anemic but was not sufficiently impressed with the possibility even to order blood work. The mother, as might be imagined, was justifiably worried, but she was also in a state of anxiety that was unreasonable and out of all proportion to the severity of the problem. Consultation with a pediatric hematologist revealed that there was no reason for concern. The mother was greatly relieved and expressed gratitude to everyone who had helped to allay her anxiety. In the process, the boy's basic problem, his lack of involvement with his world, was not put into perspective nor was his mother's anxiety. Thus, no relevant help was offered. Three years later the child was walking over desk tops at school, showing violence toward a deaf child whom he described as "not even human because she can't even talk right" (as he could not), destroying his own and other children's work, and so disrupting order on the school bus that the driver tried to have him excluded from service. When counseling was recommended at this point, the parents resisted. They insisted that the problem lay with their child who, they were sure, suffered from "hyperkinetic behavior." Many examinations supported the diagnosis of emotional problems in both parents and child, but the parents rejected help consistently and continued to shop around. They finally found a pediatrician who prescribed massive dosages of ritalin. The child, a severe depressive at this point, was as might be expected, somewhat improved on this medication; and the parents again felt somewhat relieved and reassured in the absence of any basic alteration in their relationship with their child. Their period of comfort was brief. The boy lost weight, experienced sleepless nights and continued in modified form his bizarre and unpredictable behavior in school. This was a generalized problem of parent-child interaction that required management by experts. Providing such narrowly-focused assistance was worse than ineffective. It reinforced the parents in their desperate efforts to change their child without changing themselves and seriously delayed their accepting the treatment plan that had the best chance of succeeding.

This is not to say that problem-oriented help is never indicated. It may be appropriate when the parent-child relationship is healthy, in conjunction with active parent counseling designed to improve the relationship, or as an emergency measure to alleviate an acute problem as parent counseling is being planned.

Another example will demonstrate this point. A mother of a four-year-old boy with minimal brain damage, hyperactivity and a serious communication problem was in a state of panic over her rapidly-deteriorating relationship with her child. They were in a constant hassle for control with the mother saying and screaming, "Don't!" or "Stop!" hundreds of times a day. The little boy, completely ignoring her, went wildly on his way. She obviously required much help, but it took time to arrange for that. In the meantime, the situation was going from bad to worse. As an emergency measure, it was pointed out that her present system of management was ineffective. She agreed with enthusiasm. It was then suggested that she might want to try a totally different approach, refraining from all critical comments for a period of two weeks and consciously seeking out her son's positive behavior (at least four times a day) which she might reinforce by telling him how well he was doing, spending extra time with him, or using other simple reinforcers. The mother seemed relieved to be given permission to stop using her old system of discipline. She obviously needed such permission because she thought that *good* mothers exercised almost complete control over their children, and that to ignore her son's behavior even temporarily would be to abdicate her responsibilities and become a *bad* mother. Supporting her and offering a new management scheme almost as a prescription allowed her to change as she really was ready to do because someone in authority had given approval.

This was admittedly a simplistic approach, and it may or may not have succeeded, depending upon the readiness of the mother to accept and implement the plan. In this case, it worked like a miracle. The child reinforced the mother beautifully as well as the other way around, and tensions began to subside. When mother and child were seen two weeks later, the mother was happy and jubilant with her results. She began the conference by saying, "You know, this has worked so well with my little boy! I wonder if you think it would work with my husband?" Again, she was asking permission to change! Some forward steps had been taken, and the clinician was infinitely more knowledgeable about the mother's requirements in counseling.

The same general approach may often be used with less serious, transient, developmental difficulties in childhood provided underlying parental concerns, anxieties and needs are not overlooked. A bright, well-educated, somewhat older mother of a first child, a precocious, beautiful three-year-old, will illustrate this failure. This mother called in some desperation after having failed to reach Dr. Spock and several other nationally-known child authorities with whose writings she had spent many of her waking hours. The problem was that her child was stuttering. By the time the little girl was seen in the clinic, she was whispering. In response to her mother's ill-chosen *cures* for the nonfluency, the child had given up vocalization although she continued to use masses of whispered verbal output. It was a simple matter to restore her to full function, and the mother was most receptive to guidance around the speech patterns her child was manifesting. When they left, it seemed that the tide had turned and that the speech issue had been successfully resolved. However, the mother was to keep in touch and, specifically, to call in one week. She did in a breathless, concerned voice which suggested that the stuttering behavior was at a new peak, but that was not the case. When she was asked about the speech, the mother replied, "Stuttering? Oh, that's all right! But how do I get her out of the bathtub?" We had failed to realize that each new event in this child's life constituted a major crisis for the mother, who was sure something terrible was going on that would damage her daughter's psyche permanently. The result was that this tiny little con artist was a virtual dictator headed toward worse psychic disasters than the parents had of yet dreamed. Ongoing assistance to change basic attitudes was in order in addition to help with the management of specific problems.

The goal of all work with parents is to help them function successfully and independently outside of counseling and in relationship to their child's changing status as he progresses from infancy to adulthood. With a handicapped child, whose life requirements may differ from children who are not so involved, the parents may encounter almost insurmountable hurdles that come with age. These hurdles can often be predicted and, thus, can be eased somewhat for the parents and for the child as well. For example, a young child with intractible seizures presents many problems in his growing up in both educational and emotional spheres, but it is often possible to minimize these and to help him fit fairly comfortably into a small, well-supervised, accepting society. His big encounters with reality come later on when he wants to drive a car and can't, when he experiences career limitations, when he has seizures in new situations with people who were not a part of his smaller, more protected world. His parents may find themselves once more overwhelmed by the enormity of these changing implications of their child's convulsive disorder. Again, they require guidance and may continue to need it for as long as they retain even partial jurisdiction over their child's destiny.

If this parental responsibility will be required into adulthood, then other problems will emerge with which the parents hopefully, by this time, will seek assistance as it is required, as much for their son or daughter as for themselves.

The Handicapped Child in the Family

In discussing handicapped children, we must keep constantly in mind that they are members of families which often include, in addition to parents, other children whose well-being may also be at issue. In our zeal to create a good world for the child with special needs, we too often contribute to a poor environment for the rest of the family. In so doing we destroy the foundations of family living for the child with problems. Parent-counseling should be carried out with a clear understanding of the family as a unit and with concern for the integrity of each family member. Thus, the counselor, ideally, should be aware of all the family's hopes and dreams, disappointments and burdens, and should know and care about the people involved lest the nonhandicapped members of the family become unnecessary victims of the handicapped, casualties of poor planning and helping.

APPROACHES TO COUNSELING

Clinicians have a number of options as to the type of counseling which they may elect to use. The insight therapies have their roots in Freudian psychoanalytic theory and are not usually approaches with which individuals trained in disciplines other than counseling *per se* have sufficient background for ethical and judicious use. However, such approaches as client-centered counseling set forth by Carl Rogers (34) and his followers have special applicability. These systems of therapy are designed to help the individual understand himself and his feelings in the belief that deeper insights will result in more effective and more comfortable patterns of living. The emphasis is not upon modifying the behavior itself but upon the inner human psychological structures presumably responsible for determining behavior. At the opposite end of the continuum are the behaviorists, now enjoying a rebirth of popularity through such exponents as Skinner (40), Wolpe (50) and others. This group places stress upon behavior that can be observed, described, broken into component parts and modified without access to or speculations about its origins or the feeling systems underlying it. At midpoint on the continuum stand the group who strive to develop insight as they simultaneously attempt to modify behavior.

There is little hard data to support the relative superiority of one philosophy over another. In fact, Eisenberg (15) recently asserted that witchcraft and spirit healing have about as high a success rate among people who believe in them as psychiatry does among its followers. "Any form of treatment seems to work in some cases," he said, "and there isn't any one thing that works better than anything else."

In spite of this general state of knowledge, most clinicians would find little fault with Travis' statement (46) to the effect that "therapy is learning." Nor would there be serious disagreement with Hobbs (23),

> All systems of psychotherapy involve in varying measures the five kinds of experiences that I have described. Their effectiveness will depend on the extent to which they provide an opportunity for the client to experience closeness to another human being without getting hurt, to divest symbols associated with traumatic experiences of their anxiety producing potential, to use the transference situation to learn not to need neurotic distortions, to practice being responsible for himself, and to clarify an old or learn a new cognitive system for ordering his world.

Clinicians undertaking parent counseling as a part of their professional activities would do well to remember and build upon Hobbs's philosophy. It provides a useful framework for structuring parent work regardless of clinical technique. However, most clinicians will probably select an approach that will be designed to improve insights and change behavior. The attempt will be to help parents understand themselves in relationship to their child's problem, assist them in developing insights into the interactions and transactions that occur between them and their child, illuminate alternatives and, where indicated, assist them in modifying their own and their child's behavior.

The practicing clinician does not have the option of ignoring counseling as a part of clinical responsibility since it is simply not practical, desirable, or possible to refer all patients in need of help to psychiatric facilities. More than that, in the case of handicapped children, there is a necessity for much of the work with parents to be done by a clinician who is expert in the area of disability and is responsible for the child's treatment program. The child's major problem and the management it requires are often intimate parts of the need for counseling and relate directly to the content of parent work. Thus, it becomes essential for the clinician to see the counseling process in the breadth that it deserves. The sections which follow will deal with several different aspects of the counseling process.

Information-Giving by the Clinician

The most commonly-used form of counseling at all professional levels is information-giving. Regardless of what kind of evaluation is carried out, the responsible clinician must decide what will be imparted to parents. The clinician decides what portions of the message are essential for parents to understand, how their understanding will be checked, and, if they have not understood, what steps can be taken to assure that they either develop the understanding necessary to handle the problem or modify their behavior in relationship to their child so that necessary clinical goals can be achieved.

The clinician will want to begin by determining something about the parents as people, how they view their child, and what their anxieties are. This background will help decide how to impart information, will direct attention to areas of parental concern, and will provide understanding about parental strengths and weaknesses which will influence management. The failure to be informed about parents before informing them about their child is a frequent explanation for clinical failure. *Listening* to parents discuss their child and their concerns is the best clinical tool available even though this may require a whole new orientation for the clinician who may be far more accustomed to making pronouncements, discouraging questions and cutting short parent interviews.

A few examples will illustrate this important point. A preschool girl with obvious behavior problems of a prepsychotic mother developed a gastrointestinal disturbance which was treated by the family physician. Since she was dehydrated, the physician recommended that fluids be forced. This was a straightforward necessity under the circumstances, and the instructions were precise. The failure related to poor understanding of the mother's obsessive-compulsive behavior, the need to help her through a difficult time, and then to reassess the situation to provide new instructions. Since this was not done, the mother continued to force fluids for two years; the child's behavior disorders were exacerbated; and there was never any recognition of the vast psychological urgencies which surrounded every physical complaint and its required treatment.

On the other hand, there are strong, knowledgeable parents who require little more than the best information the physician can provide. Anything short of that is a cause for disturbance. Mental retardation is a case in point. Countless parents recognize slow development in their infants, and they need desperately to talk with someone who can, first of all, assess their child objectively, provide them with currently available facts, and tell them what can and what *cannot* be determined until a later date. These parents are not helped by a clinician who discounts their observations and then tries to reassure them with some old cliché to the effect that all babies are different or that this one will grow out of it. Unfortunately, parental concern is often handled in just that way with the result that mothers and fathers become frightened, frustrated, hostile, aggressive and emotionally wounded. Neither are they assisted by the clinician who sizes up the situation at the moment and then makes a specific, perhaps poorly-founded prediction such as "This child will never walk." When the child *does* walk, as he often does, the parents immediately reject every other more reasonable clinical finding on their child. And who could blame them? They *want* a normal child, a fact that the thoughtless informer failed to take into account. Now they are angry, and their trust in professional people has been shattered. They will not soon again believe even responsible predictions that are provided by careful clinicians whose counseling job has been made more complex by prior events. How much better to acknowledge the slowness as real, to suggest careful watching, and to offer help to the parents such as training programs for high-risk babies and their mothers.

Other failures in the information-giving area are legion. A father who worried everybody about radiation levels when cinefluorography was recommended for his son was very nearly referred for psychiatric help before anyone found out that he was a radiation physicist whose knowledge of the field far surpassed that of the clinician who had ordered the studies. A mother who refused to have her child admitted to the hospital for needed surgery seemed to be behaving in a negligent manner until investigation revealed that she had overheard a discussion among surgeons about what surgical procedure would be best for her child. Her interpretation of this conversation was that the surgeons did not know what they were doing. Therefore, she was afraid to trust her child to them. Had the original recommendation for surgery included some discussion with her about the possibilities for using one of several procedures and the reasons for deciding upon the one to be undertaken, the mother might have been saved unnecessary worry and massive misunderstanding even if she failed to understand all the technicalities.

Even the simplest of instructions to parents must be viewed in terms of the parents as people. An extremely permissive parent may be unable to adhere without help to a precise medication regime while an authoritarian parent may find it almost impossible to allow a child to decide how much or how little food will be eaten simply because a clinician advises that action. Between these two extremes are the parents who will do well with simple instructions provided they understand them. The clinician's art is in knowing the difference and in being able to modify and change clinical tactics when parents require a different approach.

It is difficult to specify all aspects of this clinical art so essential in the evaluation of the environmental aspects of handicapping conditions. Feinstein (17) addresses himself to this issue as a part of his discussion of clinical judgment in therapy,

The multiple human personal attributes considered in the environmental decisions are often too complex to be cataloged, analyzed, and rationally dissected by any conventional contemporary logic. The clinician's approach to evaluating the patient exclusively as a person is still an artful aspect of care that depends on human perception and understanding. These components of clinical care are properties of heart and spirit, of instinct and psyche, and cannot be easily identified, assessed, or quantified by ordinary methods of reasoning.

Throughout all contacts with parents, the clinician is constantly faced with the necessity of evaluating them as human beings, their responses to particular stresses, and their ability to mobilize their strengths in the solution of their problems. This applies even in the seemingly simple function of giving instructions. Thus, clinicians must seek better ways of instructing (teaching) and of evaluating effectiveness.

When instructions are a bit complex, it is often useful to summarize them for the parents at the end of the interview and to present them in writing so that they may be taken home for future reference. Parenthetically, a simple self-carbon form can be set up for this purpose so that there is a written record of the instructions for the permanent file. This wrap-up summary is one way for the clinician to be assured that instructions are clearly and concisely presented. It also allows an opportunity for the parents to ask questions about anything that seems unclear to them. However, the system is not foolproof, and other precautions are usually necessary as well.

Telephone follow-up, when possible, is helpful since many parents have more questions after they get home and have had a chance to think than they had at the moment of impact. This plan also offers a partial solution to the problem of the parent who is fearful of asking *dumb* questions or who is reluctant to *bother* the busy clinician with his problems. Another way to assist parents is to encourage them to telephone the clinician freely if they feel the need.

This aspect of parent-counseling is not designed to simplify the clinician's life, only to assure that parents are managed more effectively. Their troubles loom large in their lives even when the clinician is not impressed with the enormity of the problem.

Fortunately, a competent and well-trained paraprofessional can be most helpful in programs of this type and can successfully assume at least a part of the clinician's burden without sacrificing the close contact with parents. This system tells the parents of the clinician's ongoing interest and assures them of the availability of support and help. It reflects an attitude of concern that is all-too-often missing in large, somewhat impersonal settings where many children are under care.

Once information having implications for the child and his family has been given and careful follow-up has been planned, reassessment of the situation and further discussions with the parents upon subsequent visits should be provided. The need for this is clear if, for example, the child is diabetic and must be followed methodically in order to ascertain the effectiveness of treatment. The very nature of the problem assures a certain surveillance, and there is an almost built-in mechanism for determining something about the parents' abilities to understand and handle their child at home. However, not all handicapping conditions in childhood are life-threatening, and it is then easier for the parents to close their eyes to reality after the initial examination, discussions and recommendations. For this reason, in connection with any problem, it is usually advisable to arrange for a follow-up visit or visits in order to be certain that the parents are cooperating and managing reasonably well and that they are helped to take the next step.

Follow-up should be done even if the particular clinician is not the appropriate source of long-term assistance, and particularly if the child and the parents require service elsewhere. Referral is often an easy out for the busy clinician, but it can spell disaster for a child if the parents, for whatever reason, are unable to execute the plan.

When information, instruction-giving and careful follow-up prove insufficient to accomplish what is required, the clinician is then faced with a further job of assessment — that of determining what additional help may be useful to the parents. In this connection the word *useful* is of paramount importance. The goal is to find an approach that will assist parents to understand their problems better, that will enable them to change their own behavior if that is required, and that will be acceptable to them. It may even be destructive to make recommendations which, for any reason, parents cannot execute. The wise clinician will be able to judge what can or must be undertaken presently, what should be delayed until appropriate preliminary goals have been achieved, and what must be postponed indefinitely. For this reason, the clinician should be aware of and willing to adopt alternative procedures based upon an assessment of the whole situation. There is often a wide chasm between telling parents about the nature of a child's problem and getting them to the point where they can either live with it or take action to change it. Follow-up on initial encounters will help the clinician decide what type of further intervention is indicated. Sometimes the parents are in a state of grief and loneliness that makes them poor candidates for understanding even simple things or for referral to other agencies. Other forms of assistance must be found so that supportive and preparatory intervention can take place on the level of the parents' perhaps temporary needs. In this connection it is essential, as in all aspects of counseling, for the clinician to seek feedback from parents so that they themselves provide active data in the evaluational process.

Parent Intervention

Parent intervention can often be a helpful adjunct to professional nurture. As was pointed out by Irwin and McWilliams (24), parents can be useful to other parents. Here, the use of *trained* parents on professional treatment teams might be considered. These parents may, upon request, make hospital visits when a handicapped child is born so that the parents of the new baby can meet someone who has walked in their shoes and who can talk to them in general terms about the nature of the problem without diagnosing or making specific recommendations for management. Since every parent who comes to this special experience brings to it his own previous self and background, it is impossible to predict ahead of time what the major concerns will be, or even if they can be verbalized initially. What is important is that troubled parents discover that someone cares about them and will take the time to *listen* to them and to extend help in their terms.

Trained parents (or paraprofessionals) may also be of special help during clinical evaluations of children. Many parents are reluctant to ask questions about the things they do not understand. They are afraid that their questions are *dumb,* that they are somehow on trial, that their parenting is in question, or that the clinician is too busy. In some cases, they are simply too frozen to hear, see, speak or think. Later, in interaction with a concerned parent, perhaps over a cup of coffee, they can express themselves and begin to piece their personal puzzles together. The trained parent, on the other hand, can alert the professionals to special needs so that they can be met as promptly as possible.

These adjuncts to professional care may be viewed as intermediary between the parent and the clinician. They are used in an effort to reach parents who may otherwise be unreachable because of fear, resistance, guilt or simple lack of sophistication.

A word of warning is essential in this connection. The clinician who sees the route of using parents (or paraprofessionals) as a helpful one should be aware of the pitfalls. The system requires a careful clinician able to select parents wisely for this kind of interaction and willing to teach them some rudimentary approaches to other parents. In addition, the parents who undertake such a mission must be able to look beyond their own problem and simply lend quiet support. This system has been used successfully in many areas, but it has required work, tact and supervision. The clinician responsible for programming of this type must recognize at the outset that the most troubled parents are sometimes the most eager to seek solutions to their own difficulties by *helping others.* Thus, again, the clinician must be capable of interpreting the real message that such a parent is communicating, and of assisting that parent to reach a more satisfactory resolution of personal dilemma. The effective parent is the one who has either found solutions or who has accepted the child's condition and is reality-based in terms of its implications for both the child and the family. The effective parent must also be an easy, involved listener, able to refrain from talking too much, giving advice, making judgments or projecting personal feelings.

Programs of this type seem to be most successful when the

contacts are made by a few parents with whom the clinician can remain in an ongoing relationship, perhaps using group process as a technique for continuing in-service training and as a means for assessing effectiveness.

Parent Literature — Bibliotherapy

Many parents, particularly those oriented toward reading and personal problem solving, seek literature which discusses their child's problems. They are almost always successful in their search, whether the clinician thinks it wise or not. There are hundreds of books, articles and pamphlets available to parents of normal and deviant children, and they attack a wide variety of issues ranging from normal development, sex education, drug abuse and education through special problems such as bed-wetting, feeding, learning disabilities, mental retardation, sensory handicaps and physical anomalies.

These materials are a mixed blessing at best. They are often so brief as to be misleading. They frequently include too much too soon, or they are written from the point of view of a specific treatment philosophy which may be in conflict with what is planned for a particular child. Such dangers were pointed out by Wylie and McWilliams (51, 52). However, in spite of these short-comings, some parents are comforted and a few are helped by having something in writing to which they can refer. McDonald's *Bright Promise* (26) is an example of a publication that has enjoyed many years of popularity among parents.

Other materials dealing with specific problems found currently in a number of department stores include Apgar and Beck (1); Brutten, Richardson and Mangel (6); Cameron (7); Delacato (10); deVries-Kruyt (11); Doman (12); Dreikurs (13); Easson (14); Finnie (18); Frazier (19); French and Scott (20); Joseph (25); Nichtern (29); Shiller (38); Siegel (39); Stewart (44); Ulrich (47); Wagner (48); and Wender (49). It is apparent that if parents wish to read about their child's particular handicap, they will find no dearth of information. Fortunately, those with a strong desire to read often raise the issue themselves and, in so doing, open the door for additional counseling.

Once again, bibliotherapy does not simplify the clinician's responsibilities as reading material for parents is sometimes thought to do. Rather, the use of it requires that the clinician be well versed regarding the offerings in particular fields and that, initially, those things considered to be most objective, least misleading and biased, and most compatible with the overall treatment protocol being projected or carried out be made available. In addition to these precautions, the parents should be given the opportunity to discuss what they have read and to resolve any conflicts that may have resulted. This interaction with a knowledgeable person should be available also to the parent who seeks and reads on his own, perhaps with insufficient background to be discriminating.

This educational activity may be conducted as a part of other forms of individual counseling or may be incorporated into a parent study group composed of parents with similar concerns and interested in exploration through independent reading. This arrangement saves time for the clinician and provides an opportunity for exchange among parents under professional leadership.

The reason for these suggested precautions is not to monitor what parents read. Rather, it is to help them make the best use of general materials as they relate to their unique situation and to be certain that they understand both what is and what is not applicable to their own child. In addition, parents must eventually learn that advances in management are not always reflected immediately in materials prepared for parents or even in professional textbooks, and that certain biases on the parts of the authors are bound to influence their presentations.

As Slavson pointed out (41), it is doubtful that reading materials by themselves do very much to help parents, particularly significantly-troubled parents, handle their difficulties more effectively. However, in the presence of appropriate guidance, such readings may help them to feel less alone and may contribute to their general knowledge about the problem they face.

It is essential to reiterate, however, that parents are people and that they cannot always understand or respond to what they read as the writer intended, nor can they be expected to shed their own personalities and suddenly begin to handle their feelings and their children in conformity to an alien system. Again, the middle-of-the-road parent is likely to do somewhat better in this regard than is the parent who represents either extreme. It is obvious that the clinician concerned with counseling must have access to many possible routes in addition to providing information either verbally or in written form. Counseling, whether done individually or in groups, is most successful when it is custom-crafted to individual measurements. The failure to recognize this is one of the primary sources of clinical failure throughout the helping professions.

Parent Groups

Most professional people working with children and parents agree with Auerbach (2) that parents can learn through discussion. There are many types of parent groups now in existence.

Some groups have been established by the parents themselves who are bound together by a mutual need for comfort, support and assistance. The more successful of these groups have active professional advisory boards and attempt to provide informal, but on-going, education for their members. Some parents who would be reluctant or unwilling to accept personal counseling can be reached at least partially through such organizations. The informal, quasi-social atmosphere of the meetings is less threatening to them than are more personal clinical contacts. Parents who attend these groups may become better informed and, hopefully, more accepting of their own situations. Unfortunately, many parents seem to use the group primarily as a mechanism for venting hostilities or for personal crusade, sometimes ill-conceived and often yielding questionable results.

On the other hand, such parent groups have often been in the vanguard of, and responsible for, important changes in public programming for handicapped children. The right-to-education laws now on the books of many states are undoubtedly the direct result of the activities of the various state associations for retarded children. Contacts with such groups are, in some instances, valuable in preparing parents to take other steps which will involve them more personally in the counseling process.

The use of parent groups is one more approach to counseling that does not simplify the clinician's involvement. In fact, it complicates life because of the necessity to know and work with the parent group being used. Some groups are not clinically useful because of the nature of their programming. Others are organizations of disgruntled parents who have banded together in a kind of a mass denial. They represent parents who require assistance themselves and so are poor adjuncts to clinical programs. Since these groups represent such a wide spectrum of usefulness, the clinician must be sufficiently knowledgeable about them to choose wisely in any given case.

A second type of parent group may be established by a clinician who wishes to find an economical means of orienting a number of parents to a particular problem, or giving them an opportunity to profit and learn from each other's questions and concerns, of using the group therapeutically in both assessing and changing parent attitudes, and of preparing certain of the parents for more individualized counseling at a later date. This plan has frequently been used with some success in speech and hearing clinics where it is possible for the parents to meet with a staff member while their children are in communication therapy. The plan also has been effective in relation to such chronic diseases as cystic fibrosis, hemophilia, leukemia, diabetes, kidney disease and many others.

These groups appear to be most successful when they are broadly-based and are designed to deal generally with parental concerns rather than with narrowly-defined topics. Major disorders in childhood, like childhood problems, are initimately related to all aspects of development and to parent-child attitudes, interactions and transactions. Thus, it is almost never desirable to focus on a single area to the exclusion of other pertinent issues which may have significant influences in the child's environment and, thus, on his illness. It is clear that modes of behavior assumed by the parent in specific situations may be incompatible with his responses in other situations. This leads to discomfort on the part of the parent, confusion for the child, and a weakening rather than a strengthening of parent-child relationships. Thus, it is seldom enough to stimulate a parent to do something unless the

clinician is certain that he can accomplish it consistently and well
in an overall atmosphere conducive to the success of the total
clinical plan. Group counseling designed to encompass general
concerns is one approach. However, under certain circumstances
the clinician may wish to limit the group to parents of children
with similar disorders. For example, parents of blind children
might be managed better in a special group than in a situation
where many different handicaps impose too wide a variety of
special, perhaps unrelated, problems.

A third type of parent group is one run by trained parents such
as that discussed by Irwin and McWilliams (24) where parents
work under the direction of a responsible professional person.
This type of programming is somewhat difficult to manage because, as in the case of parent adjuncts in clinical settings, it
requires using the services of some parents but not of all parents
who wish to be group leaders. This method has been used successfully, however, by having the professionals establish rigid criteria
to which parents, usually mothers, working with parents must
conform.

Criteria for selection of parents who would lead groups were
detailed by Irwin and McWilliams (24). The parent leaders should
have a handicapped child of sufficient age to have undergone the
bulk of his rehabilitative procedures or for the parents to have
come to terms with and accepted the irreversible parts of the condition. They should have had a special training program offered
by staff knowledgeable in the appropriate clinical area and including work in group dynamics. These parent leaders should
also have a good understanding of the problem in general and be
able to see the condition as larger and more variable than their
own child's disorder.

It is this last criterion that is most difficult to meet because it
becomes necessary to hand-pick parent leaders and to say *no* to
those who are still too personally involved to make good leader-
counselors. An example of this is the mother who was trauma-
tized by her feeding experiences with her Pierre-Robin infant and
who could not accept the fact that not all babies with clefts encounter the *same* distressing episodes. She simply could not believe that *any* cleft baby could be fed in less than two hours. Her

reference point in all situations was her own experience, and her own feelings always stood between her and the other parents, even in the training group. She was obviously not ready at the time she wanted to undertake the training. She required much more assistance with her own anxieties. However, she was eventually able to work through her own feelings and then had the potential for excellent leadership. Another mother had not been able to discuss information about her cleft with her own ten-year-old child but had a missionary zeal to *help* other parents. She had to be discouraged.

This kind of counseling cannot be developed without careful thought and without full knowledge of the dilemmas it may create for the professionals involved. On the other hand, properly planned and executed, such programs can be extremely rewarding and can, in a nonthreatening environment, gradually lead anxious parents to accept more specific help in clinically-oriented settings.

Still another type of group that the clinician may wish to use is not so clearly mission-oriented as those previously described but is usually designed to help generally with the problem of parenting. A number of such programs are available in many communities. They run the gamut from adult-education classes such as those discussed by McWilliams (27) that are offered by colleges and universities either on general problems of child rearing or on more specific areas of concern through programs of group discussion (2), parent schools (5) and structured instruction in such things as Gordon's "Parent Effectiveness Training" (22). These approaches represent varied philosophies of working with parents. They appear to have real value for relatively successful parents who are seeking improved methods of handling children's problems and their own that seem to emerge during times of crisis. Parents who seek training programs, often on their own, either are already capable of fairly reasonable insights or recognize their need for help but are still reluctant to risk a clinical encounter. These parents may do all right with a new technique with which they are comfortable and which proves to be more flexible and effective than the old unschooled patterns of behavior. In a few instances, parents who are fearful but, nonetheless, relatively strong and basically insightful are able to use such experiences as stepping stones to other, more personal sources of assistance for their children and themselves.

There are certain parents, however, for whom such approaches actually may be harmful, and the clinician must be alert to them. They are the parents who have no natural insights into their child's behavior or into their own and who are unable to apply a technique successfully because they do not have the love, compassion, understanding and humility that are required. Thus, technique is simply technique. The child winds up the victim as he has always been, and his parent suffers under the delusion that he is using the best in child rearing tactics.

Again, it is clear that an approach to problem solving must be rooted in the personalities of the parents. For example, it would be folly to try to change an authoritarian parent into a permissive one even if permissiveness were more acceptable to the clinican. It also may be folly to work permissively with a parent whose whole previous orientation has been authoritarian. Permissiveness may be a goal but probably not a first clinical tool. Parents must be approached and helped in their own terms to become as effective as they are able to be and as open in their expressions of love and acceptance as possible. Tragically, it may also be essential to help them and their children cope when these emotions are missing. A technique is simply not enough to accomplish that.

Regardless of the type of group counseling undertaken, the clinician must remain alert to the characteristics of the parents who will comprise the groups. This sytem of management, while most effective for parents capable of such interaction, may, like all other approaches, be undesirable for parents whose requirements differ either because of their own or their children's differences. In a discussion of child-centered group guidance of parents, Slavson (41) emphasizes this point,

> ... the most important single condition for the success of Child-Centered Group Guidance of Parents is the proper choice of members who can gain from this method. It is my contention, derived from examination and treatment of several thousand patients, that the predominant number of failures in all psychotherapies is largely due to the inflexible application of one

method in a blanket fashion.

Consultation

Thus far, we have been dealing here with counseling as it is carried out by professional people who are not trained primarily as counselors but whose clinical practice demands that they counsel. This implies that such clinicians will be able to recognize those areas in which they ought not to offer even the first word of specific advice, but often this is not the case. It is an unwise pediatrician who provides educational guidance in the absence of test data and knowledge about a particular school program. Equally naive is the belief that it is possible to tell by looking that a child is or is not mentally retarded, learning disabled or emotionally disturbed, and that treatment of both parents and child can be based on such a verdict.

Everyone, at one time or another, needs help. The pediatrician may well need to seek out the classroom teacher as a source of assistance and will do so willingly if there is sufficient insight into personal shortcomings in the educational field. In this area, the pediatrician is not the expert and must be willing to accept as equals those who are. By the same token, the classroom teacher may sometimes require guidance that only the pediatrician can provide. The school nurse may require the opinion of the ophthalmologist before sending home a report of normal vision in a child obviously wearing corrective lenses. The psychologist may wish to confer with the language pathologist and audiologist before undertaking a counseling program related to a perhaps erroneous diagnosis of mental retardation. And so it goes — professional interaction is required with no room for petty jealousies or for a pecking order that assumes one profession to be either superior or inferior to another. A team, informal though it may be, emerging as the need dictates, is a viable approach to counseling and may make the best possible resources available to parents and children.

Consultation of this type takes time and patience, but it can be accomplished even by telephone. In complex cases, face-to-face staff conferences may hold the best answer. However, this is not always necessary and, if unwisely used, can be a great and expensive waste of professional time. Used with discretion, the system may result in better understanding among professionals and in more expeditious management of the parents and their child.

Referral to Other Agencies

Beyond what can be accomplished by the clinician working both directly and indirectly with parents, referral to other agencies should be a part of the plan when problems appear to be deeper than the child and the special disabilities. Communities differ in the availability of such helping services, so it is essential for the clinician to be aware of the possibilities in a particular situation. The qualifications of the people to whom referrals will be made must be well-documented, and communication must be established with them on a regular basis. This kind of exchange can help to avoid confusion for parents and assure a unified approach to the child's management. It will also establish at the outset that the clinician making the referral expects to remain in the clinical picture and to participate actively with whatever agency will carry on the major work of counseling.

In certain instances, the referring clinician may, in consultation with the parents, decide that some other source of help should be central to the child's and parents' management. For example, a developmental disabilities clinic might be better able to provide the services required for a multiply-handicapped child than would a general pediatrician. A cleft palate center might be better equipped to provide an integrated management program than would a plastic surgeon functioning independently. A deaf child and the involved parents might be more totally served in a comprehensive audiological-otological setting than by an otologist who would have to make referrals for all sorts of special needs including educational planning. In these instances the referring clinician might either bow out of the case or play a role secondary to that of the agency accepting the referral. The decision is based upon an objective appraisal of the requirements of the situation and a decision as to how clinical responsibilities can best be met. The data that influence decisions will differ from case to case, and so will the conclusions reached. For example, a pediatrician may have served a major function when parents have been helped to make the decision to accept assistance in a developmental clinic and when they have sought and carried out the first contact. There then may be no real reason for the pediatrician to remain active with the case since the required counseling and direction can be provided in the new setting. On the other hand, if the pediatrician has a special rapport with the family, has a history of assisting them with their other children, or is viewed by the parents as a source of strength when they need it, it might be a crucial tactical error to withdraw totally even though, with this particular problem, there will be a reduction in activity and involvement.

Again, referral to other sources of help does not always make life simpler for the referring clinician who must be aware of the strengths and weaknesses of community resources and must be able to assess their appropriateness in a given case. This requires as much interaction as often as possible with other agencies and the sharing of observations with them. Some referral sources are valuable and can be counted upon to respond in professional terms to the problems presented to them. Others, unfortunately, are worse than neutrally useless. They are negatively useless, which often means that they have the potential for being destructive. Thus, the clinician who makes referrals should be alert to the nature of the facilities available.

ASSESSMENT OF RESULTS

The clinician who undertakes any form of counseling, regardless of discipline, does so with certain goals in mind. The pediatrician who is counseling a mother about the feeding of a normal baby who is gaining poorly may use as the yardstick of success the baby's reaching and maintaining a normal weight. The ophthalmologist may want the child to wear an eye patch consistently and without emotional upset. The pedodontist may be aiming for a child free of anxiety in the dental chair. The endocrinologist may be striving to develop an environment in which the obese child is both permitted and able to monitor food intake. The neurologist may be concerned with preparing both parents and child for the child's entrance into a developmental class with the gradual loosening of the apron strings that such participation requires. The psychologist may be faced initially with helping parents resolve guilt or denial or both as they come to terms with mental retardation. The speech pathologist or audiologist may be involved with any one or combination of these problems when severe communication disorders are the focus of treatment. The classroom teacher may have the goal of altering parents' attitudes toward homework or grades. Any one of these individuals may be striving to get the parent to accept a referral to a social worker, a psychiatrist, a mental health unit or a child guidance center.

Whatever the profession, whatever the goal, the counselor must decide whether to see the parents once or over a period of time on a regular or irregular basis. Once is probably not enough if the counselor is to determine anything about the effectiveness of the counseling. On the other hand, long-drawn-out encounters that are not resulting in progress or that are out of proportion to the nature and severity of the complaint are probably not much better. The time of both counselor and parent should be effectively used or the treatment plan should be changed to assure the achieving of minimal preliminary goals.

While it is true that there are impossible parents in the world, that some are not sufficiently concerned for their children's welfare to make change likely, and that some are too frightened to become involved, it is also true that clinicians, being human, often explain counseling failures largely in terms of parent failures. During periods of assessment the clinician must be willing to examine both the parents and himself. Inability to *like* a particular parent may result in the inability to establish rapport. A permissive clinician may be unable to deal effectively or sympathetically with a parent who is authoritarian; and the parent may be utterly lost in nondirectiveness. Being unable to respond positively to Blacks or Roman Catholics or WASPS or Jewish people, or poor people or rich people, can be clinically disastrous.

The successful clinician recognizes these personal limitations instead of laying all failures at the doors of parents. It takes a responsible, able, honest clinician to accept such attitudes as resulting in ineffective counseling, to admit failure and to help the parents seek help elsewhere. This is another of the reasons, of course, that anyone who undertakes counseling requires many tools including flexibility, a sense of humor and the ability for personal objectivity. Accepting successes and living with failure can both be difficult for the clinician. However, since the honest assessment of clinical results is an integral part of therapy, it is clear that the counselor must be sturdy enough to admit both success and failure.

The evaluational process that is essential is usually best carried out with the help of parents as well as through observation of the child. The clinician who attempts to make an independent judgment about the achievement of goals may be fooled and only temporarily ego-satisfied. Therefore, access to the perceptions of parents will provide a means of objectifying observations of the child. Counseling is not successful, for instance, if an enuretic child still wets the bed most of the time even though he may have previously wet nightly and if his parents now punish him only most of the time instead of all the time. The goal has not been achieved, but there is minimal movement in the desired direction. That may represent success early in counseling, but it may also suggest failure if too much time is being utilized, if the minimal improvement in bed-wetting has been accompanied by the development of new behavioral problems, or if age is proving to be a more effective therapy than the clinician.

There can be no doubt of the parallel that exists between clinical and scientific processes. Both demand observation, recognition of the problem, definition and execution of a process designed to answer the question or change the existing condition, assessment of resultant data, interpretation of findings and seeking alternative approaches if tested solutions are inadequate. The clinician who is willing to adopt this clinical rigor and apply it in work with parents is almost bound to succeed by one route or another.

SUMMARY

The clinician who deals with children on any level must accept the responsibility for dealing also with their parents. Thus,

62 *Professional Approaches with Parents*

parent counseling in some form is basic to the management of all children whether they be normal or deviant. The clinician may choose from many available alternatives. Hopefully, the requirements of the parents will be more important in the selection of an approach than will be any preconceived or ill-conceived notions of what counseling is or should be. Successful counseling can be carried out in a variety of ways by a variety of people. The trick is to find the best way to help a *particular* parent reach goals that can be stated and assessed and modified over time.

REFERENCES

1. Apgar, V., and Beck, J.: *Is My Baby All Right?* New York, Trident Pr, 1972.
2. Auerbach, A. S.: *Parents Learn Through Discussion.* New York, Wiley, 1968.
3. Barker, R. G.: The social psychology of physical disability. *J Soc Iss, 4*:28-38, 1948.
4. Baruch, D. W.: *New Ways in Discipline.* New York, McGraw, 1949, p. 8.
5. Brocher, T.: Parents' Schools. *Psych Comm, 13*, 2:1-9, 1971.
6. Brutten, M., Richardson, S. O., and Mangel, C.: *Something's Wrong With My Child.* New York, Har-Brace, 1973.
7. Cameron, C. C.: *A Different Drum.* Englewood Cliffs, P-H, 1973.
8. Coffman, E.: *Stigma, Notes on the Management of Spoiled Identity.* Englewood Cliffs, P-H, 1963.
9. Cowen, E. L., Underberg, R. P., and Verillo, R. T.: The development and testing of an attitude to blindness scale. *J Soc Psychol, 48*: 297-304, 1958.
10. Delacato, C. H.: *The Ultimate Stranger, The Autistic Child.* Garden City, Doubleday, 1974.
11. deVries-Kruyt, T.: *A Special Gift: The Story of Jan.* New York, Wyden, 1971.
12. Doman, G.: *What To Do About Your Brain-Injured Child.* Garden City, Doubleday. 1974.
13. Dreikurs, R.: *Coping With Children's Misbehavior.* New York, Hawthorne Books, 1972.
14. Easson, W. M.: *The Dying Child.* Springfield, Thomas, 1970.
15. Eisenberg, L.: *In Pittsburgh Post-Gazette.* May 31, 1974.
16. Engel, M. (Ed.): Studies of children from kindergarten through eighth grade; report of Task Force II, in Joint Commission on Mental Health of Children, *Mental Health: From Infancy Through Adolescence.* New York, Har-Row, 1973, pp. 99-194.
17. Feinstein, A. R.: *Clinical Judgment.* Huntington, Krieger, 1967, p. 28-29.
18. Finnie, N. R.: *Handling the Young Cerebral Palsied Child at Home.* New York, Dutton, 1970.
19. Frazier, C. A.: *Parents' Guide to Allergy in Children.* Garden City,

Doubleday, 1973.

20. French, E. L., and Scott, J. C.: *How You Can Help Your Retarded Child.* Philadelphia, Lippincott, 1967.
21. Freud, S.: *Collected Papers* (5 vols. 3rd ed.). New York, International Psycho-Analytical Pr, 1946.
22. Gordon, T.: *Parent Effectiveness Training.* New York, Wyden, 1972.
23. Hobbs, N.: Sources of gain in psychotherapy. Presidential Address, Div. of Clin. Psych., A.P.A., 1961. Reprinted in E. F. Hammer (Ed.): *Use of Interpretation in Treatment,* New York, Grune, 1968, pp. 13-21.
24. Irwin, E. C., and McWilliams, B. J.: Parents working with parents: The cleft palate program. *Cleft Palate J, 10*:360, 1973.
25. Joseph, S. M.: *Children in Fear.* New York, HR&W, 1974.
26. McDonald, E.: *Bright Promise.* Chicago, National Society for Crippled Children and Adults, Inc., 1959.
27. McWilliams, B. J.: Adult education program for mothers of children with speech handicaps. *J S H D, 24,* 4:408-410, 1959.
28. McWilliams, B. J.: Psychosocial development and modification. *ASHA Report Number 5,* 1970, pp. 165-187.
29. Nichtern, S.: *Helping the Retarded Child.* New York, G & D, 1974.
30. Noland, R. L.: *Counseling Parents of the Mentally Retarded.* Springfield, Thomas, 1970.
31. Noland, R. L.: *Counseling Parents of the Ill and the Handicapped.* Springfield, Thomas, 1971.
32. Noland, R. L.: *Counseling Parents of the Emotionally Disturbed Child.* Springfield, Thomas, 1972.
33. Paradise, J. L., and McWilliams, B. J.: Simplified feeder for infants with cleft palate. *Pediatrics,* 1974 (In press).
34. Rogers, C. R.: *Client-Centered Therapy.* Boston, HM, 1951.
35. Rogers, C. R.: *On Becoming a Person.* Boston, HM, 1961, p. 56.
36. Schwartz, A. H., and Landwirth, J.: Birth defects and the psychological development of the child: Some implications for management. *Conn Med, 32*:457-464, 1968.
37. Shields, D.: *Effects of Clients' Social Class, Race, and Religion as Perceived by Hospital Speech Pathologists.* Doctoral Dissertation, University of Pittsburgh, 1974.
38. Shiller, J. G.: *Childhood Illness.* New York, Stein & Day, 1972.
39. Siegel, E.: *The Exceptional Child Grows Up.* New York, Dutton, 1974.
40. Skinner, B. F.: *Science and Human Behavior.* New York, Macmillan, 1953.
41. Slavson, S. R.: *Child-Centered Group Guidance of Parents.* New York, Int Univs Pr, 1958, pp. 8, 230.
42. Spock, B.: *Raising Children in a Difficult Time.* New York, Norton, 1974, p. 15.
43. Spriestersbach, D. C.: *Psychosocial Aspects of the Cleft Palate Problem.* Iowa City, University of Iowa, 1973.
44. Stewart, M. A., and Olds, S. W.: *Raising a Hyperactive Child.* New York,

Har-Row, 1973.
45. Tisza, V., and Gumpertz, E.: The parents' reaction to the birth and early care of children with cleft palate. *Pediatrics, 30*:86-90, 1962.
46. Travis, L. E.: The psychotherapeutical process. In L. E. Travis (Ed.): *Handbook of Speech Pathology and Audiology.* New York, Appleton-Cent, 1971, pp. 229-242.
47. Ulrich. S.: *Elizabeth.* Ann Arbor, U of Mich Pr, 1972.
48. Wagner, R. E.: *Dyslexia and Your Child.* New York, Har-Row, 1971.
49. Wender, P. H.: *The Hyperactive Child.* New York, Crown, 1973.
50. Wolpe, J.: *The Practice of Behavior Therapy.* New York, Pergamon, 1969.
51. Wylie, H. L., and McWilliams, B.J.: Guidance materials for parents of children with clefts. *Cleft Palate J, 2*:123, 1965.
52. Wylie, H. L., and McWilliams, B. J.: Mental health aspects of cleft palate: A review of literature intended for parents. *A S H A, 8*:31, 1966.

Chapter 3

PSYCHOEDUCATIONAL TREATMENT FOR PARENTS OF AUTISTIC CHILDREN

Nanette L. Doernberg, Mary B. Bernard, and Carol F. Lenz

S TRANGE, elusive, bizarre, inaccessible — these are
the rare children about whom so much has been written and so
little has been understood; these are the children who suffer from
early infantile autism. Nosological and etiological confusion and
disagreement have marked the thirty years since Kanner outlined
the symptoms of what he believed to be a profound abnormality
of social response and described as "extreme autistic aloneness"
in very young children. He concluded his brilliant, seminal paper
with the following words,

> We must then assume that these children have come into the
> world with innate inability to form the usual biologically pro-
> vided affective contact with people, just as other children come
> into the world with innate physical and intellectual handicaps.
> If this assumption is correct, a further study of our children may
> help to furnish concrete criteria regarding the still diffuse no-
> tions about the constitutional components of emotional reac-
> tivity. For here we seem to have pure-culture examples of *inborn
> autistic disturbances of affective contact* (18).

However, perhaps due to the strong influence of psychoanalysis in the field of childhood mental illness at that time, this clear
statement of biological origin was minimized and emphasis and
attention were focused on his conceptualization of parent character and its role in the etiology of autism (14, 34).

Kanner's new volume, *Childhood Psychosis: Initial Studies
and New Insights* (19) bring together his writings on this subject.
One sentence in the paper, "Early Infantile Autism Revisited,"
states, "At no time have I pointed to the parents as the primary
postnatal sources of pathogenecity" (20). In general, his later

articles have pointed more toward a biogenetic etiology and have specifically denied that parents are totally responsible. Rimland (28), in his review of this volume, says, "Kanner repeatedly emphasizes the point made in his very first paper: autism is an *inborn* disorder usually present from the beginning of life, 'refrigerator parents' notwithstanding."

Current theoretical stances range from those which posit primarily psychodynamic etiologies with special emphasis on the quality of mothering (3, 22, 26, 36), to those which hold that autism may result from various combinations of environmental and constitutional factors (15, 29), to those which consider biological causes both necessary and sufficient to account for autism (32, 27, 37, 38, 35).

Some do not believe that autism is truly different from other childhood psychoses,

> On the basis of these observations and deductions, we now consider that childhood psychosis is a syndrome and the clinical subgroups which are mentioned in the literature depend on the age and stage of development of the child at the onset of psychosis, his underlying protoplasmic endowment, and the nature of the interpersonal environment in which he finds himself. In brief, a variety of etiological factors which eventuate in one final common pathway that becomes clinically apparent as a common syndrome of childhood psychosis is more consistent with our experiences than the concept of unique etiology — unique syndrome (24).

Others state strongly that autism has only certain commonalities with schizophrenia, such as abnormal social relationships and withdrawal, but that there are many significant differences between the two (39). Rutter (33) said, "Autism has nothing to do with schizophrenia."

This brief overview is sufficient to indicate that there are still many points of view in the field. Issues of causation and classification have not been resolved. Excellent reviews are available elsewhere (1, 32, 35). It will probably be many years before there is consensus on causation and treatment. Meanwhile, clinical practices continue to be based on this range of theoretical orientations.

This chapter delineates a program for parents of autistic

children from the viewpoint of autism as a constitutionally-based defect which is not a variant of childhood schizophrenia. The focus will be on the implications of this position for clinical practice, using work with parents as a treatment approach to children.

Identification with an organic viewpoint does not negate the importance of the environment, which can do much to exacerbate or ameliorate the original *givens.*

> Of course, the argument that autism is not primarily due to psychogenic factors does not mean that environmental influences are unimportant in the development of autistic children. On the contrary, they are as susceptible as are other children to family and other influences, and it is necessary to use these in treatment (33).

Moreover, with our present state of knowledge and skill, a basic constitutional defect is not susceptible to remediation or correction by direct treatment. To date there have not been significant physiological treatment successes. Psychopharmacological interventions are being intensively explored, but the data await further study (4).

Therefore, it is essential that environmental treatment approaches be developed which deal with the day-to-day problems of autistic children and their families. While we seek further understanding of biological components, we *must* work with the environment. Since parents *are* every young child's principal environment, we work directly with them so that they may become optimum influences for their child's maximum development within the limitations of his constitution.

Behavioral Characteristics of Autistic Children

The children have been described in detail in the literature (5, 6, 7, 8, 9, 10). We use Rutter's delineation of the syndrome,

> In short, infantile autism is a disorder present from early infancy, in which the three cardinal features are: A failure of social development (of a specific type), a deviant and delayed language development, and various ritualistic activities (33).

Aberrations of Social Development

In his description of a failure of social development of a specific type, Rutter specifies the following characteristics:

> Appearance of aloofness and distance and apparent lack of interest in other people, failure to join in group play, the avoidance of eye-to-eye gaze, little variation in facial expression, infrequent exhibition of emotions or humor, and a relative lack of sympathy or empathy for other people (31).

The course of the social-emotional development of autistic children does not follow or parallel the timetable of normal children. Their isolation, remoteness and feeling of separateness distinguish them from all other children and are the qualities most difficult to understand because they cannot be related to our experience with any children of any age.

There is a quality of asynchronism about them. On the one hand they seem infantile in their total dependence, disinhibition and unawareness of environmental expectations; on the other, they lack spontaneity and seem *old*, self-sufficient, sober, rigid and joyless. In this sense they are *no-age* children.

Aberrations of Language Development

In autistic children, language development is often markedly delayed, and frequently there is no expressive language at all. Even minimal understanding of word or gesture is often absent. Ability to understand seems to vary inexplicably from time to time. Often there is no evidence of *inner language*; often they show no ability to associate, categorize or sequence objects, sights, sounds or events.

Some children develop the ability to use a few words or stock phrases or sentences appropriately, but are not able to expand and generalize their repertoire. Some are able to use the expressions they know only in the environment in which the association was originally acquired. They are so concrete that the abstraction inherent in the word is not understood, i.e. a ball is only this red ball, or even more specifically, this red ball in this particular room.

Additional speech and language problems include immediate and delayed echolalia, and repetition of television commercials and other rote-learned material without regard to context. Voice quality is often abnormal — guttural, uninflected, high-pitched, whispering or hollow.

Aberrations of Behavior

Behavioral manifestations include banging or mouthing objects, lining things up or stacking them, twiddling, spinning objects, excessive attachment to useless materials (such as string or a straw), hand-flapping, screeching and finger mannerisms. A need for sameness may be shown by a child's panic reaction to the most trival changes in his environment, such as the change in the position of an object on a table, while at the same time he seems unaware of the presence or absence of his mother and will contentedly go off with a total stranger.

A particularly confusing aspect of autistic children is that some show areas of skill which are significantly out of keeping with their general level of functioning (30, 25, 23). Some do complex puzzles. Others are able to sight-read but without meaning. Some remember details that would be overlooked or forgotten by a normal child of the same age. Some who drink all liquids but milk from a glass will go to the refrigerator, get the milk, warm it up, prepare their bottle and settle down to drink it. Others exhibit memory for complex rote material that is out of keeping with their general inability to connect the past with the present (30).

All in all, although there are differences of opinion as to the cause and treatment of autism, there is general agreement that these children are baffling, confusing and extremely difficult to change no matter what treatment approach is employed.

PROGRAM SETTING

At the Early Childhood Center (ECC) preschool children (2 through 7 years old) who present with extreme emotional, social and behavioral deviation are seen. About ninety children and their families are referred each year for extended evaluation and short-term treatment (from a few weeks to a few months, never more than a year). Many of the children have been diagnosed as autistic.

Although ECC occupies its own small building, it is part of the Children's Evaluation & Rehabilitation Clinic (CERC) of the Rose F. Kennedy Center for Research in Mental Retardation and Human Development, Department of Pediatrics, Albert Einstein College of Medicine, Yeshiva University. Children are referred to the Early Childhood Center by interdisciplinary teams at the clinic after a thorough multidisciplinary work-up has been done.

The staff of sixteen at ECC represents diverse racial, religious, socioeconomic and educational backgrounds. Therapists' training is primarily in early childhood education, child development, psychology or special education. The director is a psychologist with experience in early childhood and special education. Supervisors and psychologists are persons with backgrounds which include speech pathology and occupational therapy as well as special education.

PARENT EDUCATION PROGRAM

In the Parent Education Program (PEP), one of the programs offered at the Early Childhood Center, parents observe a one-hour weekly session during which the therapist works intensively with their child on a highly individualized program. Primary goals of the PEP sessions are to offer parents a model of interaction; to expand each parent's understanding of his own child's functioning; and to offer alternative approaches to training, discipline and teaching at home. Another goal is to teach parents how to become skillful observers and teachers of their own children so that they may offer them the most appropriate home environment possible. Each child's psychoeducational program is continually revised as more is learned about him both from direct observation and interaction, and from his parents. In addition to observing, parents have the opportunity to talk with PEP supervisors and with the director of the center if there is something they would like to discuss. Between weekly sessions there is the opportunity for telephone contact with staff members if the need arises.

One of the goals of PEP is to make appropriate referrals, using the knowledge which has been gained during the families' participation in the program. Another goal is to share what has been learned about the child with the clinic since the staff has an opportunity to observe a child in an ongoing, informal, nontest situation. However, the key concept is to help the children by helping the parents, which, in effect, changes the child's environment.

In addition to observations and weekly individual discussion, parents meet in small groups with the senior author, who knows each child. The purpose of these groups is to generalize weekly experiences, share parental and professional knowledge, and participate in a group interaction in which it is safe for parents to express their feelings about their child and his problems.

The director is a catalyst in the group. It is her role to create a climate in which parents can interact constructively and speak openly and directly with each other. Care is taken to keep the group functioning along agreed-upon lines. Defenses are respected, and focus is on conscious material. If it seems that another type of intervention might be appropriate, parents are referred for psychiatric evaluation.

The leader serves as a source of information about normal and abnormal child development, psychological testing, general child rearing practices and the adaptation of these practices to the special development patterns of these particular children. She uses concrete examples of child behavior to illustrate abstract principles. At the same time, parents are helped to develop a frame of reference for understanding their children. A kind of armature is constructed on which they can build a philosophy and practice of child-rearing, suited both to the needs of their child, and compatible with their feelings and life-style.

SPECIFICS OF WORK WITH PARENTS

Parents of *mentally ill* children are in a unique situation, one which is extraordinarily complex. Not only must they deal with the daily problems of any parent whose child is not normal, but they must also deal with a guilt that has been imposed by themselves and by others (2, 17, 35). The lay literature is replete with references to parents who are inadequate and have been the cause of their children's troubles. The people with whom the parents of an autistic child interact are not likely to be sophisticated enough to question this. Parents of autistic children also have the special problem of living with a difficult child who is nonresponsive to them as people, and who provides little or no feedback, intellectual or affective.

Since the writer is working from the theoretical position of autism as an organic disability, she counsels these parents in much the same way as we would counsel parents of youngsters with other serious and permanent handicaps such as blindness, spina bifida or cerebral palsy. This is not to say that the disabilities are comparable or that the symptoms are in any way similar, but only to emphasize that parents should not be considered responsible for autism any more than they should be considered responsible for these other handicaps.

Disavowing parents' original responsibility as causes of the handicap does not in any way disavow their responsibility to rear their children in the best possible way, nor does it deny that their behavior will influence their child's development. In other words, she works on the principle that within the framework of biological possibility, autistic children can be well or poorly-adjusted, and well or poorly-brought-up, just as their families can be well or poorly-adjusted to the fact and result of the handicap. Therefore, it is entirely reasonable to deal with family patterns which may perpetuate and encourage unacceptable behaviors or fail to teach and develop more desirable ones.

Parents of autistic children are individuals and are subject to the same emotional ills and instabilities that others may suffer. It should be noted that they do not appear to have higher-than-average tendencies to suffer from schizophrenia, unlike the parents of adult schizophrenic patients and of children who develop true schizophrenia in later childhood (38). They *do* appear to have higher-than-average intelligence if true autism is considered and not autistic-like behavior (18, 19). They bear an additional burden both in the home and in the community because of their child's deviance, and especially from people's reaction to it. They need help.

The work with parents has been conceptualized as centering in four core areas. These are restoring esteem, inducing insight, giving information, and guiding and directing.

Restoring Parents' Self-Esteem

All parents of autistic children come to ECC emotionally battered, intellectually confused and physically exhausted. Most have been exposed, implicitly and explicitly, to censure and criticism for their child's disability. They have read the popular press (11) and they have heard that they have consciously or unconsciously been the cause or major contributors to their child's illness. They are unlikely, as are their critics, to have read the less accessible, undramatic scientific studies that bring this position into serious question.

The first thing that this writer does when these parents come to her is to tell them about this body of opinion. She says that she believes that the weight of evidence supports the hypothesis of an organic cause for autism. She assures them that she does not think that they created their child's basic problem although they may be inadvertently contributing to it out of confusion, ignorance, anger and pain.

The writer has tried to make definable and operational the principal of showing respect to parents. She serves them coffee. She tells them that she is sorry that they have to deal with this very painful problem and that she will do her best to help them. She tells them that she sees them as experts on their own children, and that no one has the information about their children that they do. She tells them that she and they must work together if either are to be successful in helping their children. She adds that she does not always interpret the data as they do, but that she will share the exploration of alternative explanations with them.

Before she allows trainees to observe a PEP session, she asks permission of the parents to do so. She also asks the parents' permission to include a professional visitor in their group discussion.

One very angry parent, whose relationships with every agency had been marked by fighting, broken appointments, and general disruption, was astonished when I asked her if it was all right to have an observer in the room. She quickly said, "Yes." Two months later she said to me, "You treat people with dignity here. I feel important. At other places I feel that I am treated like dirt, like I'm not there, or like I'm a specimen to be studied. Here I feel like a person."

The writer listens to parents, really listens. When parents bring their observations to her, it is up to her to put their data together in a way that allows the development of hypotheses about their children's behavior and the ways in which she can help the parents learn to modify it. Some case material can illustrate this point,

Susan Jane was a ninety-pound six-year-old. She was not toilet-trained, nor did she seem to have any receptive language. She had no expressive language. She screamed and bit herself and, when left by herself, she rocked and spit. Her mother, a devoted, conscientious woman with five normal children, found herself completely puzzled by her daughter's behavior.

As we began to know each other, the clinician learned that every time Susan Jane screamed, her mother put some candy in her mouth to comfort her because she felt sorry for her, and it was the only thing she could think of that would make her feel better. Mrs. Cole immediately understood when it was pointed out to her that, by doing this, she was really teaching Susan Jane to scream. She stopped reinforcing her screaming and it diminished markedly.

One day, while sitting in the clinician's office talking, Mrs. Cole said, "I don't understand Susan Jane. She will only *eat* Shopwell and Gristede ads, but she does not *eat* A & P or Grand Union ads." This statement is so bizarre that it is difficult to take seriously. Susan Jane's mother seemed to be a stable, reality-oriented woman, so the clinician listened to what she said and tried to figure out what it might mean.

The conversation was reported to the child's PEP therapist, and together they puzzled over its possible significance. Susan Jane had shown no interest in any materials of any kind, but they had noticed that when she came into the office, she stopped screaming and rocking and intently studied the bulletin board, which had no pictures on it. Her mother's statement and the clinician's and therapist's stored observation together led them to wonder if Susan Jane had somehow learned to discriminate printed material.

Before the next PEP session the therapist brought pictures of everyday objects and the printed words which identified them on separate cards. She offered them to Susan Jane, who immediately matched the first three. During that one-hour period, Susan Jane matched sixty pictures with the appropriate labels while her mother, her therapist and the clinician watched with astonishment. It would never have occurred to any of them that this primitive child had such a skill.

It is not being suggested that this showed a high level of cognitive ability, but it did give the clue that this child needed help to develop very basic communication. Her mother was asked to print the family word for toilet on a piece of plastic (since the youngster ate paper) and to take Susan Jane to the toilet with the piece of plastic. Within a very short time she learned to get the plastic to take to her mother when she needed to go to the bathroom, and she became toilet-trained. Other signs for needed objects were added to her vocabulary. Her frustrations diminished, and her screaming ceased.

Thereafter, Susan Jane spent two years in a class for seriously disturbed children where she accepted the group structure. She subsequently went to a class for retarded children where she participated well. She is able to live at home, and her family sees her as a pleasant member. They are realistic about her ability, and do not assume that this strange, splinter skill indicated other hidden talents.

This case is presented to emphasize the importance of listening to parents and trying to decipher the meaning of their comments, no matter how strange they may sound.

By sharing thoughts and findings with parents, the writer indicates that she is not trying to preempt their children by withholding, editing or revising information to which she believes they should have access because it pertains to their children. One of the most frequently-heard objections to past professional services is that parents feel they have been treated as though they were stupid and incapable of understanding the situation.

In this same vein, she tells parents that she will show them the written reports on their child, and she does so. She recognizes that these reports may be subject to misunderstanding or misinterpretation. She is alert to possible confusion, and she translates anything that may be unclear. She monitors herself so that she may be aware of how she sounds to parents, and she tries always to hear herself from their vantage point, keeping in mind their background and style of verbal expression.

An enlightening example of possible misunderstanding occurred in an interview with a child's pediatrician, his parents and the senior author,

> A four-year-old classically autistic child and his family had been in the PEP program for nine months. His mother and father had gained considerable understanding of their child's developmental pattern and were very tentatively beginning to recognize his retardation. The pediatrician began the conversation by saying, "During these last few months, we have learned more about Chester. We now know that there is much he really does not understand and much he really cannot do, and he is beginning to look like he is retarded as well as autistic."
>
> I sensed a stiffening in both parents, who were very proud of their child's handsome appearance. I interrupted the pediatrician and asked him to explain what he meant by saying Chester "is beginning to look like he is retarded."
>
> The pediatrician, of course, was using "looks" as a synonym for "seems;" but Chester's parents interpreted it as a reference to their child's appearance. Had this not been clarified at the time, the rest of what we said might have been discounted or rejected. Chester's parents would have accurately denied that their child appeared retarded and would have had doubts about the rest of what was said.

If something in the report is not understandable, the writer urges parents to point it out and ask questions. In his own reports he refrains from using professional jargon which is not useful in true communication with laymen.

She suggests that it is up to her to offer a useful program, and that if parents do not find this one to be helpful, she does not think that they should waste their time by coming. She does say that, if they do elect to participate, she expects regular attendance since she has learned that without the parents' cooperation, she cannot have an effective program. She expects parents to telephone any time they are not able to come to a session or a parent group meeting. If they do not call, she calls them. Sometimes this is perceived to be intrusive and is met with irritation or outright anger. Frequently, when the writer has called to ask why parents have not attended a meeting, she has been scolded and told that she did not understand how complicated their lives were. Although she has always agreed with this statement, she has persisted in expecting their attendance and in *chasing* them.

Ultimately, in every case this outreach approach has seemed to assure parents that they are really valuable and that the staff at ECC is interested enough to pursue them. A high value is placed on their time and that of the staff by telling the parents that they should not come if the staff does not prove itself to be useful, but also by saying that it cannot afford to reserve time for them if they will not make use of it. Occasionally, parents are asked point-blank if they would like to discontinue the program and are told again that this is completely their decision to make. This direct and outspoken interaction often is successful with parents who have consistently failed to keep appointments at other agencies.

In her discussions with parents, the writer tries to start where they are. When she and the parents first meet, she asks them a number of open-ended questions. These questions encourage expression of both their realistic expectations and their most optimistic wishes. She asks them to identify and describe the behavior that annoys, irritates or angers them most, and that they would like her to try and help them change. The writer also asks a *magic wand* question which encourages their expression of nonreality-bound wishes. Usually when she says, "If we had a magic wand, which we most certainly do *not*, where would you like us to wave it?" The answer is, "If you could only teach him to talk." This response usually indicates a limited understanding of the overall situation. These two types of questions very often give us both a practical starting point and an idea of the parents' perception of the extent of the child's disability.

One of the most dramatic and unlikely examples of how it helps *to start where the parents are* occurred as follows:

A mother came to the program holding a screaming little boy

in each hand. In addition, she had a shopping bag full of diapers, and a shopping bag which contained a toilet seat, since
one boy was not toilet-trained and the other could only perform
on *his* seat.

After the staff member took the children in for their evaluation and their mother and the clinician sat down to talk, she
asked her how she could help her. She responded immediately,
"If they would only drink something besides apple juice for
breakfast."

Why did this mother choose such a trivial matter to bring up
first when it was so obvious that there were major problems with
each of her children? There were many possibilities. It may have
been that she was so embarrassed by her children's behavior at the
moment that she wanted to present them as being more normal at
home and present their problems as being very insignificant. It
may have been that she was testing the clinician to see if she would
take her seriously. It may have been that her total situation was so
overwhelming that she was only able to extract a detail as a starting point for her discussion. It may have been that the mechanism
of denial was so strong that she was truly unaware of the enormity
of the problem.

In any case, they started with apple juice. The staff was able to
guide and support her through this change as a result of which
she was reassured that she would be treated with respect and that
she was indeed capable of changing her children's behavior in
some way, no matter how small. From apple juice they pro-
ceeded to toilet-training and to intervention with the continuous screaming.

It should be added that this was one of the very few parents
with whom the staff had worked over the last ten years who was
psychotic. She had multiple hospitalizations during the period
of time they worked with her. Despite this serious instability,
she was able to make use of the intervention and was able to
change her own behavior with her children significantly, which
enabled their behavior to be modified.

Both children were diagnosed autistic and were classic examples. The older one *read* any printed material and quoted verba-
tim entire newscasts. The younger one had no speech, avoided
eye contact, had many established complex rituals, and was
totally unresponsive to people.

The Professional's Realm of Interaction

When meeting with parents in groups, the writer introduces the subject of professional feelings and professional limitations. She explains that she rarely, if ever, can make things all right, but that she can usually help parents to improve matters by working closely with them. She introduces what is often a brand new, startling idea — the idea that professionals who work with these youngsters experience, although to a lesser degree, the same confusion, frustration and sometimes anger that parents live with intimately. She tries to dispel the myth of professional omniscience and omnipotence.

Much about autism is unclear, and one must function in a condition which presents a high degree of uncertainty and ambiguity. The writer urges parents not to try and force professionals into premature, often inaccurate predictions or, alternatively, unrealistic optimism and minimization of the severity of the problem by demanding answers when none can be given at the time. She tries to make herself more personal and less remote, more available for parents to identify with her.

Parents have come to the clinician because of concern about their special child. This writer does not feel that this gives her the right to inject herself into all areas of their personal life. However, she does not feel that her responsibility would be fulfilled if she were to focus on the child's needs alone. She has defined the area of proper interaction with parents as that which touches on their relationship with their child and how that relationship affects the rest of their life.

Frequently, she finds that issues over child management are central to a marital problem,

> One vivid example of this was when a four-and-a-half-year old's parents came in together with their child, Robert, but sat rigidly with their backs to each other while they discussed him, and referred to each other only in the third person.
>
> Robert's behavior was symbolic for each of them, but each was interpreting the other parent's reaction to his behavior in terms of its meaning to himself. For example, Robert spent a great deal of time jumping on his father's bed. Robert's mother

felt that this was one of the few things that he enjoyed, and therefore he should be allowed to do it. Robert's father was angry and felt that Robert's mother was showing lack of respect for him when she allowed their child to do this.

In further discussion, it developed that Robert's father had not had his own bed as a child, and that this symbolized to him his dignity as a man. He had never expressed this to his wife, or possibly even to himself. When she understood this, she agreed that it was important that the child not be allowed to continue this behavior. She was eager to be given ideas which would help her manage the problem. The marital relationship improved considerably as a result of the changes in Robert's behavior.

It is stressed here that it is not appropriate, necessary or desirable that parents submerge their interests or those of the rest of the family for the questionable benefit to their autistic child. It is emphasized that the normal siblings should not, in effect, be penalized for being normal by losing their right to their share of their parents' attention and their right to their proportion of family concern and accommodation. Parents should be assisted in creating a climate in which their normal children are encouraged to express anger, fear and embarrassment about their autistic sibling. Not only are the normal children helped by these parental changes, but when parents give their children permission to express negative feelings about the special child, they also give it to themselves in a sense. This is especially true when the parents are partially denying their own ambivalent feelings or acknowledging their anger but feeling very guilty about it. When they are urged to encourage their children to speak out, their anger is sanctioned more forcefully than by just telling them that it is natural.

Parents are often unaware of how difficult it is to be the normal sibling of an autistic child. Consider the following example:

Jerry, a beautiful, blond six-year-old boy, had two exceptionally-attractive, well-mannered brothers, eight and ten years old. They spoke of Jerry with affection and understanding, even when he ripped up their school work and interfered with their social plans.

The clinician remarked to Jerry's father that the older boys must get so furious at times, that they wished Jerry were not a member of their family, and that it must be difficult for them to always maintain control. Mr. H. looked surprised and disbelieving. He said, "Oh, no, they never get angry at Jerry. They love him. We all love him." The clinician suggested that, as he and his wife well knew, love and anger were not mutually exclusive. The conversation continued without further reference to the older boys.

About a month later, Mr. H. came in the clinician's office and said, "I want to tell you something. Once a week we have a family round table, when we talk about anything we feel like, especially things that are troubling us. Last week, I said to the older boys, 'You know, sometimes Mom and I get so angry at Jerry, even though we know that he can't help himself, that we really feel like killing him.' There was total silence, and then Bobby said, 'We feel that way sometimes, too, but we thought that we were wicked.' And then they burst into tears."

Parents' rights to sleep in their own beds, to occasionally leave their child with a responsible sitter and to go out of the house in pursuit of their own recreation, and their right to have a few minutes of privacy in a busy day are emphasized. Often the writer has found that the ECC staff members are the first professionals with whom the parents have come in contact who deal directly with the grinding daily work associated with living with an autistic child and of the necessity of an occasional escape from it.

The staff devotes a great deal of space to this concept of helping in the restoration of parents' self-esteem because they perceive it to be the cornerstone of all of their work. Naturally, parents are very grateful for the help they receive in removing the unbearable burden of guilt, and so they start from this vantage point in their work with parents.

In a sense, the ECC represents a special element of society, one which is trained and experienced with children like theirs, and which, therefore, has a potentially powerful influence on parents' perceptions of themselves. They represent an aspect of society which can approve, support, disagree, limit, guide and redirect when necessary. They have learned that if they are unable to develop a relationship of trust between them, the rest of their work is not likely to be effective. If parents do not feel positive toward this program, they can make only limited use of it and are less able to derive benefits from any aspect of it.

Inducing Insight in Parents

Both in individual conferences and in group meetings, feelings are recognized and discussed. Conscious or nearly-conscious material is dealt with, primarily that which is rather directly related to problems around the child such as home-management, parental difference of opinion about the child's ability and the best way in which to manage him, sibling interactions and difficulties with extended family community. Interaction is deliberately limited to areas appropriate for this group. The ground rules are explained to all group members before the first meeting.

When, as occasionally happens, a group member shows a need for more intensive therapy, the writer suggests this and offers to make the referral. This is usually done when there seems to be potential danger or when the parent recognizes the need for deeper and more intensive therapy, as is frequently the case with prolonged, serious depression.

> Joe's mother presented herself to the clinician by declaring that if she told her there was something wrong with her child, she would bounce her off the wall. She had brought her child to the clinic because of a severe speech delay and other behaviors which she did not understand. Joe was the fourth child in an intact, devoted family. The three older siblings and the mother denied any possibility of major handicap, especially retardation.
>
> As they worked together in the PEP program, and especially as the group began to interact with Joe's mother, father and aunt who frequently came to the meetings, the question of possible retardation was raised. Joe's mother became angrier and angrier and threatened to kill Joe, her other children and herself if he was retarded. At the same time, she began to cry in group meetings, and it was evident that she was beginning to recognize the severity of her child's handicap and was unable to deal with it.
>
> The group was sensitive to her pain, and several spoke of their own feelings of fury and of their concern that they might not be

able to control themselves. The leader suggested that it was not necessary for her to try to deal with her feelings by herself, that more intensive help was available, and that the group felt that she needed it. She accepted a referral for psychiatric counseling.

Giving Information to Parents

It is imperative that more be done than just help parents feel better about themselves and become more aware of their feelings. The writer also considers it her responsibility to share her knowledge with them and to give them information about their children which will ultimately enable them to deal with the total situation more effectively. The following concepts are frequently difficult for parents to deal with and require sensitive exploration and discussion.

AUTISM AND NORMAL DEVELOPMENT. One of these areas of confusion is the relation of atypical development to normal development. As a rule, the focus has been so intensively on a child's abnormality that it is almost forgotten that he is more like other children than unlike them, no matter how strange he may be. Most parents understand something about normal child development out of their own experience, but fail to relate what they know to this particular, different child. When parents begin to think about behavior on the basis of developmental levels instead of chronological age, much of it becomes more understandable, less threatening and easier to handle. They are asked to try to forget their child's calendar age for a moment and judge his age according to how he behaves. Often, they themselves recognize that he does not act as old as his considerably younger sibling. This helps put things into perspective for them.

AUTISM AND MENTAL RETARDATION. This conceptualization inevitably leads to a consideration of the relation of autism to mental retardation. Much of the literature suggests or states that autistic children are of normal or superior intelligence or potential. Parents often have the impression that when the autism is removed, a normal child will emerge. However, there is ample evidence in the literature to indicate that many, if not most, autistic children are retarded (30).

Retardation is a difficult concept for a parent to consider, even when his child is stigmatized and when the etiology is clear, such as it is with Down's Syndrome for example. Autistic children who are also retarded are usually normal in appearance and often exceptionally attractive. In addition, they do some "bright" things (30, 17, 11) which makes it even more difficult for parents to think in terms of retardation.

Often, parents have the impression that autism and mental retardation are mutually exclusive. If they believe that their autistic children definitely are intellectually normal, they may become baffled and angry when they think the child can understand and perform on a much higher level but that he will not. Many parents have angrily rejected the suggestion that their child does not really understand what they want of him or that he is unable to do it. They favor the ultimately more optimistic position that he is just phenomenally stubborn. Most parents find it easier to live with the idea of a stubborn child than a defective one since stubbornness may be amenable to disciplinary intervention.

> Eric was an attractive, alert-looking, four-year-old boy. He was the only child of young, immature, anxious parents who denied any serious problem but did acknowledge that he was difficult to manage and that his speech was not normal.
>
> Neither parent seemed to be familiar with children or to know anything about child development or child rearing. They seized avidly any information or advice they heard from relatives or friends. They constantly compared Eric's present behavior to their own past difficulties, pointing out that they outgrew them and that they were now normal. They confabulated and fabricated "expert" opinions which they said had assured them that they had a normal child. They constantly referred to the smart things Eric "came out with" at home, and to his bright, intense look which he had had from infancy and which his pediatrician said indicated superior intelligence. His parents saw Eric as deliberately withholding and refusing to perform.
>
> In fact, Eric, at four and one-half years, was functioning at about a two-year level in all areas except speech, which was at a lower age level. He had no expressive language and understood only a few concrete commands.
>
> Very gradually, with much painful effort on everyone's part,

Eric's parents began to understand the concept of retardation. They and many parents had thought that retarded children could do nothing and learn nothing and would forever be at their present level of behavior. Their own observation belied this. As it was explained what retardation meant, they were able to come to terms with it and were able to accept the result of formal testing which confirmed the clinical impression and their own judgment of their child's developmental level.

The American Association on Mental Deficiency's definition of retardation, which makes no etiological nor prognostic statement, is explained. It is descriptive only (16). It is stated that IQ scores have been found to be stable and reliable indices of future functioning in the majority of cases (21). Intelligence testing and how it is done are discussed. Standardization is explained in response to parents' frequent statements that their children are different in a test situation than they are at home.

AUTISM AND DEVELOPMENTAL LEVELS. In connection with the concepts of both normal child development and retarded levels of development, each child's level of functioning is identified in the four key areas of self-help, socialization, communication and preacademic skills. Parents are encouraged to identify their children's levels from their own observations. Often they experience an *Aha* phenomenon when they recognize that their autistic child is functioning on a considerably younger level than a younger sibling.

It has been learned that when parents have a more realistic level of expectation for their child's functioning, they are able to adapt their interaction more suitably. They can then make more realistic and fulfillable demands, help their child to respond to their more appropriate stimulation and affection, see their child achieve some success, feel approval for the child and for themselves, and endure less frustration in their day-to-day experience.

Parents are encouraged to offer their children a great deal of physical contact and simple affectionate interaction of an intrusive nature. It is explained that the child is not able to make the link to the parent, and that the parent must dramatize and extend his wish to relate to the child. Often, parents are afraid of infantilizing their children and are trying to relate to them as they would to another child of his age. This may be done in an effort to convince themselves that the child really is like another child of that age. Of course, it is not possible to develop a relationship in this fashion. To be meaningful, an interaction must be developmentally appropriate.

It is understandably difficult for parents to interact with a big four, six or eight-year-old in a way that would be more usual for a toddler, and they need a lot of reassurance and support to be able to do this comfortably. Lap-sitting and cuddling do not seem natural at these ages, and it is especially difficult for the parents because physical contact with them is often avoided or rejected by the youngster. Parents need to know that they are not hurting their child by encouraging it.

Parents must be taught how to teach their children appropriate skills. First, the skills to be taught must be identified, and then they must be analyzed into small, discrete increments and built step-by-step. It is essential to determine whether the child is developmentally ready to learn a given skill.

A five-year-old boy, the son of two physicians, was wearing diapers and seemed to have no understanding of the use of the toilet. He was dry for several hours at a time. When he would wet himself, he would go to the dresser drawer, get his own clean diaper and bring it to his mother or to the housekeeper and posture himself so that he could be changed easily. In discussion with his parents, they didn't think that he could ever be toilet-trained, and neither of them felt they could take time from their busy practices to spend what they considered sufficient time to accomplish this. Felix had indicated that he had sphincter and muscle control and that he had sufficient understanding to know when he was wet.

We suggested the following: let diapers be eliminated since they are a license and expectation to wet; keep the child in dry training pants; praise him for performance; and change but do not scold him when wet; put him on the toilet at short, fixed intervals and watch him carefully in between. If he indicated a need to go, he should be taken immediately. Felix's absence of toilet-training was keeping him from inclusion in a nursery school for younger children.

His parents were skeptical but willing to try when told that it would only take a few days of mutual effort to achieve toilet-training. This turned out to be the case, and the implications were far-reaching. The child was accepted in the nursery school. His parents began to believe that his behavior could be changed for the better as a result of their thoughtful intervention. They felt more competent and less angry and helpless. They became more alert to other areas that might be susceptible to change. They gained a bit of confidence in professional advice and eliminated a major source of friction between them.

AUTISM AND VARIABILITY. One of the most confusing aspects of these children is their extreme variability. Almost every parent reports that his child can do things at one time and yet cannot or will not do them at another. This variability is particularly confusing in the language area. Parents say that they know their child understands them because he has responded to exactly the same words at other times. Parents also say that they know their child can speak because at other times he has used the appropriate response.

Since the ECC's total approach to parents is based on an organic model of autism, they hypothesize a physiological basis for this variability. The child's ability to perform to that of a flickering light. This analogy is a homely one and may not hold up when more information is available about the neurology of autism, but it is serviceable at this time and easily understood. In other words, sometimes when a light switch is flipped or the stimulus is given, the connection is made and holds firm, and the light or ability to understand and perform is stable. At other times the light goes on and then goes off, and at still other times it continues to flicker and is unstable. Sometimes the variability in their child is more understandable when it is likened to the adult experience of not being able to think of a name that one knows or a word in a second language which he speaks, but not too reliably. It seems that sometimes these children have it all together more than at other times just as parents report, and these differences are greater than those found in a normal child. The idea of a nervous system that does not always deal with stimuli in the same way is understandable to most.

DIRECTING AND GUIDING PARENTS

Parents need direction, they need structure and they need to understand their children's needs for structure. Because of the frequent classification of autism as a mental illness or a form of schizophrenia, there is much confusion about limit-setting and its meaning to the child, especially since there is a significant body of literature that suggests that too many limits and too little loving and giving may have been a major cause of the child's problem. In addition, identification of autism as a syndrome came at about the same time as the trend toward more permissive child rearing. Parents who really believe in greater freedom and range for their children and themselves find themselves dealing with children who cannot tolerate this freedom, and who panic and are unable to make choices. Parents need help in recognizing that their autistic child's needs for direction are not the same as the needs of other children. They also need help in interpreting these differences to their normal children and to people in the community.

Parents respond to concrete direction and suggestions for structuring their children's lives. For example, it is not at all uncommon to learn that the autistic child is sleeping in his parents' or his sibling's bed. It is also not at all uncommon to learn that when he goes to bed he insists that the whole household go to bed with him. Inadvertently, and with good intentions, parents have allowed their children to tyrannize the household. What is intended as a kindness to the child turns out to be more of a confusion. Another problem in this area is tantrum behavior. Many parents say that they cannot bear to hear their child scream so they will give him anything to solace him.

One parent said, when asked why her son, Maurice, slept in her bed, "I love him so much and there is so little he can do that I can't deny him anything." A different point of view was suggested — that because she loved her child, she wanted to help him as much as she could to live in a world with other people. In order to do this she had to establish certain guidelines for him and help him learn that he must follow them. One of these was to sleep in his own bed; another was to eat from his own plate instead of running around the table and snatching food from everyone, which made him most unwelcome. As a general principle, socially unacceptable behavior that is not redirected or stopped will limit the child unnecessarily. Ultimately, the greater kindness is to teach the child a new pattern, and parents need support and guidance in order to be able to do this.

The writer does not believe in hurting a child at any time. Most parents have already discovered that hitting is ineffective and only increases tension and guilt. They often feel that they *should* be hitting their child to teach him somehow to be more like other children and are derelict in their duty if they do not do this. It is enormously helpful to them to be told that the most effective way to eliminate unwanted behavior is to ignore it totally.

Parents are taught the principle of extinction, especially in dealing with tantrum behavior. This is suggested only when tantrums are clearly related to an identifiable environmental situation such as not being allowed to take out the contents of all the dresser drawers and strew them around the house. It is emphasized that it is inappropriate and even cruel to ignore crying that is caused by the child's pain, fright or illness. It is desirable that a child seek and receive attention and comfort under these circumstances, and his efforts to contact another human being at such times are to be encouraged. The clinician should make certain that parents understand the distinction between this kind of behavior and that which is caused by the child's inability to understand and accept reasonable behavioral limits. Ultimately, it is kinder to the child if the parents help him learn that tantrum behavior is an ineffective way of gaining his objective since such behavior will not be tolerated by others.

The child's variability and instability make it especially important that expectations are appropriate, consistent, clearly-defined and presented in such a way that they can be understood by the child. For example, this means that parents cannot say no in a gentle voice with a smile, but must look and sound stern if the word is to acquire meaning for the child. These youngsters are not sensitive to environmental cues, especially human ones, and emphasis is necessary.

Parents need information about community services. One of the goals at ECC is that they leave the program with a greater ability to be good consumers of services for their children and themselves; parents should know which organizations can help them, which legislators are familiar with the problem and will take action, which school programs are available. They are urged to speak out, to stimulate the development of services, and to join parent groups which are trying to alert the public to the problem.

SUMMARY

In short, by working with the motivations, strengths and skills of parents, the children are helped. Parents are the major influences in their child's environment. In the overwhelming number of cases, preschool autistic children will spend most of their time at home, and it is in the home that they have the greatest opportunity to get the direction and love they need to grow as fully as possible.

Throughout this chapter, the writer has stressed interaction with parents, and tried to put into words some of the feelings which she believes must be the bedrock of any effective parents intervention. She has not continually pointed out the need for a warm and concerned household because this seems to be axiomatic. By working with parents from the standpoint of mutuality rather than treatment, one functions as friendly, supportive professional with whom they can identify and to whom they can turn for an open exchange of opinion and information, expert advice and an affective response to their difficulties.

During the past eight years the program presented here has been offered to several hundred families. Results have demonstrated that there are measureable changes in both children and families as a result of this limited psychoeducational intervention (12). The writer recognizes that she is working with a self-selected group — namely those families who can and will become involved in this program. She knows that the program is not equally effective in helping all families; she also realizes that the service is useful in different ways to different families.

The basic position from which it works — namely that these children are biologically impaired, not maltreated or insufficiently loved — is one that is antithetical to many clinicians. It is obvious that this position is most acceptable to parents, and just the statement of it can do much to establish the beginnings of a good relationship. This treatment approach is presented here with the hope that it will serve to stimulate thinking and encourage the development of interventions which will enhance the functioning of autistic children and alleviate the suffering of their parents.

REFERENCES

1. Bender, L.: The nature of childhood psychosis. In Howells, J. (Ed.): *Modern Perspectives in International Child Psychiatry.* New York, Brunner-Mazel, 1971, pp. 649-678.
2. Berlin, I. M., and Szurek, S. A.: Parental blame: An obstacle in psychotherapeutic work with schizophrenic children and their families. In Szurek, A. and Berlin, I. M. (Eds.): *Clinical Studies in Childhood Psychoses.* New York, Brunner-Mazel, 1973, pp. 115-126.
3. Bettelheim, B.: *Love is Not Enough.* Glencoe, Free Pr, 1950.
4. Connel, P. H.: Medical treatment. In Wing, J. K. (Ed.): *Early Childhood Autism:Clinical, Educational and Social Aspects.* London, Pergamon, 1966, pp. 101-111.
5. Creak, M.: Psychoses in childhood. *J Ment Sci, 97:*545-554, 1951.
6. Creak, M.: Schizophrenia syndrome in childhood. Progress report of working party. *Cerebral Palsy Bull, 3:*501,1961.
7. Creak, M.: Juvenile psychosis and mental deficiency. In Richards, B. W. (Ed.): *Proc London Conf Sci Stud Ment Def.* Dagenham, May and Baker, 1962.
8. Creak, M.: Childhood psychosis: A review of 100 cases. *Br J Psychol, 109:*84-89, 1962.
9. Creak, M.: Schizophrenia in early childhood. *Acta Paedophsychiatr, 30:*42-47, 1963.
10. Creak, M.: Schizophrenia syndrome in childhood. Further progress report of working party. *Dev Med Child Neurol, 4:*530-535, 1964.
11. Creak, M.: Diagnostic treatment variations in child psychosis and mental retardation. In Menolascino, F. J. (Ed.): *Psychiatric Approach to Mental Retardation.* New York, Basic, 1970, pp. 140-149.
12. Doernberg, N., *et al.: A Home Training Program for Young Mentally Ill Children.* A Monograph. League School for Seriously Disturbed Children, Brooklyn, New York; Public Health Service Research Grant Number MH 022 4503, The National Institute of Mental Health, 1968.
13. Eberhardy, F.: A view from "the couch." *Child Psychol Psychiatry, 8:* 257-263, 1967.
14. Eisenberg, L.: Introduction. In Rutter, M. (Ed.): *Infantile Autism: Concepts,*

Characteristics and Treatment. London, Churchill Livingston, 1971, pp. 2-5.

15. Goldfarb, W.: Therapeutic management of schizophrenic children. In Howells, J. G. (Ed.): *Modern Perspectives in International Child Psychiatry*. New York, Brunner-Mazel, 1971, pp. 685-705.

16. Gross, H. J. (Ed.): *Manual on Terminology and Classification in Mental Retardation*. American Association on Mental Deficiency: Special Publication Series No. 2. Baltimore, Garamond/Pridemark Press, 1973.

17. Hermelin, B.: Recent psychological research. In Wing, J. K. (Ed.): *Early Childhood Autism: Clinical, Educational and Social Aspects*. London, Pergamon, 1966, pp. 159-173.

18. Kanner, L.: Autistic disturbances of affective contact. *Nervous Child, 2*: 217-250, 1943.

19. Kanner, L.: *Childhood Psychosis: Initial Studies and New Insights*. Washington, V.H. Winston and Sons, 1973.

20. Kanner, L.: Early infantile autism revisited. In *Childhood Psychosis: Initial Studies and New Insights*. Washington, V.H. Winston and Sons, 1973.

21. Lockyer, L. and Rutter, M.: A five-to-fifteen-year follow-up study of infantile psychosis: III. Psychological aspects. In Chess, S. and Thomas, A. (Eds.): *Annual Progress in Child Psychiatry and Child Development*. New York, Brunner-Mazel, 1970, pp. 445-471.

22. Mahler, M. S.: On child psychoses and schizophrenia: autistic and symbiotic infantile psychosis. In *Psychoanalytic Study of the Child*. New York, Intl Univs Pr, 1952, pp. 286-380.

23. Menolascino, F. J., and Eaton, L.: Psychosis of Childhood: A five year follow-up study of experiences in a mental retardation clinic. In Chess, S. and Thomas A. (Eds.): *Annual Progress in Child Psychiatry and Child Development*. New York, Brunner-Mazel, 1968, pp. 525-539.

24. Menolascino, F. J., and Eaton, L.: The description and classification of infantile autism. In Churchill, D., Alpern, T., and DeMeyers, M. (Eds.): *Infantile Autism*. Springfield, Thomas, 1971, pp. 71-97.

25. Mittler, P.: The psychological assessment of autistic children. In Wing, J. K. (Ed.): *Early Childhood Autism: Clinical, Educational and Social Aspects*. London, Pergamon, 1966, pp. 145-158.

26. Rank, B.: Adaptation of the psychoanalytic technique for the treatment of young children with atypical development. *Am J Orthopsychiatry, 19*: 130-139, 1949.

27. Rimland, B.: The etiology of infantile autism: The problem of biological versus psychological causation. In *Infantile Autism: The Syndrome and its Implications for a Neural Theory of Behavior*. New York, Appleton Cent, 1946, pp. 39-66.

28. Rimland, B.: Review of L. Kanner, *Childhood Psychosis: Initial Studies and New Insights*. *J Autism Child Schizo, 3*: 88-92, 1973.

29. Ruttenberg, B. A.: A psychoanalytic understanding of infantile autism and its treatment. In Churchill, D., Alpern, G., and DeMeyers, M. (Eds.):

Infantile Autism. Springfield, Thomas, 1971, pp. 145-184.

30. Rutter, M.: Behavioral and cognitive characteristics of a series of psychotic children. In Wing, J. K. (Ed.): *Early Childhood Autism: Clinical, Educational and Social Aspects.* London, Pergamon, 1966, pp. 51-81.

31. Rutter, M.: The description and classification of infantile autism. In Churchill, D., Alpern, G., and DeMeyers, M. (Eds.): *Infantile Autism.* Springfield, Thomas, 1971, pp. 8-25.

32. Rutter, M., and Bartak, L.: Causes of infantile autism: Some considerations from recent research. *J Autism Child Schizo, 1*: 20-32, 1971.

33. Rutter, M.: Childhood schizophrenia reconsidered. *J Autism Child Schizo, 2*: 315-337, 1972.

34. Schopler, E., and Reichler, R. J.: Psychobiological referents for the treatment of autism. In Churchill, D., Alpern, G., and DeMeyers, M. (Eds.): *Infantile Autism.* Springfield, Thomas, 1971, pp. 243-264.

35. Schopler, E., and Reichler, R. J.: Parents as cotherapists in treatment of psychotic children. *J Autism Child Schizo, 1*: 87-102, 1971.

36. Szurek, S. A.: Psychotic episodes and psychotic maldevelopment. *Am J Orthopsychiatry, 26*: 519, 1956.

37. Wing, J. K.: Diagnosis, epidemiology, aetiology. In Wing, J. K. (Ed.): *Early Childhood Autism: Clinical, Educational and Social Aspects.* London, Pergamon, 1966, pp. 3-49.

38. Wing, L.: *Autistic Children,* New York, Brunner-Mazel, 1972.

39. Wing, L.: What is an autistic child? Reprint in *Newsletter: National Society for Autistic Children.* Metropolitan New York Chapter. *6*: 4, 1972.

Chapter 4

A DEMONSTRATION HOME APPROACH
WITH HEARING IMPAIRED CHILDREN

AUDREY SIMMONS-MARTIN

WHILE educational programs for parents have existed for as long as there are records, the concept that the family is the most powerful educational delivery system in the life of any child, and especially the hearing-impaired infant, is relatively new. Originally, early education programs placed emphasis on parents' increased understanding of their handicapped child and on their performance of certain tasks for the general well-being of the child. Gradually, however, the scope of interest has widened to take in a broader understanding of the parental role.

The infant's capability for assimilating and processing information in his very early years as well as his capabilities for emotional and physiological involvement have been clearly documented. The influence of the early growth and development of an infant on his adult potential are much too important to be ignored. It now is clearly recognized that parents serve to shape these early experiences.

In many ways, the greatest need of a handicapped child is a parent who can understand his problem and adjust to it. He needs parents who, as a result of this understanding, foresee what his needs will be.

Parent involvement is more than *information receiving* in the program at Central Institute for the Deaf. The Parent-Infant Program aims toward increasing parents' understanding and developing their competence in dealing with their children. Of course these goals are to be applied realistically. Parents will gain from involvement in a variety of different ways, depending upon their needs and readiness. The clinician may not be able to bring about drastic changes in the personalities of parents; she may also be unable to effect dramatic changes in certain parents' child care practices which have their roots not only in individual knowledge, but in the parents' own upbringings. However, she must provide parents with greater knowledge of children, of the handicapping condition of their child, and of themselves in order to enable them to alter some of their own practices.

The basic approach in the Parent-Infant Program at Central Institute for the Deaf is to give parents an understanding of their handicapped child and to help them seize every opportunity to further the necessary warm interactions with their infants daily, hourly, in their own homes. Rather than going into the child's home, the parents bring the child to a home demonstration center where they can have meaningful experiences typical of those in their own home.

Just as parents universally help their infants learn to listen, to communicate and to learn, so must the parent of the hearing-impaired child. In order for them to utilize critical moments in their child's life for this very important interaction, it is well to involve the parents in the habilitation process at the earliest possible moment. Unlike many, however, the writer does not believe the child's future is permanently fixed by a particular age of eight, ten or eighteen months. Intervention can be useful at later ages. Rather, the reciprocal and interacting behaviors of the parents can be more easily shaped if they have not had an opportunity to develop undesirable patterns. In this respect the program would like to be a preventive rather than a remedial one.

While the long-range goal of the Parent-Infant Program is for the child to reach the maximum level of which he is capable, the immediate aims are for parents to provide the stimulation necessary for that achievement. At the same time the parents are dealing with the infant's needs as a child, they are also coping with hearing impairment as a handicap. Few if any parents escape the questioning, "Why?" "Why me?" "Why my child?" but it is hoped that they can be moved on to the other questions, "What do I do?" and "How do I do it?"

The interval of time between the asking of the *why* questions to the raising of "What to do?" and "How to do it?" can be shortened, the writer believes, if strong positive guidance is offered the family and the mother in particular. Teacher-counselors stand ready to offer positive suggestions, firm directions and effective models. They tap the child's abilities and give pertinent information. The very moment a parent is ready for affirmative action, the process can begin. The parents' feelings as well as their support have significant bearing on their child's progress. The trauma of having a handicapped child is not quickly resolved.

REACTIONS OF PARENTS

Most parents move through several stages in the acceptance of their child. The person doing the intervening needs to be sensitive to parental feelings and recognize how far in the process of acceptance a family has moved.

Stage I — Shock

Although the parents may have diagnosed the handicap long before the professional evaluation, they nevertheless experience shock when it is confirmed. Every parent wishes for an idealized child who is normal or even superior to himself. If the child is handicapped, the most adjusted parent encounters a crisis reaction. During the period of numbness resulting from the shock, parents tend not to perceive sharply and clearly. They may show a great deal of docility. Lowell (3) reports that at this stage parents retain little if any of the important crucial information given them. The implication is apparent that the teacher, clinician or intervener must provide for much repetition of information. Important points should be written for the parent if possible, and in a form they can read and discuss later.

Stage II — Panic/Bewilderment

Shontz (8) refers to the next stage as panic whereas Schlesinger and Meadows (7) call it bewilderment. Just as the terms imply, parents are confused. They frequently seem unable to plan or to understand the situation. In their panic they may doubt the diagnosis even though it confirmed their own. They frequently seek other opinions, and trouble is compounded when they meet conflicting reports.

While the wish to shop about is understandable, parents should be channeled to competent sources. Where there are divergent management theories, parents should be so advised. At this time, particularly, the intervener should be a counselor. The intervener should be one who listens wisely and guides with honesty. The counselor is accepting of the parents' dilemma and at the same time able to state facts in objective terms from which parents can glean the important information. Remembering that parents' emotional factors may interfere with their understanding, the counselor clearly and comfortably leads the discussions about hearing loss and ways people can assist. The face-up-to-it approach must be avoided because it will only result in parental defensiveness and rejection.

Stage III — Retreat

When the situation becomes overwhelming it is natural to want to escape, so the stage of retreat or denial follows. Parents may even overtly reject the child at this time and seek custodial or daily programs which will relieve them of their responsibility. They seem unable to follow suggestions that they are given. They want someone else to do everything. At this point parents may say, "You teach him," along with "I don't know how," or "I don't have time." Other terms of avoidance are common. Interveners certainly must not stand ready to assume the teaching job, however great the pressure.

Parents in this stage are often so caught up in their own emotional needs that they are unable to focus on ways to help their child. They may deny the handicapping condition and report numerous examples of how the child heard or how he talked if the handicap is deafness. Obvious denial of the handicap and any of the procedures relative to it, e.g. a hearing aid or distinct speech patterns for easy lipreading, might be rejected. At this stage the intervener is wise to be an interested listener who talks about the child rather than the handicap. The intervener should utilize this stage to talk knowledgeably about the universal parental role. Such discussions can be supplemented with films, slides or books which focus on parents' roles with children. Discussions on the role of parenting are most appropriate.

Stage IV — Realistic Expectations

At this stage, parents are able to achieve realistic expectations and give appropriate help to their child, but with acceptance comes sorrow. Many parents report it is as if "they had just buried a friend." It is probably true mourning for the child who might have been. Now parents are ready to roll up their sleeves and plunge into the task of parenting. Even though the intervener may have been ready to initiate educational techniques earlier, the time was better spent in frank discussion with parents tempered with acceptance and warmth.

At the stage of realistic expectations, parents will quickly and eagerly learn techniques. Lots of positive reinforcement for the parents and lots of opportunities to demonstrate growth are in order.

It should be noted that all parents do not follow the same sequence of feelings nor go through all stages. Some parents may be on their way to accepting the handicapped child, but this does not mean that they have overcome their own personality conflicts. They may still be bitter, guilty, anxious or sad. They may scapegoat each other, the doctor, the circumstances or even the agency rendering service, which is a natural target in the parents' search for blame.

Not to be overlooked is the fact that parents' vulnerability to scapegoating may lie in the unknown cause of their child's handicap. Even with acceptance there are parents whose expectations are too high and others whose are too low. Michaels and Schucman (4) describe mothers who not only accept the child's handicap, but appear to approve of it. These low-expectancy parents view the child's dependency as giving meaning to their own lives. Their efforts are bent toward discouraging the child's acquisition of self-sufficiency. The unhappy consequence of the high-expectancy parent is the child's inability to please him. Repeated exposure to failure and parental disapproval have serious effects on the child's emotional stability. It is extremely important that those parents be reassured that progress can be made. They need to see others who have progressed and to have frank discussions with the parents of achieving older children.

Some of these parents are guilt-prone. They continue to view the handicapped child as a symbolic punishment for real or imagined wrong-doing or even wrong-thinking. The parents may have not wanted that child or considered not having it. In general, the heavy burden of guilt carried by parents seems to be tied to an assumption that they somehow are always responsible for what has happened to their child. It is interesting that parents who feel relatively certain that their child's condition was caused by rubella or who have adopted their child do not describe the intense feelings of guilt as do the others.

It is quite common, too, to see another much-favored defensive mechanism. This is the almost obsessive overprotection used by parents of handicapped children. Whether it springs from a parents's deep unconscious need for absolute dependency of the child upon them or from their own guilt feelings, it must nevertheless be dealt with before the child can mature.

Often father and mother are not at the same stage or experiencing the same feelings simultaneously, so the problem for the intervener is compounded. The important point is that the intervener should try to assess the feelings of both parents and be sensitive to the presence of these feelings.

THE FAMILY

The total family milieu may be of such a nature as to alter entirely the paternal or maternal attitude toward any individual child. Sickness of the mother or of the family members or economic crisis within the family setting naturally put strain on the parents' attitudes. If these crises are brought on because the child is handicapped, certainly relations can be affected.

Importantly, in the family setting there are siblings who need consideration and inclusion in the total picture. A series of studies relating to this problem in regard to retarded children in the family has been done by Farber (1). He found greater adverse conditions resulting from a high degree of dependency and from superordinate roles eventually assumed by the normal siblings, irrespective of the handicapped child's place in the family sequence. The handicapping condition affected not only the parents but the entire family as well.

Some parents may deprive the rest of the family while they spend an inordinate amount of time with the handicapped child. This danger exists even when parents are truly involved in trying to aid the child. Family participation might provide the appropriate balance.

The number of children and the handicapped child's rank in the family also affect parents' relation with the siblings and the child. A handicapped child who is the oldest can receive more of the mother's time than one who is the youngest of a large family. Research findings are just becoming available regarding mother-child interaction patterns in a home setting rather than in a laboratory. Rosenberg (6) and others have found that mothers of firstborn infants interact significantly more often with their infants than mothers of several children. Documentation of the early *enrichment* environment of firstborns is particularly interesting in that the intellectual advantages of the firstborn and only children have been reported frequently. Quality of parenting is an area in which White (10) recently has been reporting, and it is that with which the teacher in the family of a handicapped child is concerned.

Families of handicapped children nevertheless are, first of all, families and thus have feelings similar to those of any family. In other words, parents and siblings of the handicapped have the needs, hopes, desires, wants and frustrations of all families as well as unique attitudes because of the handicap. Therefore, all parents and families cannot be treated alike any more than all handicapped children can be treated alike. In order to involve parents in the process of educating their handicapped child, a variety of techniques, activities and approaches designed to meet their individual needs have to be utilized.

Unfortunately, many parents do not possess information and understanding as to the importance of early stages of learning, nor do they understand the need for sensory stimulation for deaf children. Frequently parents lack knowledge of child development, are not informed about behavior management, and do not understand the handicapping condition nor how to ameliorate its effects. Certainly there are few who are aware of ways language is acquired and the parents' role in its acquisition. Contrary to the notion that parenting is instinctive, evidence is accumulating that it is learned.

Because of the variables, each family group needs to be considered as an individual group for a large part of the intervention. Not only do parents have individual needs that must be recognized, but the identification of the handicap may occur at any time. There can be no waiting until the child is six months or six years. The parents need help *immediately*. The task of the intervener is to enter into the parent-child transaction to modify the naturally-occurring dynamics and produce the necessary change.

PARENT-INFANT PROGRAM

Since 1958, there has been a program for parents of deaf infants at Central Institute for the Deaf in St. Louis, Missouri. Over that period of time, procedural changes have been made, but the goal for each child, that he attain his maximum capability, has remained constant.

Originally, parents came together to receive information and directly intervened with the child himself. It became clear that parents needed such information, but it also became clear that they needed to know how to shape their child's behavior. Rather than being observers, as they were earlier, the parents' role has shifted to that of dynamic participators. They focus on their roles as managers of their child's behavior, shapers of his language development and sources of cognitive and sensory stimulation.

Individual Conferences

With infants there could be no formal teaching situations, so a natural approach was adopted. All parents have many opportunities in their homes, moment-by-moment, for shaping language behavior. There is dressing, washing, feeding, playing and cooking. Therefore, the Central Institute for the Deaf initiated the home demonstration center which is housed in an old house converted into two very modest apartments. The rooms are furnished in *Early Desperation* and are far from prestigious. Nevertheless, they are warm, inviting and comfortable. The house has kitchens, living rooms, bedrooms, baths and playrooms. There is an outside yard. All appliances work with some degree of regularity. The refrigerators, while not laden, are adequately full and, similarly, are the cabinets and closets. In short, nothing is contrived.

Into this setting comes the family group — the child, his parents, siblings, grandparents, surrogate parent, etc., for a weekly session with the teacher/counselor or intervener who is a teacher of the deaf. The individual sessions are scheduled for an hour but may extend longer. The parent, usually the mother, engages the child in some activity comparable to their own home activities. During this time, the intervener attempts to help the parent seize every opportunity for language input.

In their own homes, the mothers are teachers in the broadest sense. Therefore, in the home demonstration center, the mother demonstrates how well she is progressing while the intervener comments appropriately. It is obvious that the latter has to be skilled in creating an atmosphere of ease, transforming apprehensiveness into creative energy and helping the parents feel the need for interaction with their child.

Such adult-child interactions provide scanty and unsystematic linguistic data whereby a normal child learns a vocabulary of sounds, words and a complex system of morphology and syntax by three years of age. It is the writer's experience that hearing-impaired children can learn language also, although delayed in time. The task for the parent is to seize every opportunity to structure the appropriate label for the child, importantly the label for what *he*, the child, is *experiencing*.

The features of a home environment are highly perceptual, and those perceptual features have verbal labels associated with them which in turn assist in the storage of both concept and language. If the parent provides the information at the appropriate moment, the child will receive the data whereby he, too, can induce language rules. For example, *pulling* is a concept which has

linguistic form,
  pull the toy
  pull the chair
  pull the shade down
  pull your socks up
  pull your sweater down
  pull the drawer out
  don't pull mommy's hair, etc.
The action is a tugging motion which all of the expressions have in common.

The hypothesis is that the word *pull* experienced in a variety of situations can be more readily learned by the child than the word experienced many times but in only one situation, as for example using *pull* only with pop-it beads. There are some interesting data available which confirm this hypothesis (2).

The appropriateness of the activity is part of the teacher/counselor's direction. Sometimes the task or tasks she has planned for the hour are discussed with the mother prior to her demonstration with her child.

Since the emphasis is upon parents being first-rate parents rather than second-rate teachers, the focus is upon the *process*, not the curriculum. The activities are household tasks, child care and typical daily tasks. Because of the range of experiences as well as the variety of situations and needs presented by the parents and their child, it is evident that the teacher/counselor assumes a variety of roles. These roles include being

1. *A listener* because parents may have no one else with whom they can discuss their concerns about their child

2. *A model* who demonstrates activities and interaction with the child for the parents to imitate

3. *A reinforcer* because she supports everything positive that the parent does

4. *A reality tester* who helps the parents test out the reality of a situation as it concerns themselves or their child

5. *An activity director* who gives ideas to the parent who is unsure of what to do

6. *An interpretor* who puts professional jargon into language that parents can understand

7. *A resource person* who keeps abreast of the latest knowledge in child development, hearing, hearing aids, medical advances and any other topic related to their child

8. *A teacher* who communicates rationale and objectives to the parents. This is last but by no means least.

One of the basic characteristics of the individual conference is its inherent flexibility in terms of time and content. The time can be arranged from week to week if parents have other obligations. It can be made to follow an audiologic or psychologic evaluation so that the findings can be discussed. The content can be very specific but always highly confidential. The language of the teacher/counselor can be geared to the cognitive level of the individual parent. The intervener may even need to demonstrate with the child to clarify still more the significances of a principle for that particular parent.

There are guidelines for the teacher/counselor to help implement these roles. The teacher/counselor should

1. Make the parent feel comfortable and accepted.

2. Be as patient with the parent as she expects the parent to be with the child.

3. Be genuinely interested in the parent and meet his/her individual needs.

4. Be friendly, yet objective, thereby avoiding too close personal relations.

5. Refrain from making moral judgments or showing surprise, disgust or rejection.

6. Focus only on the habilitation of the child and the parent as the child's real teacher.

7. Avoid trying to do psychotherapy; if the parents need further help, they should be referred to a mental health professional.

8. Express genuine interest in the parent and what that parent is doing, especially as it relates to hearing, to language and to cognitive growth; the intervener offers parents much positive reinforcement.

9. Summarize each session for the parent so that he/she can realize what was accomplished and what is to be done.

10. Keep records of each session and record all information as

soon as possible the same day.

Strategies Used by The Teacher/Counselor

The intervention curriculum is a *process* whereby the teacher/
counselor attempts to modify the naturally-occurring dynamics
of the hearing-impaired child's home for the child's benefit. In
the course of the process, parents are taught certain strategies
which cluster around (1) hearing and hearing aids, (2) receptive
language, (3) expressive language and (4) reinforcement.

Because parents are individuals with a wide range of needs,
each is helped individually to perfect his or her own style or
strategy. Some parents are given specific instruction; some are
given models; some have set experiences to imitate. For all of the
parents, however, videotapes have proven useful in leading them
to develop their own unique strategies and skills.

Uses of Videotape

Videotapes have proven particularly helpful in effecting
change in the parents' behavior. After a model described by Nardine (5), parents, or usually the mother and child, are taped in the
home demonstration center at regular intervals. Immediately following the taping the mother views the filmed sequence and
evaluates herself. In this way she becomes aware of her strengths
and abilities as well as her weaknesses. She and the teacher/coun-
selor can then discuss meaningfully her interaction with her child
and that of the child with her. Self-criticism is much easier than
subjective evaluation by the intervener. Further, the taped experience can be played and replayed to extract the maximum from the
session. As a result of viewing themselves, parents improve their
existing teaching strategies and develop others. Skill at parenting
seems to be learned more readily through this type of microteach-
ing than the traditional vicarious procedure.

The videotapes also have proven to be beneficial in helping
parents see where they have been and how they have progressed
over time. Most parents receive much reinforcement when they
observe their progress. These tapes serve as tools for conferences

when other family members are present. They also serve to communicate what has transpired at the sessions when the other members were not able to attend. When parents can monitor their interaction style, they self-correct and carry over into their own home the principles and strategies encouraged in the home demonstration center.

INFORMATION GIVEN TO PARENTS

Parents of hearing-impaired children need information in four major areas — hearing and hearing aids, receptive language, expressive language and reinforcement. These will be discussed below.

Hearing and Hearing Aids.

Important to an early intervention program is close association with an audiologic clinic. The Parent-Infant Program is fortunate in being part of Central Institute for the Deaf where the speech and hearing services cooperate closely. The intake evaluations are made in those clinics, and ongoing retesting and follow-up management with reference to hearing aid use continues after the child is scheduled in the Parent-Infant Program.

The audiologists meet regularly in weekly staff meetings with the home demonstration staff and maintain records with regard to hearing levels. They inform the staff of the auditory sensitivity of the children, enabling the teacher/counselor to make judgments concerning the intensity of signals which the child requires. They select the hearing aid which is to be lent to the parent, and guide the final selection of the one the parents purchase.

Without a doubt, if a program of intervention is not fortunate enough to have a clinic with these services, they should adopt one. Teacher/counselors needs to work closely with audiologists in order that the child receives the best possible help. Furthermore, parents need wise audiologic guidance. The audiologic assistance needs to be ongoing and available whenever parents have a need.

Fundamentally, parents must become experts on hearing problems and their own child's problem in particular. They need to know why surgery, chiropractic, acupuncture and the like will not restore hearing that does not exist. Importantly, they need to know how to utilize the hearing that does exist to the maximum. They need to be able to interpret the audiogram and explain it themselves to grandparents and other interested relatives and neighbors.

Parents need to learn simple facts about acoustics in relation to amplification; they need to know about the relationship of the distance from the microphone and environmental noise, for example. Binaural versus monaural listening needs to be explained. They need to know how to help their child *learn to listen* to speech in the noise instead of just hanging a hearing aid on him. They need to calibrate themselves to their child's particular aid and routinely check it each time their child wears it. They need to know how to spot trouble with the aid; check batteries, cord and earmold; and attend to the child's reaction to amplified sound in various situations.

Parents need to know the limitations of their child's hearing aid, and they must become experts at compensating by (1) getting to within auditory range before speaking, (2) getting to the child's eye level or getting him to their eye level, (3) giving the child language meaningful to him when he is listening and looking, and (4) reinforcing his efforts when he listens or when he looks and listens.

Most importantly, parents must accept the aid for the great value it offers. A parent's acceptance of the aid sets the model for the child doing the same. Regrettably, some parents respond to their own feelings rather than the child's performance and reject the aid because it is a visible sign of a handicapped child. The intervener needs to understand the cause of the rejection and help parents come to terms with such feelings. This often takes time because the intervener cannot force the issue. Meanwhile, if she can demonstrate the child's response first to intonation and later to his name with and without amplification, she can speed parental acceptance of the aid.

Receptive Language

The concepts parents need to learn in this area are much too lengthy to describe in this volume, but the following are a sample of some of the strategies they are expected to use:

1. Talking about things that are interesting *to the child,* i.e. tuning into him.

2. Talking about what the child is perceiving at the moment; what he is seeing, feeling, tasting, smelling, doing are the actions that need verbal labels.

3. Labeling *his* playthings, *his* food, *his* clothing, *his* body and *his* actions — all things in the child's perceptual zone of the here and now can be labelled.

4. Using sentences, phrases and, only as a last resort, single words to label.

5. Seeing that the child's experiences are repeated and that language accompanies the activity — Repetition teaches!

6. Expecting responses to situational language — they are asked to show pleasure when the child understands whether his understanding is only of the situation or of the language used.

7. Waiting for the child's responses to language that is out of context. Parents are asked to clarify what they have said to the child only when certain that he does not understand.

8. Demonstrating along with the language used when the child needs clarification.

9. Reinforcing all of his efforts positively.

Expressive Language

Parents are given handout material on this as well as on the other three major areas. The material covers the vocal process as well as how language develops in hearing children. The major strategies parents learn are

1. Listening to the child and responding — every vocalization should get attention and reward.

2. Giving form to *his* vocalizations — parents are asked to put the child's thoughts into words. Further, they can put words to *his* feelings.

3. Giving him models for what is said — parents should

respond to the child's actions with language.

4. Teaching imitation through play, first by imitating the child.

5. Encouraging the child's imitation of parental actions.

6. Letting the child learn the *function* of language.

7. Helping him with the *content* of language.

8. Not worrying about the *form* of the language a child uses; the classroom teacher will do that.

Reinforcement

Parents need to become familiar with their own reinforcement techniques and the strategies they cover. The following items of information about reinforcement are explained to parents:

1. *Amount.* Parents need to be aware of how often they use positive reinforcement in the course of a day.

2. *Source.* All members of the family unit should realize that they are reinforcers and use reinforcement wisely.

3. *Nature.* Parents should move quickly from the concrete, such as a pat or smile, to the verbal.

4. *Direction.* Parents need to learn consistency in their reinforcement.

5. *Focus.* Parents need to know whether they are reinforcing general behavior or language and see that both receive appropriate positive rewards.

6. Not to be overlooked is the need to reinforce other members of the family group for their participation in the handicapped child's habilitation.

PARENT MEETINGS

While the assumption is wrong that parents need *only facts* regarding education and, in particular, the language education of their child, parents do need to learn about the handicapping condition. Knowing about the handicap is fundamental to their understanding. For this reason, a program of parent education is continued as an essential part of the Parent-Infant Program. Because a large group meeting is efficient in transmitting information to many persons, these are held monthly. At these didactic meetings, lectures and discussions focus on such topics as development, toys, behavior and opportunities for deaf people. Some of the speakers have been deaf adults, the school principal, child psychologists, medical people, parents of older deaf children and teachers.

Since small groups allow greater attention to individual needs of the members and more opportunity for participation in discussion, these are also scheduled monthly. At these meetings, usually of mothers, plans are made for various program activities, e.g. speakers are selected for meetings, potluck get-togethers are planned. Also, the group leader may go into more detail about a current topic using films, taperecordings and the like.

Fathers attend the larger meetings, and effort is extended to see that they also participate actively. Therefore, additional group meetings are held for them about five times a year, usually on weekends or evenings. It also should be added that attendance by grandparents, siblings and others is to be encouraged at any of the meetings. Grandfathers and sons, for example, frequently join the fathers.

Parents' Wants and Needs

In thinking about what parents gain from experience in groups, a question needs to be raised. What is it that they really *want* and *need?* There are some universal trends that have been observed. Parents want, first of all, up-to-date, accurate scientific information, in language they can understand, regarding their child's handicap, the effect that disability may have on the usual chart of normal child development, the emotional aspects of the handicap, and effects of the handicap on behavior. They want to know very practically what they can do to help their child develop to his best capacity and what they may expect this capacity to be. In other words, they want to know how to manage now and what they have to look forward to.

These are the questions parents often bring first to professional people with a very strong sense of urgency. It is only later that they reveal that they need to know more about themselves, about their own widely-conflicting but normal feelings, and about their own special level of tolerance of the demands that are put upon them. They need to have help in recognizing both where they are weak and where they are strong so that they can turn to appropriate services for help as it is needed. They also want to know the effect of a handicapped child on the family as a whole — the strain this places on the marriage, the effect on other children as they are growing up.

The impact of one parent upon other parents in group situations is not to be underestimated. There is quite a ventilation of attitudes which frequently do not come out in individual interactions between the professional person and the parent. Parents proceed in the meetings to enter quickly into significant discussions with a rather immediate sense of identification from one parent to another taking place.

Surely some of the information parents need can be made available to them through the printed word and in lectures at large meetings. Yet we must always remind ourselves that these formal presentations have their limitations, that parents will take from such reading and talks only what they are *able* to take from them, and that they may react to this material in ways that one cannot predict in advance.

Nevertheless, summaries of lectures are prepared as handouts and distributed after the presentation along with chapters from a text, *Chats With Johnny's Parents* (9). The book shelves in the home demonstration center contain the latest material for parents from newspapers, magazines and professional journals along with books on the subjects of hearing impairment, child development, etc. Frequently a review of some reading of interest is the topic for discussion at a meeting. In almost all instances, the teacher/counselor follows up on the reading to insure its comprehension.

CLASSES FOR CHILDREN

As the child matures and is ready for group education, he is placed in a part-time nursery class. Placement in a specific group within the nursery is based upon individual assessment of each child's auditory capacity, his language level and his social maturity. Instruction of the children in the various nursery classes accommodates to these variables.

Within the classes, the planning of the learning environment revolves around the children and their needs. The learning experiences and activities are designed to satisfy children's urges to invent, discover, construct, create and, importantly, to attach language to these activities. Class content includes:

1. Undirected active play involving gross muscular activity
2. Teacher-directed activities designed to develop communicative skills of listening, observing, speaking, etc.
3. Visual-perceptual and visual-motor activities which contribute to eye-hand coordination, reading readiness, etc.
4. Creative play — such activities are dramatic play, water play and painting
5. Activities related to the environment, for example, science materials and concepts and crafts
6. Games and story-telling
7. Contrived experiences to develop appropriate language
8. Language for the child's management of the environment

The specifics of the curriculum are not defined activities which are utilized over and over. Rather, specific activities are constantly changing so that they may be employed to implement learning. The *process* of learning rather than facts or subject matter should be the focus, with particular attention paid to the developmental levels of individual children.

Some of the goals of the nursery class are

1. To facilitate concept formation through experiencing concepts in a variety of situations, and to reinforce emerging concepts through repeated encounters
2. To provide learning experiences which will guide and stimulate language development, concept development and speech and listening
3. To provide a wide variety of experiences which stimulate physical, emotional and social development so as to counteract the deprivation imposed by the hearing impairment or other causes
4. To provide opportunities for intensive diagnostic teaching

in an attempt to find more effective ways of teaching spoken language to each child.

SUMMARY

In summary, the emphasis in the Parent-Infant Program at Central Institute for the Deaf is upon a process. The process is one of total involvement of the parents to help them become effective in their own home with their child. As parents, they learn strategies appropriate to their child to assist him in learning to listen, to communicate and to learn.

The intervener or teacher/counselor is alert to parents' emotional needs and relates to them on an individual basis. The format is home-type teaching with the parents the recipients of instruction. Assuming that parents' experience in this program assists learning, the objective is their active participation rather than passive observation. Not to be neglected, however, are group opportunities for ventilation and information exchange as well as observation of their child in a classroom setting. All of these experiences are guided for the purpose of helping parents to develop to the maximum and to assist their child to do so also.

While the home demonstration center is not a panacea for the problems of the hearing-impaired child, it does enable a parent to become more effective by providing meaningful experiences which govern the child's language and cognitive development.

REFERENCES

1. Farber, B.: Effects of severely mentally retarded child on the family. In Trapp, E., and Hemelstein, (Eds.): *Readings on the Exceptional Child.* New York, Appleton Cent, 1962, pp. 227-246.
2. Kol'tsova, N. M.: The formation of higher nervous activity of the child. *Psychol Rev, 69*: 344-354, 1962.
3. Lowell, E.: Parental skills and attitudes, including home training. *The Young Deaf Child: Identification and Management.* Acta-Oto-Laryngologica Suplm. #206, Stockholm, 1965.
4. Michaels, J., and Schucman, H.: Observations on the psychodynamics of parents of retarded children. *Am J Ment Defic, 66*: 568-573, 1962.
5. Nardine, F.: Parents as a Teaching Resource. *The Volta Review,* March, 172-177, 1974.

6. Rosenberg, B. G., and Sutton-Smith, B.: Sibling age spacing: Effects upon cognition. *Devel Psychol, 1*: 661-668, 1969.
7. Schlesinger, H. S., and Meadow, K. P.: Emotional support to parents: How, when and by whom. *Parent Programs in Child Development Centers: First Chance for Children*, Vol. 1. Chapel Hill, T.A.D.S., 1972, pp. 13-23.
8. Shontz, F.: Reactions to crisis. *The Volta Review*, Vol. *67*: 5, 364-370, 1965.
9. Simmons-Martin, A. A.: *Chats With Johnny's Parents*. Washington, A. G. Bell Association, 1975.
10. White, B. L.: As reported in Pines, M. Why some three-year-olds get A's and some get C's. *New York Times Mag*, July 8, 1969, p. 4.

Chapter 5

PARENTS AND SIBLINGS AS CO-THERAPISTS

Gertrud L. Wyatt

INTRODUCTION: CHANGES IN PROFESSIONAL ATTITUDES

THE treatment and education of children with developmental disorders and disabilities have changed considerably during the last decade. Therapy is no longer restricted to the consulting room of a specialist in psychiatry, psychotherapy or speech therapy; rather it is done in a variety of settings and with manifold and varying techniques. It occurs in public schools, in colleges, in a child's home, in a therapeutic summer camp, or in an available room in a church.

Together with the *setting* of the treatment program, the *participants* in the therapeutic venture have changed considerably. The professionals who were involved originally still play an important part in the diagnostic procedures as well as in the planning and often in the supervision of the treatment process. They share, however, their therapeutic roles and obligations with so-called lay people — teachers, counselors, learning disability teachers and, last but not least, the parents and often the siblings of the child.

In the United States, housewives or college students also are trained to act as aides in the remedial education of children with a variety of developmental problems. In the place of one highly trained specialist we now find the *therapeutic team*. In this type of group approach, everybody, regardless of age or background, has to play an important, unique role.

Nickerson (32) presented a survey of the manifold patterns of therapy existing at the present time. Let us mention here only a few — specially-trained nurses, speech therapists or college students visit the homes of young brain-damaged children, children with hearing loss or with severe language deficits, and demonstrate to the mothers how a particular child may be fed, stimulated, trained and played with in order to further his or her development. In the case of low income families, the mothers are given simple toys and picture books to use in the training and teaching of their child. Parents and helpers meet in the evening to see and discuss training films and videotapes, to produce simple toys and games with the help of the group leader, and through group discussion to ventilate their feelings concerning the developmentally-different child, thus gaining more insight into their own fear, anger and grief reactions. Examples of such activities are given by Levenstein (25) and Wyatt (54, 55).

Evidently during recent years we have been witnessing remarkable changes in the attitudes of professional people of various disciplines toward the parents of handicapped children. Earlier in the century such attitudes frequently were negative. For discussions of earlier attitudes see Appleton (1), Meyers and Goldfarb (29), and Schopler (43). They ranged from minimum communication with parents, based on the assumption, "They are lay people; they would hardly understand the nature of the handicap or the techniques used in therapy or remediation," to outright blaming of parents, particularly mothers. For example, "The mothers of stutterers reject their children from birth on." The mother of so-called autistic, schizophrenic or psychotic children were called destructive, compulsive people without warmth — *refrigerator mothers.*

Such negative attitudes toward the parents of handicapped children were based, in most instances, on the professional's limited understanding of certain handicapping conditions. Schopler, in his important paper, *Changes of Direction with Psychotic Children* (41), relates the blaming to the fact that "punitive confusion and suspension of rationality" are still characteristic of some approaches to severely disturbed children. In his opinion, such "intellectual absurdities" in professional attitudes, causing much social harm, are derived from "the human tendency to persist with theoretical positions and conclusions at the cost of ignoring new data." The absence of meaningful communication between professionals and parents adds severe guilt feelings to the parents' already-existing feelings of confusion, grief and hopelessness.

Two exceptionally-gifted women described their experiences as "scapegoated parents"; Mrs. Park, the mother of an autistic child (33), and Mrs. Cameron, whose child suffered from receptive and expressive aphasia (9). In both cases, the parents, searching for professional help, went through a surprisingly similar series of frustrations. First they experienced severe difficulties in finding out where professional help would be available; then, when diagnostic studies finally were undertaken, erroneous diagnoses were presented to the parents by professionals lacking in sensitivity and empathy. In follow-up meetings the parents often were treated condescendingly and in a criticizing manner while little actual remediation was provided for the children and no counseling was provided for the parents. Fortunately for the children concerned, both sets of parents, observing their children's behavior and minimal but continuous improvement at home, did not lose their conviction that their children could be taught. Both mothers, without sufficient professional support and against great odds, discovered by themselves ways to work with their children. Eventually, the aphasic child and her mother found help in a language-training center in California, where the child received excellent training combined with demonstration films for the mother. The mother of the autistic child found empathy and understanding of her problems at a child psychiatric clinic in London, England.

The experiences of these parents present a low point in the field of cooperation and communication between professional people and the parents of handicapped children. Fortunately, at present, decisive, positive changes in the treatment and education of children with special needs can be reported, combined with a new understanding of the parents' role in the treatment of their own children.

During the first half of the century two leading theoretical positions prevailed which, in many instances, were diametrically opposed to each other, each one reflecting the primary training and interests of the research worker or therapist. On the one hand we find an almost exclusively medical, biologically-oriented point of view. In this framework parents often were seen as clients only, not as co-workers in the treatment process. On the other hand, we observe an overemphasis on strictly psychological, particularly psychoanalytic, theorizing leading to the notion that parental attitudes and psychopathology are the main source of developmental disorders in children; further details of this view are given by Schopler (41).

Schopler credits Kanner for his early recognition of the fact that biological factors in the child as well as social and emotional factors in his environment constantly interact in a multidimensional manner (20). This multivariable, ecological assumption proved highly fruitful in the approach to children with special needs and their parents. Research within a multidimensional, and at the same time developmentally-oriented, framework has led to many innovations in the diagnosis, therapy and remediation of handicapped children. Within a multivariable and developmental framework it seems logical to attempt the identification of developmental deviations at the earliest possible moment in a child's life. Once our interest in children with special needs is no longer focused primarily upon school age children, but includes preschool children and even infants, it seems natural to *accept parents as the first and primary teachers* of their own children, independent of the role which physicians, psychologists and special educators may play at various stages in a child's growth and development.

The importance of a "multi-axional classification" and of early identification and intervention are well-expressed in the statement in *Human Communication* (18) as follows,

> A sizable proportion of preschool age children have problems that are complex. These are multiple-handicapped children, whose difficulties may include several degrees of biological dysfunction, deviant behavior, or memory problems relating to learning and communication ... The major communication impairments always have serious implications for learning, health, and educability. For this reason young children with developmental deviations or with disorders of communication require additional or special help just as soon as the deviation or disorder can be determined.

The new understanding of the value of the therapeutic team, including collaboration with parents, is reflected in Guerney's discussion of the new roles for nonprofessionals, parents and teachers and their contributions as "psychotherapeutic agents" (15) and in Schlesinger and Meadow's recommendations concerning the "Emotional Support to Parents: How, When and by Whom" (39). A fascinating indication of this remarkable change in professional attitudes can be found in the fact that a symposium on *The Positive Value of Parents* was included in the program of the Eighth International Congress of the International Association for Child Psychiatry and Allied Professions which took place in Philadelphia, Pennsylvania, in August, 1974.[1]

MODELS UTILIZING PARENTS
AND FAMILY MEMBERS AS CO-THERAPISTS

In the following pages the writer wishes to present and illustrate four different models of procedure which, at present, seem to be representative of the attempt of professionals to work with parents and other family members as their co-therapists. Roughly categorized, these models are

1. A behavior modification approach
2. A multistep approach, combining early identification and early intervention, with emphasis upon parent counseling and demonstration of educational techniques to parents
3. A psychodynamic, interactional approach in which mothers or both parents of young children learn how to become their child's primary therapists
4. An approach based upon the theories and techniques used in family therapy.

The Behavior Modification Approach

Readers who are less familiar with the basic tenets of behavior

---

[1]Among the members of the symposium were Dr. Irene E. Caspari, Principal Psychologist of the Tavistock Clinic in London, England; Dr. Audrey K. Naylor of the Child Development Unit of the Yale University Child Study Center; Mrs. C. V. Park; Dr. Eric Schopler of the Department of Psychiatry of the University of North Carolina; and Dr. Gertrud L. Wyatt. Their work and methodology will be discussed in following sections of this paper.

modification will find an introduction to theory and principles in the books by Eysenck (13), Krasner and Ullmann (22), Lazarus (24), Schaefer and Martin (37) and Wolpe (52).

The application of behavior therapy to a variety of problem behaviors in children has been described, among others, by Buddenhagen (7), Hewett (16), Patterson (34) and Thompson and Grabowsky (48). In recent years encouraging attempts have been made to train parents, siblings and other family members of handicapped children to act as behavior modifiers in the home. Case histories and family-training programs have been described by Bernal (2,3,4,5); Engeln, Knutson, Laughy and Garlington (12); Kozloff (21); Schell and Adams (38); Straughan (47); Walder (50); and Weinrott (51).

Out of the wealth of available literature on the subject, we present as illustration of this model the highly innovative "Training Program in Behavior Modification for Siblings of the Retarded", described by Weinrott of McGill University (51). The program was carried out at Camp Freedom, a behaviorally-oriented, educational summer camp for retarded children, located in New Hampshire. Sixty-four to sixty-eight children between the ages of six and fifteen were enrolled in the camp. The campers varied widely on the level of intellectual functioning and of academic skills, and, in addition, many exhibited pronounced behavior problems. The children had been selected for a seven-week residential program on the basis of school or agency referral, an assessment battery of tests, and interviews with their parents. In addition to the summer camp, a program for the training of parents, teachers and school administrators was carried out during the school year.

In 1972, a Sibling Training Program (STP) was established "in light of the limited degree of change one can reasonably expect to engender in the behavior of a retardate during a seven week interval" (51). Weinrott and his collaborators had observed that parents of retarded children often expressed doubts about their ability to teach and about their children's ability to learn. The aim of STP was to include older siblings of the retarded children in the training program. The assumptions made were that brothers and sisters often spend a good deal of time daily with the handicapped child; a constructive relationship between the sibling and the retarded child may serve either to augment the educational efforts of more dedicated parents or to minimize the effect of indifferent, overtired or otherwise noncooperative parents.

The siblings, ages ten to eighteen, were, as a rule, older than their retarded brothers and sisters. Parents were informed about the planned STP and were advised that the decision to join the program should be made independently by the sibling, without parental pressure. The siblings themselves were invited by a letter in which it was explained that participation in the program would not just increase their responsibility for the retarded child, making their home lives more difficult, but that, on the contrary, their understanding of behavior modification techniques would make it easier for them to live with a retarded brother or sister. It is noteworthy that eighteen out of twenty-two siblings who were invited chose to participate in the program. The precamp training was carried out at Harvard University in Cambridge, Massachusetts, and at the Walter E. Fernald State School nearby.

The siblings participating in the STP (from now on referred to simply as *the siblings*) first met informally at a barbecue during which a film showing life at Camp Freedom and an introduction to behavior modification were presented and discussed. A few weeks later the siblings visited the Fernald State School and observed through a one-way mirror how reinforcement procedures were being used with groups of retarded children. Soon after the opening of the summer camp, parents and siblings were invited for a Sunday visit to observe the management of the retarded children. Educational activities carried out at the camp included training in speech, reading readiness, sports, swimming, arts and crafts, music and games. The campers participated in all these activities on various levels of instruction, depending on their respective levels of intellectual capacity and physical ability.

Once the siblings had joined the campers, each sibling was encouraged to devise his or her own schedule for the following day, observing three activity classes and attending two group meetings each day. Early in their training, siblings were not permitted to attend classes in which their own brothers or sisters were enrolled. Gradually the siblings' attention was shifted from guided observations through one-way mirrors to interaction with campers, until finally each sibling began to teach his or her own brother or sister. During daily group meetings the siblings gained further understanding of the principles of reinforcement and the value of breaking down skills into component parts.

The results of this STP were evaluated through a "Behavior Situation Questionnaire," and later through follow-up communications with the families of the retarded children. Some of the findings should be mentioned. The camp teachers stated that because of the siblings' assistance they felt less overtired than in previous summers and more confident that the training methods used at camp would be continued during the coming school year. Parents reported that the trained siblings showed more patience with their handicapped brothers or sisters and helped in their home management. Beyond this, the siblings acted as watchdogs vis-a-vis their parents, reminding them to use reinforcement techniques in daily life. Parents also stressed that for the first time they were able to discuss freely with all family members the problems and strategies concerning their retarded children. In summary, it was demonstrated that siblings can serve as effective behavior therapists, and that their training contributed to maintaining consistent behavior between family members with regard to the needs and the education of the handicapped child.

The Multistep Approach: Identification, Demonstration and Parent Counseling

A large number of research and pilot studies designed for children with varying developmental handicaps have been organized around the following concepts: screening, early identification and diagnosis of the handicapping condition; early training and therapy with the child, simultaneous with the parents' extensive involvement in the diagnostic phase through intake, developmental and therapeutic interviews; followed by demonstration of therapeutic techniques to the parents and by parent counseling.

In the course of the counseling phase, therapists (psychologists, social workers or special educators) help parents share their feelings of bewilderment, despair and often anger about the handicapped child, and help them to cope with these feelings.

As several chapters in this book deal specifically with the therapeutic approach to the parents of brain-damaged, hearing-impaired or autistic children, and of children with learning disabilities, we will in this chapter only touch upon children in these categories. A comparison of many of these innovative programs, however, may bring to the reader's attention similarities in procedures used in spite of differences in the theoretical frameworks.

Cruickshank (11), in his pioneering work with brain-damaged children, found the parents indispensable as co-workers in the child's education. His approach to parents begins with a discussion of the diagnostic findings — a service which all too often is lacking in the series of procedures used by busy professional people working in hospitals or schools. In Cruickshank's opinion, the diagnostician owes the parents not only a clear explanation of the nature of the child's handicap, but almost must develop with them a long-range educational plan. He further recommends a minimum of stimulation in the home and a structured but not inflexible daily schedule. Parents are taught how to give their children simple directions, how to set limits on their behavior, how to provide an atmosphere of love and warmth, of order but not rigidity — in short, how to arrange a home life in which the child feels accepted as a person although his actual behavior may not always be acceptable.

Caspari and her collaborators at the Tavistock Clinic in London, England, also work closely with parents as co-therapists in a family approach to the treatment of reading disability (10). Diagnostic findings are shared with the parents who later observe through a one-way screen the teaching procedures used by an educational therapist. In psychoanalytically-oriented *feedback meetings* the parents discuss their relationships with the child and with other members of the family and begin to acknowledge difficulties in areas other than the child's reading problem. Educational therapists at the Tavistock Clinic receive specific training in this form of therapy, combining demonstration with parent counseling.

Schopler and his colleagues at the University of North Carolina developed a highly innovative treatment program for autistic children in which the parents were trained to act as "primary developmental agents" (41, 43). The parents' increased understanding of their children's handicaps, together with their active participation as members of a therapeutic team, led to substantial improvement in the condition of many children, together with marked improvement in family equilibrium.

Simmons-Martin of the Central Institute for the Deaf in St. Louis, Missouri, developed a most instructive parent-infant program with the explicit aim to teach parents, through guided experiences, how to shape the language and cognitive training of their hearing-impaired infants (45).

Within recent years we also can observe in many public school systems a more sophisticated understanding of the multiple and varied needs of handicapped children and their families. The increasing insight and the changes in educational practices have been truly astounding in many instances. The Department of Health, Education and Welfare (HEW) as well as the departments of education of various states set up task forces with the mandates to explore the conditions of, and to recommend appropriate programs for, the education of children with special needs. An example we can mention here is the Comprehensive Special Education Law proposed by the Commonwealth of Massachusetts as specified in "Regulations for the Implementation of Chapter 766 of the Acts of 1972."[2] Among the remarkable features of these regulations we point to the insistence upon (a) *early identification and intervention*; (b) use of the *team approach* in diagnostic and educational procedures; and (c) *parental involvement* at all states of diagnostic, educational and therapeutic activities.

The multistep approach appears to be particularly fitting for special education services rendered by public school systems. From 1968-70, the Wellesley Public Schools, with partial support

---

[2]Copies of the regulations are available through the State Department of Education, Division of Special Education, 182 Tremont Street, Boston, Massachusetts, 02111.

from HEW, Office for the Handicapped, developed a program for the *Early Identification of Children with Potential Learning Disabilities* which is reported by Wyatt (55). It was the purpose of this project to identify and examine those children who showed signs or symptoms of developmental delay or deviation, to initiate a program of compensatory education focused upon parent counseling and training of parents to help their own children, and at the time of school entry to plan appropriately and provide special services to children if needed. It was hoped that such early identification and training of high-risk children would contribute to the prevention of school failure in later years.

The project utilized the services of a part-time psychologist and speech therapist. Audiologists and physicians representing different specialities such as pediatrics, pediatric neurology, ophthalmology and psychiatry served as consultants and were particularly helpful in the design of the Developmental Questionnaire (55). The procedures used were organized along the following steps:

1. *Preschool.* Parents receive an explanatory letter and a developmental questionnaire, fill out the questionnaire and return it.

2. *Preschool.* Answers to the questionnaires are further explored through telephone contacts.

3. *Preschool.* A staff member (psychologist or speech therapist) meets with child and parent in their home and administers a series of informal tests.

4. *Preschool.* Children suspected of developmental difficulties are given extensive diagnostic tests. Referral to medical or mental health facilities is made if necessary.

5. *Preschool.* A parent counselor or a speech therapist meets with the parent (mother) for demonstration of methods in motor-perceptual or language training, and assists the mother in the management of the child. Children with very severe disturbances may be referred for clinical treatment.

6. *Prior to school entry.* Findings of the prekindergarten project are discussed with the elementary principals and the kindergarten teachers. In certain instances attempts are made to match specific children with specific kindergarten programs.

7. *Kindergarten year.*

a. All children receive learning readiness and hearing tests during the first half of the year. Through test results and teacher referrals, children with developmental problems who were missed or who did not participate in the preschool project are identified.

b. Group meetings are conducted with all kindergarten teachers. Psychologists and speech therapists consult with kindergarten teachers with regard to specific children.

c. All existing special services (speech, language and hearing therapy, motor training and individual or group counseling) are utilized to assist children with developmental problems and to assist their parents. Small group meetings with parents are conducted.

8. *End of kindergarten year.* Children, originally identified, who made good progress are promoted to first grade. This is termed *primary prevention.* Children who made little progress or very immature children may stay in kindergarten for another year while special services are continued.

9. *Grade One.* Children who experienced successful primary prevention should succeed in first grade, mastering the first grade curriculum. Children with severe or multiple problems, neurogenic or psychogenic in origin, may need continued special services. Certain children may be assigned at an early date to a learning disabilities teacher or a therapeutic tutor. This is secondary prevention.

Demonstration and Parent Counseling

In all cases of developmental difficulties, some form of intervention was attempted with primary emphasis upon parent counseling and training of parents to assist their own child. The methods used in intervention depended upon the child's major presenting problem and upon the degree of cooperation or *therapeutic readiness* shown by the parents, especially by the mother. Training and counseling of parents in this program were carried out by Mrs. Elaine Loomis, psychologist, and Mrs. Lois Scott, speech therapist, who met regularly with the consulting psychiatrist, Dr. Helen M. Herzan.

Intervention Type A was used in the case of children whose primary problems were found in the areas of speech and language development. In these cases the speech therapist became the primary agent of intervention. *Intervention Type B* was used with children who showed a variety of developmental and emotional problems. The psychologist was the primary parent counselor in these cases, although the services of the speech therapist were also used when necessary.

The methods of therapy used were, for the most part, developed during previous research studies, carried out from 1958-1964, partly supported by grants from the National Institute of Mental Health and reported by the author earlier (53). The basic assumptions underlying these procedures were (1) that the parents, in particular the mothers, of young children serve as the primary speech models and providers of sensory stimulation for them, and (2) that certain forms of parent-child interaction may facilitate language-learning in the child while others may interfere with it. In encounters with parents of children with speech and language disabilities, the patterns of interaction prevalent between mother and child were observed and analyzed. Then the speech therapists, through explanation, demonstration and counseling, assisted mothers in becoming more appropriate speech models for their own children.

This type of approach has proved highly effective in helping children with delayed language development, articulation problems and stuttering, provided these children did not show symptoms of hearing loss or of neurological impairment.[3]

Intervention Type B was used with children who were of average to superior intelligence. Many of them had specific deficits in perceptual, integrative or expressive processes. These children often were found to be ineffective in using their hands, eyes, ears, muscles and body. Their difficulties encompassed the processes of orientation, intake, integration, memory, output and feedback.

---

[3]For a more detailed description, see the section of this chapter headed "The Mother as Therapist."

The symptoms most often evident in these children were hyperactivity, restlessness, short attention span, difficulties in gross or fine motor coordination or in both, language disabilities and emotional or behavior problems.

Short-term psychological counseling was given to mothers of those children who proved to have developmental or emotional problems. This followed earlier contacts where questions had been raised either by the parent, the psychologist or the speech therapist. Therefore, in most cases the starting point was a simply-presented factual description of the child's performance and behavior related to the usual expectations for his or her age and for successful school adjustment and achievement. Goals, techniques and duration of counseling thereafter varied not only with the nature and severity of the problem, but of necessity also with parents' reaction to this information, with their level of understanding, their acceptance or rejection. Objectives ranged from trying to relieve an overanxious parent to helping another parent realize that her child's behavior deviated so much from developmental norms that the child should have a psychiatric evaluation. Some parents needed only a clearer understanding of their child's assets and liabilities to be able to manage his difficulties effectively on their own. Some were able to benefit from an educational approach from discussions about child development with concrete suggestions regarding management. Others, however, needed help to realize that their own ambivalent feelings were interfering with positive and effective interaction and communication with their children.

The case of Ronny illustrates this type of working with parents and siblings as co-therapists. Ronny's parents contacted the preschool project in the spring of 1969. At that time his parents and nursery school teacher were baffled by his behavior which appeared erratic, vacant and tired. The question of mental retardation had been raised. After an extensive diagnostic evaluation carried out by the project psychologist and speech therapist and also by a pediatrician and neurologist, a diagnosis of *developmental dysphasia* was reached, a condition not unlike that of aphasia. The most striking symptoms were Ronny's severe difficulties in word finding, his incorrect and awkward use of grammar, and his sentence structure. As a child of normal intelligence, demonstrated by his test results, Ronny was quite aware of his inability to communicate successfully and had begun to avoid interaction with others. Ronny's unusual condition was discussed with his parents, and he received intensive language training based upon the ideas of Johnson and Myklebust (19). Training focused upon the hierarchical organization of concepts and verbal categories such as animals, fruit, furniture, body parts, means of transportation, his own movements and actions, and so forth. The instructions were given with the use of real objects in the therapist's or in Ronny's home, also through pictures and actions. Many repetitions were necessary to develop a cognitive network of references in Ronny's memory, which eventually would facilitate his recall of words. One of the most important features in Ronny's training was the presence of his father or mother and of two older siblings at every therapeutic session.

In this manner all family members gained an understanding of Ronny's very specific language problems, and all acted as co-therapists, proceeding at home in a manner similar to that demonstrated by the therapist. Whenever Ronny could not find a word, the word was not simply given to him (which has little if any permanent effect), but instead his parents or siblings guided him toward the relevant verbal category and then assisted him in recalling the appropriate word.

When Ronny entered kindergarten the following fall and had to function in a strange environment plus meeting an unfamiliar teacher, he again regressed for a two-month period to withdrawal and avoidance of communication. At this point, the kindergarten teacher and a learning disability specialist joined the therapeutic team. For the next three school years, Ronny daily received special training in all areas of verbal, visual-motor and cognitive development — speaking, listening, formulating sentences, drawing, reading and writing. Ronny made excellent progress, enjoyed school and made many friends. His parents and siblings shared his training and enjoyed his progress with him.

By the third grade Ronny showed few if any deficiencies in expressive verbal language and was reading and writing. If Ronny had been exposed to the usual school work without previous

diagnosis and training, he undoubtedly would have been unable
to function successfully in a school situation.

At the termination of the Title VI program, the Wellesley
School Committee voted to establish the Early Identification and
Intervention Program as a regular part of the services offered by
the Wellesley Public Schools. Between 1970 and 1975 certain
modifications in the program were developed under the direction
of Mrs. Elaine Loomis, school psychologist in charge of preschool services. Although home visits undoubtedly had proved
most fruitful in the areas of establishing contact with child and
mother and of observing family interactions, they also were rather
expensive when measured in staff time and salaries. Therefore,
new screening methods were designed which now are used with
groups of children at each elementary school. A description of
these modifications can be found in the author's Title I Report
(56). An exploratory program for preschool children with *substantial handicaps* and their families is carried out at present at
the Wellesley Public Schools with partial support from the Department of Health, Education, and Welfare under a Title VI
grant.

The Mother as Therapist

From 1958 to 1964 a study was made of the verbal interaction
between children with normal speech and language development
and their mothers, as well as the interaction process between
mothers and children showing developmental disorders (54). The
basic assumption was that no deviation in a child's speech and
language development can ever be understood properly as long as
we look exclusively at the child and his symptoms. No matter
what the child's genetic endowment and physiological condition
may be, the acquisition of language by the child occurs at all
times within a system of communication. During the early years
this system is primarily activated in the "speech chain" between
mother and child as discussed previously by this author (53, 54).

Once one orders his observations within the framework of an
interactional system, the inclusion of the parents in the therapeutic team becomes an undeniable necessity. Parents, by their very

existence, are in daily communication with their children on every level of development. Observing the interactions between well-developing infants and their mothers, one recognizes the role of the mother as "the primary language teacher" as the term is used by Bullowa (8). Some mothers and fathers are indeed master teachers. Others provide inappropriate or insufficient verbal and cognitive stimulation. A third group of parents appears to be baffled and confused because their infant does not respond to the stimulation provided by the environment. In a fourth group one finds that a well-functioning family interaction system will suddenly be disrupted by an unexpected event, such as the child's or mother's hospitalization, moving, a severe illness in the family, or other events of a similar nature. Such changes may create a crisis in the life of the family (27), which under certain conditions may lead to a crisis in the young child's language development, resulting in the onset of stuttering.

The researcher as well as the speech therapist will learn much from observing the interactions in a well-functioning mother-child speech chain. Mothers of children falling in the three non-functioning groups need the assistance of a therapist or even of a therapeutic team. In all situations of disturbed parent-child interaction the procedures mentioned above will be appropriate — identification, diagnosis, demonstration and parent counseling. In some communication problems it will actually be the aim of the professional therapist to remain in the background and help the mother to become the primary therapist for her own child. Two types of difficulties in which the latter approach is appropriate are described here.

(a) *Children with severely defective articulation in the absence of hearing or neurological impairment.* Such children, at the age of four to six years, may show an interesting profile. While they may have good language comprehension, a large vocabulary and age-appropriate competence in syntax and grammar, their articulation of speech sounds is so defective that an unfamiliar person cannot understand them. Their spontaneous speech is characterized by omission of most consonant sounds; by confusion or distortion of consonants belonging to a particular category, such as unvoiced p,t,k; voiced b,d,g; unvoiced s, f, th, sh; voiced z (in his), v, th (in there), sh (in measure); m and n; and r and l. They also cannot pronounce double consonants, nor can they remember the sequence of sounds in a multisyllabic word. Typical mistakes may be *dog* (pronounced as dod, gog, or god); *curtain* (turtain, curcan, turkan); *telephone* (teyepo); *ice cream cone* (i-teeto).

In the absence of a sensory deficiency (hearing impairment) this severely-defective articulation in otherwise bright, well-developed children may be caused by deficiences in auditory processing (58) and/or by inappropriate verbal stimulation in the home. The latter is characterized by verbal input coming from a parent (mother) who speaks too much, too fast, often indistinctly, and who often uses an advanced vocabulary which does not match the child's developmental level. In short, the mother's manner of speaking "overloads" the capacity of the young child's auditory channel (17).

The therapist begins his/her work by making a home visit and observing the interaction patterns between mother and child. The therapist brings a simple preschool picture book without text and asks the mother to talk about the pictures with the child. Examples of this therapeutic approach can be found in Wyatt (54). In observing and analyzing the speech chain between mother and child, the therapist may find that the mother overloads the child with verbal stimulation, or that she uses what Reusch refers to as "tangential replies" (35), which means that she hardly listens to the child and responds to his utterances in words which do not match the child's needs or interests. In the child's absence the therapist gives the mother a brief explanation of the parent's role as speech model and primary language teacher. The therapist then demonstrates with the child present a rather simple method for improving the communications between the child and mother. The therapist shows to the mother a number of uncluttered colored pictures that can be named or labeled by the mother and child. Commercially-produced materials are unsuited for this beginning stage of training. The mother is encouraged to collect pictures of simple objects, easily found in advertisements. It is pointed out to the mother that each picture chosen must illustrate a word of one syllable, structured in the simple linguistic pattern — Consonant-Vowel-Consonant (CVC), (CV) or (CVV). No double consonants are permitted at this stage. Such one-syllable single consonant words are very frequent in everyday English, e.g. ham, house (five letters but only three sounds), hat, cat, cup, can, cap, boy, shoe, baby, hair. The mother is asked to spend fifteen to twenty minutes daily *alone* with her young child in a comfortable setting, cutting out pictures together, pasting them on a plain background, and naming them together.[4]

Once the child begins to repeat correctly some of these names, other pictures and activities may be added to enliven these *speech games*. The new stimuli may employ verbs, prepositions and, finally, short phrases, e.g. come, come here, up, down, in, go, walk, run, in a cup, coffee in a cup, beer in a can, a red hat, etc. The large majority of children love playing these word games with their mothers. Once the child gets tired of pictures the mother may use toys; objects in the house; a feeling bag which permits the child to touch objects, feel them and name them at the same time until finally double consonants can be introduced. The latter should be articulated carefully and clearly by the mother, e.g. s-kip, lip-s, b-lack; multisyllabic words come later. The mother is advised not to criticize the child when he or she is unable to correctly articulate a word, in particular not to insist on a repeated effort. The mother has to store in her own memory the fact that the child is not yet ready for certain types of auditory discrimination, or does not yet remember sounds in sequence. Whenever the child repeats correctly, the mother shows her pleasure through praise, a smile, pasting a gold star on the picture, etc. Parents are advised to play such speech games also when they dress the child, take him on a drive, or during similar occasions, but they are asked never to criticize the child nor correct him or her when the child speaks spontaneously to them, expressing needs and wants. It is useful for the parents to write the name chosen for a picture on the back of it in order to remind themselves what particular word they used during an earlier session of the speech game.

---

[4]The above method can also be used with children of other languages, although certain linguistic changes will be necessary. For example, in Spanish the simple linguistic word patterns to be taught at the early phase are words following the pattern CVCV, VCV, CVV such as casa, mesa, cubo, cada, ama, alli, dedo, muy, pie, pipa and pina, followed by pinto, pin-ta, pin-tar, etc.

This technique, which is basically simple, can be explained and demonstrated to a parent, student or teacher of young children within an hour's time. The *language trainer* (parent or preschool teacher) is asked to see the therapist two weeks later. Then the parent will demonstrate what pictures or other materials she produced and how she uses them with the child during their speech games.

The writer has used this method since the early fifties and found it highly successful with children and mothers. Eighty percent of the mothers were cooperative and imaginative in working with their children. The remaining 20 percent were either unskillful, overworked, emotionally disturbed or mentally retarded and needed help themselves. In such cases mother substitutes had to be found to play the speech games with the child. The therapist's time with child and mother is minimal. It ranges from two to three sessions during the first six weeks to one session every two or three months at a later stage. The mother experiences the satisfaction of being the helper of her own child. Approximately two thirds of the children in this group will speak normally before they enter kindergarten; another third will need continued help from the mother and the therapist during the kindergarten year only.[5]

(b)*Children with defective articulation and secondary stuttering.* The therapeutic involvement of the mother in such cases is not only desirable but indispensable. From the age of five years on, children of good intelligence who speak with severely defective articulation may at times not be understood even by their mothers or other family members. The children's interest in the world around them and their range of expressive language have become so manifold and complex that even the people close to them may not understand them any longer unless they are fully aware of the context of their utterances.

Tom, at the age of five years, three months, asked his mother,

----

[5]This type of mother-child training also can be used with preschool children who show severely-defective articulation within the syndrome of mutiple motor, perceptual and language deficiencies. Their progress, however, will be much slower, and professional training must be continued through the elementary school years (54).

"Daw me a dah." The mother had no clue for guessing the meaning of his request. Tom repeated louder and louder, "Daw me a dah!" with no apparent improvement in the mother's comprehension of his wish. Tom got increasingly angry, stamped his foot and shouted, "Daw me — daw me — d — d — d — do — it!." Finally, in a fit of anger and helplessness he turned away from his mother. Tom could not understand why his mother did not react to his request. He experienced the mother's lack of response as a hostile, rejecting act. What he actually wanted to say was, "Draw me a desk." The omission of the sounds *r, s* and *k* made his message unintelligible to the mother. During such a situation the communication between child and parent breaks down, causing feelings of distress and helplessness in both the child and the mother.

Children who frequently experience such communicative breakdowns between themselves and significant adults get increasingly angry and tense. When they enter nursery school or kindergarten they may not be understood by the teacher or other children. They react either by total withdrawal from verbal communication, or they show their anger and frustration by aggressive behavior — throwing blocks, for example.

What we as therapists have to understand fully is the fact that a total breakdown in communication between speech partners of all ages causes feelings of increasing tension and frustration. In a young child, in particular, this tension interferes with the fluency of verbal encoding, and the initial symptoms of repetitive stuttering appear, now added to the basic articulation difficulty.

The therapeutic approach in such cases by all means should include the mother. The approach to therapy is precisely the one outlined in the section above. In addition, the mother must say to the child truthfully, "Tom, I cannot always understand what you say. That makes you very angry. I will help you learn to talk so that I and everybody else will understand you. Mommy will help, Daddy will help, and the teacher will help you." Thus, the confused and frustrated child discovers that he or she is not left alone — "Mommy cares, Mommy will help me, there are people who will help me," the child feels.

Once the therapist has explained to the mother the child's predicament and has helped her understand her role in helping her child, this form of therapy proves highly successful. As the child's articulation improves, and as he or she is being understood by others and, thus, can truly communicate with them, the symptoms of secondary stuttering disappear.

(c) *The mother as primary therapist of the young stuttering child.* In the discussion of the child with *secondary stuttering*, the paradigm of a breakdown in parent-child communication leading to difficulties in the child's speech development has already been presented. This paradigm also holds true for the appearance of *primary* (monosymptomatic) *stuttering* in a young child which occurs most frequently during the critical period of two and one-half to five and one-half years. In the writer's work the mother's (or mother substitute's) role in the child's total development has been stressed repeatedly. She learned to respect the mother as the primary language teacher or speech model for her children, providing the infant with tactile-preverbal stimulation and later with symbolic-verbal input, with reinforcement or corrective feedback, expanding his words or phrases into short sentences, and, last but not least, listening to the child and responding to his or her needs in a spirit of love and, to use Mead's phrase, "mutual delight" (28). This type of daily continuous interaction develops in the child a set of trusting expectancies that are indispensable for sound language, cognitive and emotional development. A severe, unexpected or long-lasting breakdown in mother-child interaction interferes with these expectancies, to which the child reacts with anxiety, anger and tension. This response in turn interferes with the child's information processing and expressive language skills. Such a breakdown in communication is most often triggered by events beyond the mother's control such as birth of a new baby, moving, illness, death, divorce in the family or a change of job in the life of a working mother. All such events may lead to temporary separation between the child and his or her primary speech partner. In other instances the mother may be present in the flesh but inaccessible to the young child, who experiences separation or distance from the mother as a form of rejection or abandonment, to which the child reacts with increasing anger combined with increasing anxiety and a regression in speech development. The experimental findings supporting the above theory can be found in Wyatt (54, 55).

The therapist's role in such cases of primary stuttering is more complicated than that described in the two preceding sections. In working with young children, the therapist acts as an object for mutual verbal imitation. In matching words with those of the child and in providing corrective feedback, the therapist actually teaches the child patterns of communication adequate for his or her age level. By working with the mother simultaneously, the therapist makes sure that the child will have continuous satisfactory communication experiences in the home.

In working with the mother, the therapist will have to assist her to cope with her own feelings of helplessness. As time goes by and the child's speech does not improve, or even becomes worse, the mother begins to feel incompetent in her maternal role. At the same time the stuttering child's behavior, with its frequent alternation between possessiveness and jealous hostility, arouses feelings of reactive anger in the mother. Problems of discipline become particularly difficult to handle; the mother fears that any determined stand on her part will cause more intense stuttering in the child.

In working with the mother, the therapist provides her with some explanation of the dynamics of language development, of stuttering and of the manner in which the mother herself became involved in the child's communication disorder. To the mother of young children the therapist demonstrates games of word matching and mutual imitation. Therapist and mother together evaluate the dynamics of the family and consider the stuttering child's role in it. The therapist helps the mother understand the meaning of the child's behavior as an expression of his or her needs and anxieties. With the therapist's support the mother discovers ways in which she can be closer to the child, assure the child of her understanding and willingness to help, and set the stage for satisfactory mutual interaction.

The therapist teaches the mother by several means; one is through explanation and analysis of the mother's own behavior and communication patterns. Another is through demonstration of communication patterns appropriate for interaction with young children. Finally, the therapist helps the mother to understand her own feelings for the stuttering child which are intimately connected with her ability to communicate successfully.

Thus, the mother of the preschool child becomes the primary helper of her own child, supported by the professional therapist — a procedure which was found successful in 80 percent of the cases. Once the child attends school and, thus, is separated from the mother for part of each school day, the preschool procedure has to be modified. The therapist works separately with the child and with the mother in weekly sessions. Older children with advanced symptoms, particularly older boys, seem to benefit more from a male than a female therapist. During the adolescent years it is advisable to have one therapist work with the stutterer and another to meet with both parents for regular counseling sessions. Extensive case histories and forms of therapy with the parents of children of different age groups (3 years to 16 years) can be found in Wyatt (54).

Therapists who work with child and mother must be on guard not to become overidentified with either one. The therapist's primary aim must be to reestablish satisfactory understanding and communication between mother and child while the therapist remains in the background. This type of approach often makes great demands upon the tact and patience of the therapist, who should receive special training for this purpose. In the Wellesley Program all professional people participating in this work with parents — speech therapists, counselors, social workers or kindergarten teachers — have had regular conferences with a mental health professional (psychiatrist or psychologist) who assists them in understanding their own feelings and anxieties which may be aroused in this delicate work with children and parents.

(d) *Working with poor communicators.* Training the mothers of preschool children in order to improve their maternal teaching skills has also been used widely as an integral part of programs for low-income families. An experiment in improving cognitive growth in preschoolers through verbal interaction with mothers was reported by Levenstein of the Family Service Association of Nassau County, Freeport, N. Y. (25, 26). Thirty-three children, aged twenty to forty-three months and their mothers (the experimental group were visited for an average of 42.4 home sessions by a trained toy demonstrator over a seven-month period. The toy demonstrator presented each child with a total of twenty-eight selected toys and picture books called the "Verbal Interaction Stimulus Materials" (VISM). In the mother's presence the toy demonstrator modeled verbal interaction with the child, giving information, naming or labeling the toys and pictures, encouraging the mother's curiosity and interest in books, and praising her for finding teaching alternatives of her own. Pre and posttests of the experimental (E) and two control (C) groups showed that the children in the E group had made significantly greater gains than those in the C groups on the Stanford-Binet Intelligence Scales and the Peabody Picture Vocabulary Test. Furthermore, most of the mothers in the E group had become more skillful in giving information to their children, eliciting responses, verbalizing social interaction and in using books with the child. Thus, the mothers had become more successful primary teachers of their own children. Further elaboration of use of mothers as primary teachers has been discussed by the author (54).

Family Therapy Approach

In the models reported so far, mothers, fathers and siblings were included in the therapeutic team. In the following case we find an interesting modification in treatment in which all family members became both clients and agents in family therapy.

Ruderman and Selesnick, of Mt. Sinai Hospital, Los Angeles, reported a multiavenue approach to the treatment of a ten-year-old stuttering boy (36). Over a period of two years and ten months, the boy was seen in individual psychotherapy by the female social worker who saw both parents once a week. In addition, at particular times the therapist met with the whole family (the boy, his sister and his parents), and she also conducted auxiliary sessions with the boy and his father and the boy and his sister. Furthermore, in a somewhat unusual procedure the male psychiatrist, who consulted regularly with the female therapist, met directly with the boy at highly significant moments during the treatment period. Thus, although the boy worked mostly with a female therapist, the joint sessions with the father and with the male psychiatrist helped him to develop a male identification and eventually to accept the male role.

Family therapy, which developed extensively during the last quarter of a century, utilizes many techniques which might be applicable in working with handicapped children and their families. Some recent trends in this field can be found in books by Boszormenyi-Nagy and Framo (6), Ferber, Mendelsohn and Napier (14), Langsley, Kaplan and Pittman (23), and Minuchin (31).

Challenging innovations are contained in the proposal by Speck and Attneave (46) to work not only with families but with whole family networks. Speck, formerly professor of social psychiatry at Hahnemann Medical College, Philadelphia, and Attneave, a psychologist and part Delaware Indian, currently at the Harvard School of Public Health, adopted methods of "network intervention" as a way of helping families through "retribalization." Speck and Attneave's thinking of the community as a helping group reminds one of the pioneering work of the late Dr. Erich Lindemann, Professor of Psychiatry at Harvard Medical School and founder of the Wellesley Human Relations Service, Inc. (H.R.S.), a community mental health clinic. Dr. Lindemann and the staff of H.R.S. pointed to the impact of a neighborhood upon the life and well-being of families in crises, or families with special needs. In our present society and with the high mobility of many families, the so-called nuclear family frequently feels isolated, without sufficient access to relatives and neighbors. If such a family also contains a handicapped child, e.g. a brain-damaged, mentally-retarded or deaf youngster, therapeutic intervention through a team of parents, siblings and teachers still may not be sufficient. The youngster's behavior often will be misunderstood by neighbors, storekeepers or policemen. It therefore seems a challenging proposition to follow Speck and Attneave and involve a whole neighborhood in the therapeutic team.

The authors' idea of developing a supportive *tribe* is well-described in their book and illustrated through case histories. A group of up to fifty people is assembled, containing, in addition to parents and siblings, schoolmates, neighbors, relatives, storekeepers, policemen, teachers, principals and others who have frequent contact with the child or adolescent in need of assistance. This large network meets for several evening sessions given to intense discussion, interaction and psychodynamic exploration of the needs of the child and his family. The sympathetic as well as the hostile feelings of the group are ventilated. Each network session is conducted by two or three professionally-trained therapists, one of them acting as chairperson of the meetings, the others as members of the network. The group goes through various stages of mutual interaction which, at times, may become quite emotionally charged. Eventually a growing understanding of the needs of the respective family and child should emerge until the whole group finally coalesces into a tribe — a group of people with feelings of common interest and closeness to each other.

Speck and Attneave's procedures may seem bold and difficult to enact for many of us. It may, however, be well worth exploring in what particular manner and to what degree such network intervention could be adapted to families in our case in order to make a whole neighborhood positively attuned to and supportive of the family's special needs and predicaments.

FINAL RECOMMENDATIONS

An almost bewildering variety of approaches to working with the families of children in need have emerged in recent years. While the team approach seems highly promising, a few suggestions and cautions might be appropriate.

Within a team or helping group, each participant, regardless of age or professional status, has to make an important contribution to the treatment process as a whole. However, if we wish to prevent a dangerous amateurism, the so-called lay helpers will need a degree of preparatory training; and as treatment proceeds, they must have access to regular professional consultation.

At the same time the writer wishes to stress that the attitudes of the professional staff toward the various lay helpers will have a decisive effect upon the progress of therapy. In the course of the helping process, all team members will learn from each other. Thus, not only the child in need, but all the people working with the child will go through a learning process which in turn should enhance their competence and self-esteem.

Particular recommendations are addressed to team members working within the setting of a public school system. While it is most encouraging to see a state department of education develop and distribute enlightened and even sophisticated regulations concerning the education of children with special needs, we must keep in mind the following danger: Only a small minority of school systems have available at present the necessary well-trained staffs requisite to success in organizing the requested programs of early identification and intervention, special integrated education of children at all age levels, and counseling of parents. Working with parents of handicapped children is by no means an easy job; it should not be entrusted to psychologically-naive personnel, however well-meaning they may be.

The various approaches to working with the families of handicapped children will bear fruit only if state departments of education and the various school systems will provide the necessary financial means to permit the long-range training of classroom and special teachers and school administrators. We need workshops, professional meetings, internships, and other training procedures suitable for all school personnel to deepen their understanding and improve their skills in helping the handicapped child and the child's family.

REFERENCES

1. Appleton, W.: Mistreatment of patients' families by psychiatrists. *Am J Psychiatry,* June, 1974.
2. Bernal, M.E.: Training a mother. *J Nerv Ment Dis, 148*: 375-385, 1969.
3. Bernal, M.E.: Training parents in child management. In Bradfield, R. (Ed.): *Behavior Modification of Learning Disabilities.* San Rafael, Academic Therapy Publications, 1972.
4. Bernal, M.E.: A public health nursing program for training parents of outpatient retarded children. Unpublished manuscript. University of Denver, Denver, 1970.

5. Bernal, M.E.: The use of videotape feedback and operant learning principles in training parents in management of deviant children. In *Advances in Behavior Therapy*. New York, Acad Pr, 1972.
6. Boszormenyi-Nagy, I., and Framo, J.L.: *Intensive Family Therapy: Theoretical and Practical Aspects*. New York, Har-Row, 1965.
7. Buddenhagen, R.G.: *Establishing Vocal Verbalizations in Mute Mongoloid Children*. Champaign, Res Pr, 1971.
8. Bullowa, M., Jones, L.G., and Duckert, A.R.: The development from vocal to verbal behavior in children. In Bellugi, U., and Brown, R. (Eds.): *The Acquisition of Language*. Monograph, Society for Research in Child Development, 1964, pp. 29, 1.
9. Cameron, C.: *A Different Drum*. Englewood Cliffs, P-H, 1973.
10. Caspari, I.: Family approach to the treatment of reading disability. Unpublished Manuscript, Tavistock Clinic, London, 1974.
11. Cruickshank, S.M.: *The Brain-Injured Child in Home, School and Community*. Syracuse U Pr, 1967.
12. Engeln, R., Knutson, J., Laughy, L., and Garlington, W.: Behavior modification techniques applied to a family unit — A case study. *J Child Psychol Psychiatry, 9*: 245-252, 1968.
13. Eysenck, H.J. (Ed.): *Experiments in Behavior Therapy*. New York, Pergammon, 1964.
14. Ferber, A., Mendelsohn, M., and Napier, A.: *The Book of Family Therapy*. Science House, 1972.
15. Guerney, E.: *Psychotherapeutic Agents: New Roles for Non-Professionals and Teachers*. New York, HR&W, 1969.
16. Hewitt, F.M.: Teaching speech to an autistic child through operant conditioning. *Am J Orthopsychiatry, 35*: 927-936, 1965.
17. Hoermann, H.: *Psychologie der Sprache*. New York, Springer Verlag, 1970.
18. *Human Communication: The Public Health Aspects of Hearing, Language and Speech Disorders*. U. S. Department of HEW, NINDS, Monograph, No. 7, 1968.
19. Johnson, D.J., and Myklebust, H.R.: *Learning disabilities: Educational principles and practices*. New York, Grune, 1967.
20. Kanner, L.: Problems of nosology and psychodynamics in early infantile autism. *Am J Orthopsychiatry, 19*: 416-426, 1949.
21. Kozloff, M.A.: A comprehensive behavioral training program for parents of autistic children. In Upper, D., and Goodenough, D.S. (Eds.): *Behavior Modification in Educational Settings*. Proceedings of the Fourth Annual Brockton Symposium on Behavior Therapy. Nutley, N.J., Roche Laboratories, 1973.
22. Krasner, L., and Ullmann, L. (Eds.): *Research in Behavior Modification*. New York, Holt, 1965.
23. Langsley, D.G., Kaplan, D.M., Pittman, F.S., Machotka, P., Flomenhaft, K., and De Young, C. D.: *The Treatment of Families in Crisis*. New York, Grune, 1968.

24. Lazarus, A.A.: *Behavior Therapy and Beyond.* New York, McGraw, 1971.
25. Levenstein, P.: Cognitive growth in preschoolers through verbal interaction with mothers. *Am J Orthopsychiatry, 40,* 3:426-432, 1970.
26. Levenstein, P.: Mothers as early cognitive trainers: Guiding low-income mothers to work with their preschoolers. *Society for Research in Child Development,* April, 1971.
27. Lindemann, E.: The meaning of crisis in individual and family living. *Teachers College Record, 57*: 310, 1956.
28. Mead, M.: *Growing Up in New Guinea.* New York, Mentor, 1953.
29. Meyers, D.I., and Goldfarb, W.: Studies of perplexity in mothers of schizophrenic children. *Am J Orthopsychiatry, 31*: 551, 1961.
30. Miller, D.R., and Westman, J.C.: Reading disability as a condition of family stability. *Family Process, 3*: 66-76, 1964.
31. Minuchin, S.: *Families and Family Therapy.* Cambridge, Harvard U Pr, 1974.
32. Nickerson, E.T.: Recent trends and innovations in play therapy. *Int J Child Psychother, 2*: 53-71, 1973.
33. Park, C.: *The Siege.* New York, Har-Brace & World, 1967. (Paperback, Little Brown, 1973).
34. Patterson, G.R.: A learning theory approach to the treatment of the school phobic child. In Ullman, L. P., and Krasner, L. (Eds.): *Case Studies in Behavior Modification.* New York, HR&W, 1966, pp. 270-285.
35. Reusch, J.: *Disturbed communication. The clinical assessment of normal and pathological communicative behavior.* New York, Norton, 1957.
36. Ruderman, E. G., and Selesnick, S.: Multiple avenues of approach to a child with a chronic symptom: Stuttering. Paper presented at the meetings of the American Academy of Psychoanalysis, May, 1968.
37. Schaefer, H.H., and Martin, P.L.: *Behavioral Therapy.* New York, McGraw, 1969.
38. Schell, R.E., and Adams, W. P.: Training parents of a young child with profound behavior deficits to be teacher-therapists. *J Spec Ed, 2,* 4: 439-454, 1968.
39. Schlesinger, H.S., and Meadow, A.: Emotional support to parents: How, when, and by whom. *Parent Programs in Child Development Centers: First Chance for Children,* Vol. 1 Chapel Hill, T.A.D.S., 1972, pp. 13-23.
40. Schopler, E.: Parents of psychotic children as scapegoats. *J Contemp Psychother, 4*: 17-22, 1971.
41. Schopler, E.: Changes of direction with psychotic children. In Davids, A. (Ed.): *Child Personality and Psychopathology: Current Topics, Vol. I.* New York, Wiley, 1974, pp. 205-236.
42. Schopler, E., and Reichler, R.J.: Parents as co-therapists in the treatment of psychotic children. *J Autism Child Schizo, 1,* 1: 87-102, 1971.
43. Schopler, E., and Reichler, R.J.: Developmental therapy by parents with their own autistic child. In Rutter, N. (Ed.): *Infantile autism: Concepts, characteristics and treatment.* London, Churchill Livingston, 1971, pp.

206-227.

44. Schopler, E., and Reichler, R.J.: How well do parents understand their own psychotic child? *J Autism Child Schizo*, 2: 387-400, 1972.
45. Simmons-Martin, A.: Early education. Convention of American Instructors of the Deaf, Indianapolis, June, 1973.
46. Speck, R.V., and Attneave, C.L.: *Family Networks*. New York, Pantheon, 1973.
47. Straughan, J.H.: Treatment with child and mother in the playroom. *Behav Res Ther*, 2: 37-41, 1964.
48. Thompson, T., and Grabowski, J. (Eds.): *Behavior Modification of the Mentally Retarded*. New York, Oxford U Pr, 1972.
49. Wahler, R.G.: Mothers as behavior therapists for their own children. *Behav Res Ther*, 3: 113-124, 1965.
50. Walder, L.: *Teaching parents and others principles of behavioral control for modifying the behavior of children. Final report*. Silver Springs, Institute for Behavioral Research, 1968.
51. Weinrott, M.R.: A training program in behavior modification for siblings of the retarded. *Am J Orthopsychiatry*, 44, 3: 362-376, 1974.
52. Wolpe, J.: *The Practice of Behavior Therapy*. New York, Pergamon, 1969.
53. Wyatt, G.L.: Speech and language disorders in preschool children: A preventive approach. *Pediatrics, 36*, 4:637-647, 1965.
54. Wyatt, G.L.: *Language Learning and Communication Disorders in Children*. New York, Free Press, 1969.
55. Wyatt, G.L.: *Early Identification of Children with Potential Learning Disabilities*. Title VI Report, Wellesley Public Schools, 1970.
56. Wyatt, G.L.: *Early Identification and Follow-Through*. Title I Report, Wellesley Public Schools, 1973.
57. Wyatt, G.L., and Herzan, H.M.: Therapy with stuttering children and their mothers. *Am J Orthopsychiatry, 32*, 4:645-659. Reprinted in Clark, D.H. and Lesser, G.S. (Eds.): *Emotional Disturbance and School Learning: A Book of Readings*. Chicago, Science Research Associates, 1965, pp. 146-163.
58. Zigmond, N., and Cicci, R.: *Auditory Learning*. San Rafael, Dimensions Publishing Co., 1968.

Chapter 6

PROJECT COPE

Flonnia C. Taylor

INTRODUCTION

"**I** WISH we could get Missi to obey us at home as she does Miss Ann here at the center," Mrs. S. remarked to the director of the Child Development Center as she observed her child through a small window. "Does she understand what you want her to do?" the director asked. "Yes, I believe she does, but she wants to aggravate me! She is obstinate. Remember how you suggested that I move her out of our bed into a bedroom of her own? At first she cried nearly all night and was difficult to manage during the day, but now she is doing fine about that. What is more important, John is nicer to me, and we are happier having our bedroom to ourselves. I called Mrs. C. yesterday and her Johnnie is driving her up a wall, but here I notice that he's happy, plays well with others and minds Miss Ann. We both feel you helped us in our conference, but we need more of your time." The director mused for a minute and then asked, "Do you think you and other mothers would like to have regular meetings one day a week to learn more about handling your children at home?" "Oh yes," Mrs. S. quickly responded. "Until I brought Missi here I thought I'd never live through another year. Sometimes now I wonder how I can cope with her another hour."

So Project Cope was born at United Cerebral Palsy of the Bluegrass in Lexington, Kentucky. It was aimed at helping mothers to cope with their innumerable and seemingly insoluble problems and their deeply personal emotional overlay.

The Child Development Center known to Mrs. S. was staffed by people who believed in parents' knowing what the child was doing in the classroom and how the child reacted to the stress of new situations. The staff urged parents to watch their children through an observation window in the classroom, believing that child observation can lead to parent education when accompanied by appropriate guidance and stimulation.

Someone on the CDC staff noted that the first letters of *child observation — parent education* form the word *cope*, which aptly describes parents' feelings when trying to solve the multitudinous problems which a handicapped child brings into a home. A parent literally *copes* or *struggles* with the daily tasks created by the child's handicapping condition. From feeding to toilet-training, from sitting alone to walking alone, from learning how to lock a wheelchair to how to unlock braces, from pulling off a sock to pulling off a coat, from learning primary colors to recognizing his own name, from learning to share to learning how to successfully compete — all these represent some of the hundreds of problems faced by a parent trying to help the handicapped child to develop and use his potential. More patience, more self-control and more effort to induce the child to learn to do for himself are required in coping with a handicapped child than is required in training a half dozen normal children.

The parent must match herself or himself against the child's organic, psychological, mental and emotional needs; parents literally "encounter in combat" (a definition for *cope* found in Webster's dictionary) their own feelings of anxiety, guilt, depression and, frequently, hopelessness. Oftentimes a parent struggles with other members of the family, such as grandparents, who unintentionally undo the training given to the child by parent or teacher; always the parent must cope with the neighborhood and the community where rejection often is shown in such behavior as refusal to include the handicapped child in play with other children or community programs and sometimes in public school programs.

Because of the massive difficulties involved in parents' problem-solving efforts, the Child Development Center staff understood that a series of crisis situations could take place almost daily in any family unit. To handle or prevent such situations became a consuming desire on the part of the CDC staff members.

PHILOSOPHY UNDERLYING PROJECT COPE

Basically parents wish to do everything possible for the

handicapped child, but, because of their own emotional, physical and social needs, some may become child abusers. Along with the emphasis now being given to child abuse, there should be some emphasis given to understanding parent abuse. Few people recognize the frustrations created within parents by the fact of having a handicapped child. Parents literally are victims of abuse, which is brought about by the tensions created by a handicapped child. There has been community lethargy or pity for the special child, coupled with lack of consideration for the desperate situations of entire families.

For years professionals focused on the handicapped child. Parents were blamed when they did not *cooperate* or do what the professionals asked. Little attention was paid to parents' needs. Times have changed, and now much recognition is being given to parental efforts to provide a learning environment at home and to secure the best educational opportunities in the community for the handicapped child. Cognizance has been taken of parents' leadership in establishing the major national private agencies that deliver services to handicapped children. A program launched by the federal government to provide educational opportunities for all handicapped children by the year 1980 had its foundation laid some fifty years ago by groups of parents who joined hands to provide training for their own physically and mentally handicapped children.

It was in an effort to provide much-needed help to parents that the innovative Project Cope was initiated. The project was started by a private agency in the days when there were no organized parent involvement groups, when there was little or no literature on the how and what-to-do aspects of parent training, no written plans such as those which now have been provided by the Federal Office of Education and Office of Child Development and Head Start programs. Project Cope was based on psychiatric social work principles which were derived from child psychiatry, psychology and social case work. Terminology has changed during the intervening years so that *case work* now has become *counseling* or *problem-solving strategies; therapy* has become *intervention.* Regardless of terminology used, a parent in a situation of stress needs assistance at times of intolerable frustration and confusion.

PERSPECTIVES IN THE FORMING OF PROJECT COPE

Parents who have handicapped children frequently expect miracles to take place in doctors' offices or classrooms, and often after a period of time in a preschool center or classroom, dramatic changes may appear in children's behavior. To the parents these changes may seem miraculous, but such changes are brought about by skillful, knowledgeable adults. Furthermore, the people who successfully manage children can communicate with parents in such a way that some of the classroom successes can be transferred into the home situation.

The project began with meetings for the primary purpose of using child observation as a means of parent education. Meetings were designed to give parents information and to help them find answers to such dilemmas as how to accept their situation and feel good about themselves; how to manage a brain-injured or neurologically-impaired child, how to be objective about a disabled child, how to handle other problems within the family caused or magnified by the presence of a handicapped child, how to interpret the child's needs to the in-laws and to neighbors, and how to become involved in community and state planning for the sake of all handicapped children. Later the project evolved into both a counseling and an educational program for parents of preschool children. The project plan was incorporated into programs of the fifteen Child Development Center units serving approximately 500 parents annually. In addition, it influenced other agencies to start similar programs.

Such a project with parents requires leaders with skill, understanding of parents and children, an appreciation of the power of past experiences to influence present behavior, and a recognition of emotional trauma and frustration. It also takes an old fashioned, perhaps sentimental idea of dedication to the process of sharing. Leaders must be able to give supportive help, ego-strengthening help, to parents while at the same time stimulating

them to consciously work toward bringing about changes. The
leader must be a good *listener* and be able to recognize what
parents may be feeling behind the words that they choose to say.
Group leaders must be able to interact with a group of parents in
such a way that each member can communicate while no one
member dominates the discussion. The leader must have the skill
to apply parent verbalizations to the subject under discussion in
order to prevent continuous digression that is destructive to the
group.

Project Cope has the following objectives: to provide emotional support to the parent, to help parents accept their handicapped
child, to assist in parents' psychological acceptance of necessary
training, to provide parents with an increased knowledge of child
rearing practices, to recognize where the child functions below
age level and what can be done to bring about improvement, to
assist them in child management techniques, and to teach parents
how to help a child increase his functioning in areas where he
already functions at age level. Another major objective is the
clarification of goals for the child in motor, language (or communication), personal-social, cognitive and emotional areas. Still
another goal is the strengthening of home relationships.

Years of growth of the program at United Cerebral Palsy of the
Blue Grass and continuing parent involvement have resulted in a
number of activities for parents developed to meet their needs.

NEEDS OF PARENTS

Basic needs of parents seem to remain the same yesterday, today
and tomorrow. Their specific needs change as time brings the
development of more resources and opportunities and as they and
their children grow older.

Project Cope requires that during annual parent interviews a
survey be made of what may be called *universal parental needs*.
The problems of which the parents are conscious as well as problems recognized by the social worker, teacher or other personnel
must receive practical, realistic help. These needs are considered
by the agency's board of directors and its program services committee. This needs assessment forms the basis for activities that

will be planned.

The major common problem in most families appears to be an unstable home situation in which the wife feels she is carrying all of the burden, the man feels neglected because of the child, and siblings feel rejection and jealousy. This problem can have many variations, as when in-laws deny there is a handicapping condition and blame the parents for spoiling the child. Many variations appear in broken homes or when a child was born out of wedlock; these mothers are taxed with emotional problems and many leave the burden of care for the handicapped child with the maternal grandmother. Further, many fathers escape their share of responsibility by working long hours or finding other activities away from home. Lack of communication between husband and wife and between parent and children is common. Another common problem is parental reinforcement of the child's undesirable behaviors through negative attention such as yelling, scolding and fussing, or through overprotection and lack of limits. Still other general problems pertain to neighborhood and community rejection of the handicapped child, to the fears of both parents concerning the future of the child, and to the tremendous medical bills with which many parents are burdened. While each family will probably share some problems similar to those in other families, each family will also have its unique and specific problems.

All parents are encouraged to participate. Some of the parents in Project Cope are professional people; others have little or no formal education; there are those with varying degrees of education between these two poles, and there is no effort by the agency to segregate parents according to education. The philosophy that "whatever is done with a handicapped child should be done with a purpose, should have an objective, should build a positive self-image, and should be done within an atmosphere conducive to learning" is applicable to all parent programs. Regardless of the education of any parent in the group, the sessions can be conducted in such a way that each parent will derive benefit and can find the session applicable to herself or himself.

Some parents are extremely wealthy; others fall into the poverty and disadvantaged groups. Some can manage to live within their incomes; others are heavily in debt. Some can arrange for baby-sitting service, but since all cannot, the agency offers nursery service for those children not in school while parents attend meetings. Some parents do not have transportation to the meetings. In keeping with the assumption that all parents can profit by participating, the agency and parents concerned arrange transportation either by agency bus or through other parents.

An explanation of the parent program is given to parents at the time the child is evaluated at the center and enrolled. Because of many problems overwhelming them, most parents need reminders about dates for the meetings, which is done through telephone calls and letters.

ACTIVITIES INCLUDED IN PROJECT COPE

The first two activities of Project Cope, individual counseling and mothers' group sessions, started a series of activities which now include the following:

Individual Parent Counseling — as needed
Parent Project Council — monthly
Mothers' Sessions — early part of school year
Fathers' Sessions — early part of school year
Parent Club — meets five times during year
Mother-Father Joint Sessions — near end of year
Parent Orientation to Classroom — first week of school
Parent-Teacher — *Classroom Observation and Conference* — as needed
Parent-Speech Therapist Conference — as needed
Parent to Parent — mutual support
Parents as Resources — to staff, to the community
Follow Along Service — problem-solving help as long as child is in Kentucky.

These various activities will be discussed further in sections of this chapter.

INDIVIDUAL PARENT COUNSELING

Individual counseling was the first parent involvement program in many agencies. Where there is an active and proficient social work staff as many as 95 to 98 percent of parents may take advantage of the service. This is the case at the Child Development Center. Interviews are arranged in the social worker's office or in the home according to parent's desires. These contacts increase markedly after a series of parent sessions. Perhaps the support given in the sessions allows parents the freedom to bring their personal problems into open discussion with a worker. Perhaps they learn to verbalize their feelings during the session and can seek additional help. Intensive counseling involving emotional problems is provided by professionally-trained psychiatric social workers while other general problems are handled by *generic* social workers trained in the strategies of problem solving.

A *Parent Project Council* was developed to bring parents into the actual planning of parent education. Two representatives from the mothers in each class unit are invited to meet with the social work staff to plan the parent sessions. The selection of these representatives is made by the agency evaluation team which sees each child and each parent upon application for admission to the center. The criteria for the selection are the amount of time the parent has for such an activity, her leadership qualities and her willingness to participate. The parent's formal education is ignored. Leaders have come from poverty-stricken, illiterate, wealthy and professional people. One of the most attractive, influential and successful council members was a young mother with a third grade education and three children. Her extreme shyness vanished as she received approval and acclaim. Her leadership abilities were emulated by others who had little or no education.

Parent representatives organize themselves into a formal council with elected officers and defined duties which include notifying mothers of the meetings, serving as hostess in greeting new mothers, serving coffee or cold drinks, having the secretary keep notes and notify other mothers about illness of anyone in the group, or sharing information about any family crisis. This council takes its responsibilities seriously and has been instrumental in the development of other parent activities. Each year the members make excellent suggestions as they assist in making out agendas and summarizing the meetings.

GROUP SESSIONS FOR MOTHERS

Mothers' groups were started because these women have many needs which can best be met in group situations. Some of the needs have been itemized as

1. The need to feel that she is not alone in a stressful situation. The *need to belong* is as urgent in adults as in children.

2. A chance to be away from the handicapped child a few hours each week, free from feelings of concern.

3. Help in learning to observe and listen. The child's behavior speaks poignantly.

4. Help in learning how to interpret the child's behavior.

5. Although mothers have a desire to successfully manage the child's behavior, they need help in developing the skill to do so.

6. A yearning for personal approval and reinforcement can be met in well-conducted group situations.

7. Help in handling fears, guilt and depression.

8. Help in accepting a handicapped child as a person with some potential.

9. Help in attaining feelings of successful achievement.

10. Help in establishing a home atmosphere of sharing, giving and receiving by all members of the family, especially by the father of the child.

11. In broken homes the need for male companionship is obvious, and martyrdom feelings on the part of the mother are usually apparent. These mothers need help in finding strength and courage to live, to make friends, to set goals for themselves.

12. The need for help in martialing forces to handle crises.

In 1958, through the enthusiasm of a few mothers, the first mothers' meeting was arranged, and a plan of action was determined. The first group asked for weekly meetings of one and one-half to two hours to continue throughout the school year. However, from past experience, the agency director had learned that limits are good for parents as well as for children and, therefore, set a limit of eight weekly meetings for each session. The plan has not changed much over the years. The first two sessions are devoted to "Getting Acquainted and Listening." A problem, usually discipline, is studied at the third meeting. At the fourth and fifth sessions other problems are focused upon; these usually pertain to the physical needs of the child in the areas of motor behavior, speech, feeding, toileting and personal-social problems. Mothers discuss such matters as dressing, buttoning, putting toys away, etc. By the fifth session intangibles such as sibling jealousy or lack of assistance and emotional support from the father appear in the discussion. Usually the last three sessions take on a deeper, more personal note including such matters as a mother's feelings regarding herself, her husband, her children, her in-laws, marital problems and, finally, neighborhood problems and community resources. The series is closed with a review of the sessions in which all mothers participate. An evaluation form is filled out by each mother before the close of the sessions. Mothers also answer the same set of questions which were put to them at the beginning of the series. A comparison is made by the leader to discern changes in a mother's attitudes.

During these sessions the overall program for the children is discussed along with the parents' problems. Discussions include explanation of stages of child development from birth to eight years, techniques of child management, influence of family interactions, the art of developing a happy home atmosphere and a successful marriage, and the importance of childhood as a time when the handicapped person finds his unique doorway to hope and when parents find a satisfaction in opening that door.

The getting-acquainted period is as important to the success of the total session as is the first interview in portraying the image of an agency. The leader opens by welcoming everybody and introducing the mothers' council members, explaining their services and the class groups they represent. Then she asks the mothers to separate into pairs to play a game. Even as children learn through play, so can adults. *Know thy neighbor* is the name given to the game. When the mothers have grouped themselves, the leader asks each person to obtain from her *neighbor* her name, that of her husband and children, where the husband is employed, and where the family lives; she also asks the *neighbor's* favorite color, pet gripe and hobby. After five minutes the group reassembles and each person introduces her neighbor. This ice-breaker lets the women know whose husbands have the same employer or whose hobbies are the same. The discussion of favorite colors follows, usually with much laughter at the psychological meanings described by the leader. Mothers also are asked to discuss the colors most often chosen by their children. If a child consistently chooses dark brown or other dark colors in preference to bright colors, the parents are told to take a close look at his disposition, facial expression, his eyes. He could be emotionally upset, anxious, worried and unhappy, but note that this generalization cannot apply to children that are blind or have a great deal of visual impairment. Then mothers discuss hobbies from the point of view of reason for the choice. The discussion of hobbies and pet gripes gives some insight into the mothers' personalities and patterns of reaction.

By the time discussion generated by the game is completed, mothers are relaxed and ready to talk. Each mother is asked to make a placecard by writing her name on both sides of a large piece of heavy paper or cardboard, folding it in the center and placing it in front of her so that people all around the table can fit the name with the person. Usually a ten-minute coffee break here gives the mothers a chance to change seats and to get acquainted with someone in whom they have found similar interests. The hostess invites the group members to help themselves to coffee and doughnuts provided by the center or donated to the center by a civic club.

After the group is called back, the leader presents some information. For example, she may explain that brain damage may occur during pregnancy, at the time of birth and after birth from such causes as accidents, high fevers and infections. She may discuss her ideas regarding the causes of brain damage in an effort to explain to mothers that they are not to be blamed for their children's handicaps, and that no mother is given a handicapped child as punishment. Somewhere a universal law has not been followed, usually through ignorance, and the result is a handicapped child. For instance, no physician would deliberately delay a birth if he knew it would harm a child. Yet many children have been brain-damaged because of delayed birth, more of them prior to the time research revealed it as one of the causes of handicapping conditions. Also, no woman would allow herself to have a poor diet during the first two months of pregnancy if she had the means to obtain a balanced diet; yet many children are brain-damaged because of this lack of nutrition. No woman is going to deliberately expose herself to measles during the first three months of pregnancy now that we know measles is one of the great causes of brain damage, yet for many years many children with cerebral palsy were born because of the general lack of knowledge. And unmarried women would not run the risk of pregnancy if they realized that a large percentage of children born out of wedlock are brain-damaged because of poor diet, long emotional trauma and lack of early medical care.

The leader also spends a few moments extolling mothers who have handicapped children. She emphasizes that once there is a handicapped child in the family, it is important for the mother to garner her strength to find needed medical and community resources and to keep in mind that as diamonds are made by pressure, so can human beings become strong under pressure. Then a poem such as "Heaven's Special Child" (15) is read, and the leader praises the mothers for their efforts to help their children find their place in the community.

Each mother is asked to describe her handicapped child and the major problems he or she presents. As the problems unfold, one of the council members lists them on the blackboard, perhaps as discipline, speech, hyperactivity, short attention span, temper tantrums, inability to learn, poor memory, feeding problems, toileting, refusal to play with others, in-law problems, neighbors rejecting child, failure of father to help with child, sibling behavior and failure in school, etc. Frequently a mother will volunteer information regarding how she solved a particular problem with her child. Others ask questions and spontaneous participation results.

Before the first session ends, the leader explains how the problems mothers have listed may be alleviated by the agency program and discusses long-term goals and the short-term objectives of programs. With the parents' help, she summarizes the important points brought out by various individuals during the session.

A look at the blackboard shows a long list of problems. A vote is taken on the problems that should be considered first, and those that are of sufficient concern in the group to be discussed later. Those problems which are mentioned by only one or two individuals are considered in private conferences.

Only once did a mothers' group select a problem other than discipline or child management for first consideration. Parents comment on how short the sessions are and how nice it is to meet other mothers with the same problem.

From the second session on through the series the leader gives more information about the agency program, provides a period of observation of children in the classroom, and gives handouts which usually include an appropriate poem, a funny story and serious articles carefully selected to go with the topics under discussion. A questionnaire regarding her child is included in the first group of handouts to mothers.

Discussions regarding the agency include a look at the assessment tools used by the teachers such as The Lexington Developmental Scale (19), a discussion of records kept on each child, and the daily prescriptive teaching plan based on an individual child's needs. From time to time the agency's philosophy about handicapped children is given. This philosophy can be summarized by the following quotation: "When we treat a child as he is, we make him worse than he is; but when we treat him as if he already were what he potentially could be, we make him what he should be" (Grothe, 13).

Issues Regarding Parents in the Classroom versus Parents as Home Teachers

When mothers question whether they are allowed to work in the classroom, the reply usually is phrased something like this, "The answer to your question is 'no.' This agency believes it is better for the child to function part of the time away from parental influence." The leader then asks, "Aren't you really enjoying the freedom of three hours each day that you can spend with your baby or do housework undisturbed, or shop without worrying about the safety of your child? Aren't you a better wife because of this time free of worry?" Mothers usually agree that this is the case.

In recent years parent involvement programs have mushroomed, and there are two distinct schools of thought regarding them. Many programs include parents as part of the classroom staff. Some of the arguments in favor of this procedure include the need for continuity in a child's training and giving parents an opportunity to learn more about child management, child development and professional methods in training. Perhaps a foremost reason is the need for additional classroom staff and unavailable funds to meet such a need. Few agencies can afford the cost of sufficient paid staff to meet the individual needs of handicapped children in training.

The Child Development Center follows the policy that a child's best interests may not necessarily be served by parents being with him full-time. Length of time the parents spends with the child is not as important as the types of relationship and communication. Parents are not allowed to work in the CDC classrooms containing their own children. The reasoning behind the policy includes the belief that parents need to be away from the handicapped child a part of every week in order to be more relaxed and more effective parents. They need to leave the child with persons in whom they have full confidence. Their need to be away from the child includes being free of anxiety and guilt during the period of absence. Leaving a handicapped child with a baby-sitter (provided one can be obtained) may not eliminate feelings of anxiety or guilt, whereas leaving a child in a school situation provides freedom for the parent without deep concern about the child's experiences or the care he is receiving. Furthermore, most children, after the orientation period, adjust more quickly to a new learning situation with other children if a parent is not present. Finally, it is believed that the teacher-child relationship can be more easily transferred to the mother-child relationship or the father-child relationship after some of the child's undesirable patterns of behavior have been modified in the classroom. Parent education seems to be obtained more readily through systematic observation of the child in the classroom according to Haring (14), parent education sessions and the various other activities that bring parent and children into interactions that are positive and educational.

Programs which do not use parents within the classrooms extend their teaching staff through the use of carefully-selected and trained volunteers and student trainees in special education. Although parents have been included in the planning of the center's parent education services, most of them prefer not to work in the classroom. A few have expressed the desire to be with the child because of his dependency needs. Later, their own overprotection patterns were revealed. A large number volunteered to work in the agency and were accepted after their children had left the center and were enrolled in elementary school.

Methods Used with Mothers

Prior to the time mothers observe children in the classroom, the leader does not attempt to explain classroom procedures or activities. Mothers observe daily classroom activities which serve to stimulate their questions and discussion. The experiences of one group of mothers will be used now to illustrate the kinds of activities observed and discussed, and the way these discussions are geared to offering education and support to parents.

A group of mothers, after observing four-year-olds, commented on various activities they had observed. Although classes had been in progress only four weeks, it was noted that the children happily took turns and proudly showed their achievements. Mothers noted that at refreshment time the children pulled or carried their chairs to the table, sat down and waited to be served. Napkins were handed out by one child, peanut butter and crackers were served by another (some children wanted two servings but the server said, "Wait, later!") and the fruit juice was poured with the help of the teacher by the child designated as leader. Most of the children talked or communicated in some way and laughed with each other. One child had to be fed by the teacher because of poor hand coordination, but he was encouraged to try to carry a small piece of cracker to his mouth. He succeeded, and the entire group clapped when the teacher called attention to his success. One child refused to eat what was served. She asked for a cookie and milk. The child who was leader said, "Today juice day." The teacher praised the leader for his explanation and repeated, "Today is juice day." The teacher than asked, "Why do we have juice today?" The children chorused, "Milk yesterday!" The teacher said, "Yes, we had milk yesterday," and she explained that no one had to drink the juice or eat the crackers and peanut butter, but there was no substitute. When another child reached to take the juice and cracker which the little girl would not eat, the teacher explained that the little girl might change her mind and eat it, and if the other child wished a second helping he should ask the leader who was seated in the center of the half-circle table. These mothers had also seen the children working in small groups of two with finger paints. They had seen them put up their paints, take off their paint aprons, fold them and place them on a shelf, then look for their own chairs. They had seen the children go to the bathroom to wash their hands before eating. A teacher stood near the bath, but each child who could walk well went in alone. The severely handicapped were taken one at a time by a support teacher. The amazement felt by the mothers who observed these behaviors was so overwhelming they could only make such comments as "My Joey would never put anything up at home," "My Billy has never gone to the bathroom alone," "My Mary has never washed her hands in her life," "My Johnnie has never been that still that long," "My Julie always wants what is not on the table."

In this case the leader asked the mothers if they had heard what the teachers repeatedly said to the children. One mother replied, "Yes, I noted Miss Ann said, 'Joey I like the way you folded and put your paint apron on the shelf,' and Miss Evelyn said, 'Billy, I'm proud of you. You are a big boy today. You went to the toilet, you washed your hands with soap, you dried them and then placed the towel in the waste basket. I'm so proud of you,' and she hugged him as he came out of the bathroom door." The leader added that each child was praised warmly for the desired behavior. Hugs, pats and verbal praise so that others could hear it were used over and over with each child. Behavior that was not desirable was ignored if it did not hurt the child or someone else. The leader then listed some of the techniques used with the children, for example, the courtesy each staff member showed each child, saying thank you and please to children as a routine part of communicating with them, using complete sentences when speaking to a child without correcting the child for not using a complete sentence in reply. This respect was consistent with the belief that no child likes to be belittled, and learns best through observation, repetition and approval.

In such postobservation discussions as these, parent observation can be channeled into parent education. For example, the leader opened the second session with the above mothers by discussing how we influence each other by the way we react to each other. Mothers shared interesting little vignettes of their home life, and how they yelled, complained and fussed. Before time to leave that session the leader asked the group to help plan the next session by asking them to count during the coming week the number of times their children engaged in the behavior which annoyed them the most. This was the topic for the third session. Again, mothers' ways of handling annoying behaviors could be compared with teachers' ways of handling these.

Each session of this group was summarized by the leader. Occasionally the leader repeated earlier comments such as one made at the beginning of the first session — "Mothers are wonderful people! Mothers of handicapped children are extra wonderful and have much inner strength or they would break under their heavy loads. Mothers set the atmosphere in the home. When they go to pieces, the entire family disintegrates." The leader closed each session with a story. An example is the story about the five-year-old who was helping her mother set the table for Sunday dinner. She had been to Sunday School while the mother attended church service. The mother asked, "What did you learn in Sunday School today, honey?" "Oh, I lun'd 'bout Dod and how he made the wo'ld." "How did God make the world?" "Well, He made the dirt, the trees, the sky and water. Then He reached down an' took some dirt an' patted it an' patted it until He made a man just like Daddy. He thought the man was lonesome, so He put him to sleep and took out his brains an' made a woman jus' like you, Mommie."

At the session at which discipline was the main topic, parents were asked to describe the various kinds of discipline they used most. Forms of discipline ranged from scolding or deprivation of an enjoyable activity to spanking. In each case discipline meant punishment. The leader suggested that mothers consider the words *disciple* and *discipline*. The group was silent for a while. Then discussion started and gradually became enthusiastic as the mothers considered disciple, meaning follower or learner, and connected it with teacher and love and sacrifice. Eventually the group concurred with one mother who said, "Discipline should mean showing love by giving instruction, *not* punishment."

The discussion then moved to how to give instruction to a handicapped child who may not understand the meaning of the words the mother uses or who has already sized her up and knows how to get attention even if he must be annoying in order to get it. The leader recalled some of the statements made by these mothers in past meetings which could be appropriately used and which showed strengths. This technique is used to build a feeling of self-confidence in mothers and a willingness to try again. It also stimulated others to voice opinions which included such statements as, "I ask, I tell, I yell, and finally I let him do what he wishes when he wishes." One parent quietly volunteered that, after watching a teacher at the center the previous year, she had been talking slowly and using gestures to her little girl, who is a child with spastic cerebral palsy. If she says to the child, "Bring me *one* large spoon," she raises one finger and then points to the cabinet drawer which contains the spoons. She also makes a drawing in the air of a *large* spoon. If she said, "It's time to go to bed," she would point to the clock and then the bedroom. She confided that since she had placed her child on a regular routine program for bed, meals, bath, toileting and even dressing, she had less trouble managing her in other activities. The child had learned to put on her underclothes by herself after the mother laid them out on the bed in order, and could put on one or two dresses that were easily fastened and her coat. She could put on socks and shoes, but sometimes she placed a shoe on the wrong foot. It was pointed out how right the mother was because a spastic child becomes very tense and rigid under pressure, but when there is a routine the child feels less pressure.

The parents continued to discuss *structure* and *limits* as a part of discipline. Many mothers had given up on trying any kind of routine or placing any kind of limits. Consequently, many four-year-old children were going to bed at 11 p.m. or later and getting up at 7 a.m. They had no regularly-scheduled meals except the refreshment time at the center. Parents questioned how to bring about a change in objectionable behavior and establish a more relaxed routine. The discussion then focused on the teacher's techniques in bringing about changes. Parents had observed that teachers followed good behavior with attention and affection. The teacher gave a mild disapproval for objectionable behavior, such as giving a child who misbehaved the choice of stopping the undesirable behavior or leaving the group or play activity. If a child was aggressive toward another child to the point of hurting him, a teacher intervened and sent the aggressive child into another activity or removed him from the group but gave extra attention to those children who were behaving nicely.

Emphasis was placed on what may be called Bucker's and Lovaas' (3) theory that one follows the consequence he wishes to strengthen with reinforcing events, and one follows the responses he wishes to weaken with punishing events. The withholding of all forms of reinforcement can be a useful form of punishment at times. Tangible reinforcers such as being allowed to pull up the window shade mean a great deal to small children.

Children learn through their senses. They learn and remember pleasurable experiences. They learn through games, and parents need to learn how to play games that give constructive experiences. Holt (16, 17) describes education as the games of trying to find out how the world works. Parents oftentimes are too busy, too tired or too serious to play a game with the child in a spirit of joy or foolishness to allow one thing to lead to another until the child feels he is important and that he has an effect on another human being in an exciting and happy atmosphere.

It was pointed out that children are supersensitive to the emotions of adults, especially the people they love. They learn how to manipulate adults. They can punish; they can please. They understand much more than they can express. Adults forget this fact, and by talking in front of them, the adults reinforce the very behavior they would like to change.

Mothers shared the results of their assignment, describing during the third session the number of times an undesirable behavior took place and how they handled it. They verbalized ways to apply the child management principles that had been observed and discussed. If parents remember that the things they *do* help to determine the way they feel, they may try to be cheerful, learn to play games and, above all else, *talk* to the child as one person who has respect for another.

The mothers' sessions are as stimulating and challenging to staff as to parents. Each session brings out new reactions and individual problems. Perhaps the session on the tiresome everyday tasks that must be lived through with each child is one of the most challenging and most practical. For example, many mothers have problems with toilet-training a handicapped child. One mother expressed despair and anger at her child for "doing nothing on the potty," but wetting the living room rug each day and looking up at her with a roguish grin. Another mother helpfully told how she placed a toy, her child's favorite bear, on the potty chair in the living room, and he found it there. In a couple of days she moved the chair toward the bathroom a few feet, placed the bear in it and some toys around it. The child picked up the bear, sat in the chair and played with the toys. Each day she moved the chair nearer the bathroom. One day she placed the child on the potty chair with his pants down and suggested that he tinkle. He did not. The next day she tried again, this time with success. She patted his arm and called him a big boy. Little by little the chair was moved toward the bathroom, and finally into the bathroom. By this time the mother had timed this game to the child's bowel movement, and training was completed.

Feeding can be a problem. A child may be capable of feeding himself but will not eat at the table, or he will eat only certain foods. Parents often ignore his needs or cajole, coerce and scold without success. Again, the way to cope with this problem may be found in the observation room. Teachers *expect* a child to eat what is before him. They set the example and make a lot of fun out of eating activities. For example, in one room there were six children who would not try new foods. At Halloween time the class went to a farm and picked some pumpkins. The following day they made a jack-o-lantern, which was the centerpiece for the table. At the "Trick or Treat" party they had apples, nuts, juice and special cup cakes with faces which an artistic mother made. Some of the children had never eaten a raw apple or nut. Some of the children followed the teachers' examples and talked about "How 'licious." Finally, one by one, the others tried a piece of apple and a nut. Later, they cooked a pumpkin and made a pie for Thanksgiving. Even the children who previously would not try new foods ate and enjoyed the pie. One little girl explained to her mother that she had learned "how to make a pie and then how to eat it." Parents who express a dislike for a food, or parents who say in front of the child, "John does not like green beans!" are reinforcing John's behavior and food fetish.

Organically-involved children are subject to the same emotional reactions about food as are other children. A five-and-a-half-year-old boy with cerebral palsy, still on a bottle and in diapers when he came to the center, learned to eat regular food like a normal child within five months and was toilet-trained within the year. The biggest problems were not the child's but the parents'. For example, at a school picnic the child was whining that he wanted only milk. The mother could not endure the whining, asked a teacher to take over with the child, and left. The teacher said, "When you eat your sandwich, you may have your milk." The teacher ignored the boy and started a conversation with another child about the content of his sandwich, how good it was and how nice it was to have him at the picnic. It was not long before the cerebral-palsied boy asked for a sandwich and soon said, "See, I ate it all up!" He then was given a cup of milk. This incident exemplifies not only the commonality of problems among children and their parents, but also how teachers can model behavior, shaping techniques for parents.

Clothing can cause a real struggle between parent and child if the clothes are not large enough or are not appropriate for the awkward efforts of a child with fine motor problems. Clothes can also cause parent-child struggles if a mother feels too rushed to take the time necessary to let her child try to dress himself or too rushed to give him only that amount of help that will permit the child to succeed at the task.

All the problems of feeding, dressing, etc., can be made intolerable by the emotional turmoil which can accompany them. A handicapped child is an emotional problem to others and to himself. Only when parents are helped to consciously control their emotions and their actions can tasks of daily living become acceptable and pleasant.

Films are also shown to mothers' groups. Films depicting the various stages of development of normal children from birth to eight years are shown during the series of meetings to help mothers know what *normal* behavior to expect and what goals to set. A film on overdependency appears to impress deeply all parents who see it despite its age and old-fashioned style in clothes. In the film the emotional impact made upon a child by an overpossessive mother influences his adult life to such an extent that he has insufficient self-confidence to apply for a job for which he is well-trained. His youthful pattern of forcing his peers to look after him carried into adulthood, leading to difficulty in making and keeping friends. Many mothers see themselves in the film and seek help to handle their guilt feelings, their anxieties and their subconscious rejection. Following the session in which such films are shown, often there is an avalanche of requests for individual counseling.

The sessions which seem to bring a turning point in the behavior of mothers are those in which they are able to verbalize their own feelings, their hostilities toward their husbands and relatives, and their personal fears and conflicts. A wise leader guides these discussions by asking pertinent questions regarding past experiences and by dropping bits of philosophy or psychiatric principles. For example, when a mother complained that her husband "came home from work, ate supper, read the paper, watched TV and went to bed without speaking more than a word or two," another young woman asked, "How did he ever propose?" The first woman smilingly said, "He could talk then, but three children later he has forgotten how." At this point one of the mothers who had been in the program the previous year spoke,

One year ago I felt like you do, but after a session like this I
decided it takes two to make a happy marriage. Maybe I

expected him to read my mind. Maybe he wanted me to talk
about things in which he was interested instead of always
complaining about or reporting on the children. I decided to
make Friday night *our* night. I fed the children early and sent
them in to watch TV. I explained that tonight belonged to
Mother and Daddy, and they were to remain in the living room
while we ate. I prepared the dishes my husband likes best; I put
on my prettiest table cloth, lit candles and dressed myself in my
most feminine outfit. When he came home, I met him at the
door. I kissed him and asked him to read the paper in the study
for a few minutes while I served dinner. When I called him he
was surprised to see the soft lights, the lovely table and no
children around. I explained that I felt I had neglected him, had
been giving too much of myself to the children. He was *the*
important person in my life. I asked him to imagine we were
dating again, and I waited for him to pull the chair out and seat
me. You'll never believe this, but that night changed our lives. I
asked him about his work; I was enthusiastic and
complimentary. Little by little he loosened up and began to talk
freely as he did when we were young, some eight years ago. We
talked far into the night. And Friday night has been *our* night
ever since. Now *he* talks and I praise. He also compliments me
more than he ever did. He comes home earlier and does less
night work in the study. Sometimes we simply sit on the couch
holding hands while all of us enjoy a TV program. We have
made Sunday a family "do-it-together" day and the children
love it. Girls, we need to remember that the man in the family is
the head and the woman the neck, but the *neck* turns the head!

The mothers applauded this lengthy comment and asked questions about other ways to influence their husbands. Answers were
readily given, especially on the subject of interpretation of the
wife's needs, amid laughter and in an atmosphere of healthy
companionship. It is interesting to note that the Friday night date
story is repeated by some mother year after year.

So often wives expect to change their husbands' undesirable
behavior by nagging and fussing. Human beings respond better
to the positive approach. The old saying that "Honey rather than
vinegar catches the fly" has a spark of truth applicable to many
persons.

The following is another example of the content discussed in mothers' groups: A mother brought up the problem of her in-laws' lack of understanding of the problems of her handicapped son. The leader asked if any mother had solved this sort of problem. One young woman said she solved it by forcing herself to calmly explain to her parents that her son is a handicapped child according to the doctor and other professional people. She explained that she was told that children do not often outgrow handicaps, but that without intervention they may grow into them more and more. She said she had noticed that as her son grew older he grew more frustrated because he knew he could not do what other children his age did. She said she had to talk to herself a month before she found enough courage to tell this to her parents, and to say that since the boy was her child she must decide what to do. She asked for her parents' cooperation in following her instructions about what to do with the child. She told them that if they did not care to cooperate, she would have to stop their visits to her family and her visits to them. She added that this experience was easy compared to what she went through with her husband's parents. She reported that her husband would not help her, but at least he did not interfere. She also reported that his parents made quite a scene, but she held firm. To the many questions on how it was working, she replied that so far the child was much better, although her guilt feelings so great that she sometimes becomes physically sick.

The leader may take such a cue to focus on physical reactions to emotional stress. In response to the above case, each mother was given an opportunity to reveal the ways she handled stress. Some admitted they had migraine headaches but that they had never before attributed them to emotional stress. Others complained of sinus and ulcers, and one mother acknowledged that she had come to believe her colitis attacks had always followed unhappy or stressful situations.

Such physical complaints can frequently be related to patterns children develop and parents reinforce. A child copies mother's headaches, or tummy aches or nausea when he can receive extra attention, stay out of school or successfully compete with baby for mother's attention. Mothers in the group being discussed commented that their children often used the *weapon* of illness in the summer, but that since the Child Development Center opened, the children had too much fun to want to miss school. Mothers stated they had to force children to remain home at times when they ran high fevers.

The final session for mothers is always a long one because the mothers try to converge on all the problems which have and have not been discussed. Neighbors' rejection and community resources are two important areas.

In recent years the terrible experiences to which handicapped children were once subjected by neighbors have been quietly vanishing. Sometimes it is still necessary for mothers of handicapped children to invite their neighbors in for coffee and incidentally interpret the kind of handicap the child has, his and their feelings and needs. When neighborhood adults can be helped to accept a handicapped child, they can help their children become more accepting and more understanding.

CDC has developed a list of all community, district and state agencies with a brief description of their services as handouts for parents. Other materials given to parents include *Parents Are Teachers* (1), *The Learning Child* (5), *Child Behavior* (11), *Beyond the Best Interests of Children* (12), *How Children Learn* (16), *What Shall I Tell My Child?* (27), *What Makes a Marriage Happy?* (24), *Building Your Marriage* (7), *Brain Damage in Children* (2), *New Light of Hope* (22), *The First Five Years of Life* (10), and magazines such as *The Exceptional Parent* (9), *Children Today* (4), and *Journal of Learning Disabilities* (21).

A review of the entire series of mothers' sessions serves several purposes. It gives the leader an opportunity to obtain a miniview of budding friendships. For example, at the end of one series of sessions a mother approached another woman, who was a foster mother, with the proposition that since their sons were best friends perhaps they could have lunch together. This luncheon was the beginning of weekends together for the boys and a friendship that has grown despite the fact that the boys now live in different communities, attend different public schools and are of different races. The foster mother has since adopted her foster child and declares that the other mother helped her toward the decision.

The final discussion in the mothers' group also helps the leader glimpse changes in mothers' personalities. Further, a second questionnaire is administered. When the second questionnaire is compared with the first one administered to mothers prior to the group sessions it shows changes in attitudes, in understanding and in patterns of handling stress situations. Finally, an evaluation done at the final session helps the leader evaluate topics that seemed most useful to a particular group. The evaluation sheets are not signed.

In the final session, mothers comment on the satisfactions received in group discussion, on the feeling of not being alone with their problems, on the strengthening of home relations, and on the increased knowledge of child management. Such comments have become the base for continuation of parent education in its present form. Mothers' comments and evaluations have reinforced recognition of a need for Project COPE.

GROUP SESSIONS FOR FATHERS

Early in the project mothers requested that fathers be given the opportunity for experiences in education similar to theirs. One interpretation of the mothers' request seemed to be "Help us articulate to the fathers our children's special needs; help us to close the gap between what we do actually and what we want to do ideally. Teach us as a team how to manage our child's behavior so we can love him and so others can accept him. Teach us how to communicate with our husbands and teach them how to communicate with us and with our children!"

In the early years of Project COPE many mothers complained that the fathers of their children would not talk about the handicapped child, did not expect anything from the child, and refused to be with the child more than a few minutes a week. Since much of our society has refused to accept the handicapped child, it seems logical that fathers would find it difficult to accept the child and to express feelings about the daily problems they encounter. Mothers who find professional people who accept the challenges of helping the child to develop his potential and of helping parents change their attitudes and the child's environment are eager to have their children's fathers also discover such experiences.

Some fathers also asked for special sessions to learn why their wives were so enthusiastic about the mothers' program. So, requests from both mothers and fathers prompted the initiation of group sessions for fathers. Fathers' meetings are always for two hours, scheduled each Sunday afternoon and on a week night for four weeks. Additional sessions can be arranged at the request of the group. The men have a choice between either of the meetings each week. Once the date and hour is set, most of the men are coerced by their wives into attending the first session. Each year a few men find excuses not to attend until personally invited by the agency administrators.

The format for fathers' groups differs slightly from that used in the mothers' groups. The agency leader usually arranges for a father who has attended a series to be present at the first meeting in order to describe his experiences. Each man present is asked to introduce himself and give a description of his handicapped child, specifying any major problems he has with the child. The father who has had experience in such groups usually breaks the ice by describing his child, discussing the agency program as his child has experienced it and the changes that have taken place in the child and in the home. Frequently, this father explains his original hang-ups, his escape from home problems, his guilt feelings, his projection of blame on the doctor, or on his wife, or on her family. He describes the help he received from conferences with the teachers, the social workers and other staff members. This father can usually highlight important outcomes in terms of the changes in his wife after the mothers' meetings.

Sometimes a second father, experienced in the agency organization, volunteers his testimony, followed by the new fathers who are guided to briefly and concisely pinpoint the child's major problem as they see it. Most of the time their early understanding is limited to a recognition of a physical problem such as a speech or motor handicap. As fathers can verbalize more, they later express their deeper concerns. As the fathers describe their children and their concerns, the leader makes a list of the problems; illustrations used from time to time in her discussion are based on these problems.

Most of the fathers' sessions emphasize such problems as child management; their frustration about their children's inattention and inability to do what other children their age can do; and problems with the mothers' nagging, fussing and scolding everybody in the family. Eventually the fathers talk about their concern over the high cost of medical services, the extra bills brought on by the handicapped child, and the future of the child. A frequent question asked is, "Who will support the child if something happens to me?" Insurance for the handicapped person still is a major problem. Before the series ends, the leader directs fathers' discussion into the parent-parent relationship and the parent-child relationship.

The first session is not only a get-acquainted session, but an introduction to agency objectives and procedures. Tapes and slides of children are effectively used. The purpose of each activity with children is explained while the leader interprets some of the staff's philosophy about learning.

At this first meeting, the leader emphasizes that teaching methods are often at fault when a child fails; often failure is not a reflection of the child's inability to learn. The home atmosphere (or total environment) can be distracting to the child, or it can create and maintain opportunities for the child to use his capabilities to alleviate his handicapping condition. For example, if a child has to be destructive or noisy in order to obtain the attention of his father, he may hit or knock something, knowing that he will be noticed. If the father takes the initiative, such as playing a game within the child's abilities, and helps the child succeed at least part of the time, the child will make a stronger effort to please his father with more acceptable behaviors. The leader questions what father can afford *not* to take a half hour or an hour each day to spend with his child in a special way? A list of activities for father-child time is one of the handouts.

The second session is built around the physical activities a father can engage in with his son or daughter. Stages of physical development from rolling to skating are demonstrated by a physical education teacher or by a physical therapist. The types of equipment which can be made at home are shown and building instructions are given to those who want them. Often a demonstration is given by pretending a man is a child — a boy who is afraid to climb. He can be started in a simple game with his Dad on an old ladder lying flat on the ground or floor. Learning to step between the rounds, then on the rounds, then *in-out* can be fascinating to a child with a motor problem or one with fear of such physical activity. In time he will master this game. The ladder can then be raised to four inches and the child can climb it without danger. An eight-inch wide plank can be added to the equipment and propped up on an eight-inch block. The child walks up and jumps into his dad's arms. Then the plank can be raised to twelve inches, then two feet, later to three feet. As the child masters each height he is ready for the next, but what is most important is that he is with his dad; he sees approval in his dad's face; he is *glad* he is a boy and will become a man just like Daddy. Similar activities are good for little girls and their fathers.

Discussion of the fathers' actual participation in activities with the children reveals that in most families *fathers do not have time, work hours are too long to allow playtime, or their mother handles all that.* When group leaders suspect that fathers may be avoiding interaction and communication, they ask pertinent questions to stimulate thinking and to encourage communication. Group leaders also are teachers and can impart information through case stories or bits of philosophy. When fathers complain of their wives' irritability, a question which startles many is, "Could you look after your handicapped child all day for seven consecutive days and retain your sweet disposition?" Reluctantly they describe their reactions to the child and interactions with him. To the question, "How can you expect your wife to carry this burden?" many fathers reply, "Women are different!" Other fathers discuss this subject until most in the group will admit they had not seriously considered their wives' reactions and needs.

To the question, "What about your child's needs?" again many fathers express the belief that the child's needs are met by the mothers and with the money they earn to support the family. With the help of other fathers, the leader emphasizes the problems pertaining to the emotional development of the child. The child's identification of his or her sex and the basis of adult heterosexual adjustment, according to many child researchers, is laid in the early relations with parents. A little girl can dislike being a girl if she sees that her father has no respect for her mother, if he continuously finds fault with her mother, if he has no method of communicating with her. In this connection the following is illustrative:

One of the fathers told the group his three daughters, ages four, five-and-a-half and six-and-a-half, insisted on wearing pants and having Daddy bathe them and put them to bed. They vied with each other as to who sat in the front seat of the car with Daddy. Mother had to sit in the back seat. They did not like for mother to do anything with them. He drove them to school, but the mother picked them up. He spent part of each evening with them. He spent Sundays with his family. He tried to be a good father, a good provider.

Later, in a counseling session, he admitted that he found it embarrassing to show affection toward his wife in front of anyone. He revealed that he criticized his wife a great deal. He had not been aware of it until the fathers' meetings had caused him to take a close look at his home relationships. He and his wife had not been anywhere together without the children during the last four years. He became fearful that his little girls would become adult homosexuals.

Through the counseling sessions he made a plan of attack on the problem. He decided to place the three girls in the back of the car, explaining that Mommie had patiently accepted the back seat for a long time. It was time to take turns. Mommie would sit in the front seat with Daddy. Over the weekend he took his wife out to dinner and to the theater. Little by little the man changed his pattern of behavior toward his wife. He complimented her meals and her appearance in front of the children. Finally, he was able to kiss her in front of them.

The children gradually changed. They asked for some new dresses and began to ask their mother to do things for them and with them. The Follow Along Service shows that after five years, the pattern of femininity in the girls is much stronger. They also are doing well in public school. The family group participates as a group in many activities, and the parents have taken vacations together, leaving the children with grandparents.

It is well to note as have Irwin and Marge (20), that the relationship between a person's communication patterns and emotional structure is complex and that failure to communicate may result from an individual's inner conflicts.

The two final sessions for fathers usually are an extension of the discussion of family interaction, emotional conflicts and marital problems. Fathers also have a chance to discuss classroom matters with their children's teachers. Each father goes to the classroom of his child, and there the teacher explains her program, illustrates some of her techniques in child management and learning. The father's questions are answered and he is encouraged to share home experiences.

The entire fathers' group reassembles at the last session. They give their evaluation of the series of sessions, make suggestions for follow up, and pick up the handouts.

PARENTS' CLUB

As an outgrowth of mothers' and fathers' sessions, parents organized the Parent Club. They elected its officers and formed committees. The club has a three-fold objective — to provide social activities, to provide additional educational opportunities through the use of speakers in various professional fields pertaining to the many factors parents must consider (such as future educational opportunities for handicapped children, insurance for the handicapped, etc.), and to develop projects to increase their identity as a group and provide some avenue both for self-realization and for leadership for their children. Staff members attend meetings of the club when invited. Some parents continue in the organization long after their children have left the agency.

Family picnics, small social gatherings and social events for the entire club have been promoted. Each meeting ends with a social hour with refreshments. Speakers have included pediatricians, psychologists, state school superintendents, legislators, insurance salesmen and many others.

Two of the far-reaching results of the Parents Club have been (1) its influence on the passage of state legislation, i.e. establishing a Bureau of Special Education and a law permitting public schools to purchase services from private agencies for children whose needs were not met within the public school program and (2) its fund-raising projects. Funds raised by the club have been used for special equipment which all parents or their children could use, a well-stocked library with such items as *Exceptional Children* (8), *How to Parent* (6), *Parents are Teachers* (1), film strips and projectors for teachers' use with children, playground equipment and a professional camera for the agency's use in publicity.

Our experience has shown that a parent club can be a vital part of an agency program. In order to function effectively, however, such a club must have proper stimulation, encouragement and recognition.

MOTHER — FATHER JOINT SESSION

There always are some parents who ask for more group meetings. They are encouraged to arrange meetings in their homes for discussion of common problems and to share their conclusions with their social workers. These parents are advised that, in addition to their informal home meetings, they will be invited to a series of three joint mother-father sessions during the seventh or eighth month their children are in school. The purpose of such sessions is to provide opportunities for parents to make suggestions for future services from the agency, evaluate their own progress in providing a learning environment in the home, and bring out other problems on which they would like help from other parents.

These mother-father sessions provide many answers and much satisfaction to the staff. These are the sessions where parents take a backward look and set future goals.

Agency staff arranges tentative dates for these joint meetings, notifies the parents ten days or two weeks prior to the meetings, and assumes the leadership role in the opening session. Parents usually take over the discussion. Prior to closing the third and final session, the staff leader summarizes the comments, emphasizes positive changes in parents and children, and points parents toward their future goals.

PARENT ORIENTATION TO THE CLASSROOM
AND PARENT-TEACHER CONFERENCES

Regardless of the number of times a parent has been to a school or had conferences with the agency staff, there is an aura of the unknown in every new situation, in meeting a new teacher, in visiting a new classroom. It is to the advantage of both the parent and teacher to have the unknown become known, to discuss the year's general plan and some of the details in the daily schedule, to have a clear interpretation of agency policies, and to detail some of the home problems parents face. The teacher has a responsibility to portray to the parent a graphic picture of some of the overall objectives, methods used to obtain them, and the meaning of the team approach to the developmental and educational needs of the child. The teacher, therefore, discusses some of the learning problems the child must overcome and what techniques are used to bring about changes. Parents are given the responsibility to share with the teacher their expectations of the child, of the school and of themselves.

In the give and take process of discussion, the base of the team approach is formed. Discussion of one tool used by all teachers in the Child Development Center provides a concrete foundation for parent-teacher interaction. The basic tool used by all teachers is the Lexington Developmental Scale (19), an assessment instrument which provides a clear profile of the child's current status in relation to normative data. This instrument indicates what skills the child must acquire in order to overcome the lag between what he does and what he should do at this age level. Discussions of the scale are always a stimulating experience for parents. The teacher has the opportunity to talk about stress situations brought on by a handicapped child and to discuss possibilities for behavior management. Many parents, of course, do not have the necessary knowledge or skills to bring about the results they desire, and their frustrations are increased by their inability to handle pressure situations. They need help in the management and the use of the resources such as the teacher and agency staff which are available to them. They need help in understanding the basic laws of the relationship between behavior and emotional responses.

It is necessary to remember that whereas in the classroom it is comparatively easy to control the process of reinforcement and contingencies of reinforcement, in the home there are more complex, emotionally-charged situations. Parents need help in recognizing the fact that all people are actively engaged in controlling and being controlled daily. Parents need guidance so that they may be aware of the methods they use in stimulating responses and in reinforcing those behaviors they desire in their children. More often than not, parents discover that they have unintentionally reinforced the very behaviors they would like to change. For example, many children develop patterns of restlessness at the table because the atmosphere is not made pleasant by the adults; children may be ignored, or the conversation at the table is beyond their comprehension, or perhaps there is negative attention paid to how they eat or what they eat. With help, parents can modify such behaviors in themselves; then parents and teachers can work hand in hand to teach the exceptional child to manage his or her own behavior, remembering that the handicap can interfere with the normal learning and maturation processes.

Both the home and classroom environments must provide reinforcement for children as growing and learning beings. The handicapped child has a right to be loved and educated by people who understand him, who appreciate the tremendous effort he must make to do ordinary things, and who consider it a privilege to help him achieve success in whatever he undertakes. The handicapped child has a right to live in a world with people who accept him, who do not pity or ridicule him, but who offer love, work, play and fellowship. As do other children, the handicapped child comes to appreciate those who enrich his life with laughter and tears, who show joy in his achievements and sympathy when failure seems too great to bear. Words are easily spoken or written, but putting actions into practice requires stimulation, encouragement, opportunities and appropriate protection. The child's learning from his or her environment depends upon what he observes, recognizes and understands.

The nonnurturing parent spends little time with the child, little or no time talking, playing games, stimulating or challenging his thinking capacity. The child so deprived has difficulty forming significant relationships and knows little about how to behave so as to gain or sustain approval. He has little or no motivation to learn or succeed because he expects punishment, failure and attention for misbehaving.

Through use of the Lexington Developmental Scale (19) the teacher helps the parent to observe, to assess the child's status, and then to develop ways to approach the child to remediate his handicapping condition. The teacher and professionally-trained staff observe, test, evaluate and formulate a plan for the child's developmental growth in *gross motor behavior,* i.e. large body movements such as sitting, head control, crawling, creeping, walking and so forth; *fine motor behavior,* which includes grasping, holding, releasing and eye-hand coordination; *language behavior,* which includes all forms of communication, especially verbalization; *cognitive development,* i.e. the development of mental skills; *personal-social behavior,* i.e. those behaviors which reveal a child's reaction to his sociocultural environment; and *emotional development,* which refers to his basic image of himself, his security and his ability to control his emotions within the normal range for his age group during interaction with others. All of these areas are assessed by the Lexington Developmental Scale (LDS).

The teacher recognizes the importance of parent involvement in every aspect of a child's development and, at the same time, is aware of the special needs of the parent. A teacher who is skillful with children may use that skill in being supportive with parents as she gains their cooperation and involvement.

A typical group conference in Project COPE between a teacher of a first grade readiness class and parents includes the following agenda:

A. Mimeographed materials are distributed and each is discussed.
   1. Parent is told what to bring to school.
   2. Example of daily schedule is given out.
   3. Material about handicapping conditions is given out.
B. Forms to be filled out and returned to school are distributed. These include

    1. Daily schedule
    2. Medication child is taking
    3. Parents's comments and expectations for child
    4. LDS Chart (part parent completes at home)
C. Parent is given explanation of program.
D. Miscellaneous
    1. Speech therapy arrangements are made in the office.
    2. Arrangements are made for telephone calls to teacher.
    3. Reasons are given for preference that girls wear shorts or slacks to school.
    4. If there is to be any change in the plans for transportation, the parent is asked to pin a note onto the child.
    5. Children may bring anything they want to school to share, i.e. talk about, as long as it will go in their tote bags. This sharing gives the child a valuable experience in expressing himself before the group as a whole.
    6. Children will not bring food to school unless individually wrapped and enough for the whole group.
    7. If a child has a birthday during the school year there is a simple celebration at snack time and the child may bring refreshments for that day (enough for the entire class); the parent is asked to send some candles for the cake.
    8. The public school policy regarding *snow days* is explained, and the parent is asked to listen to the radio if in doubt.
    9. Arrangements may be made for observing, with the following requests being carried out:
        a. That the visit is scheduled with the teacher several days in advance; it will in turn be cleared through the office.
        b. That visits not be planned until several weeks of school have elapsed.
        c. That visitors plan to stay the entire morning so they can see the day as a whole.
        d. That visitors write down their questions during the morning; a follow-up conference with the teacher will be planned.

10. Parents are asked to notify school when a child is sick, and to let the teacher know in advance if the child is to be absent; this often makes a difference in plans for trips, tests, etc.

Whereas parent orientation sessions are held in the evening, parent-teacher observation conferences are held during the school day.

A sample letter from a teacher to parents regarding an observation-conference appointment follows:

Dear Parents:

After delays for various reasons, I have been able to clear the dates listed below for parents to observe our room and to have individual conferences.

We hope it will be possible for the fathers to come for a portion of the morning — and especially for the conference. This will give you both a better understanding of what we do in the classroom, plus an explanation of the particular areas of strength and weakness that we have observed in your child. The conference is generally scheduled for 11:30 to 12:15, but if another time will suit you better, please let me know. We ask the mothers to stay an entire morning in order to get a sampling of the entire program.

It seems to work better not to mention to your child that you are coming. If you bring him, just park your car after you let him out. Then come in (after the buses have unloaded) and come straight to our observation room. Keep the door closed as any light in that room makes your presence more apparent through the glass. Turn on the microphone if it is not already on. Please bring a list of any questions that you want to discuss at our conference and add to this list any that you have concerning what happens during the morning.

Sign your *name* opposite the date you prefer, giving a first and second choice, and return by your child as soon as possible. I will confirm your final date by a note sent by your child.

Looking forward to seeing each of you on your conference date.

Sincerely,

_____

Teacher

Attached to this letter is a list of dates. Parents can select a conference date of their choice.

One or both parents may come for any conference. Usually a social worker accompanies them to the observation room, serves coffee or tea and explains the day's activities. The teacher joins them for short intervals during the session, and has a long, uninterrupted conference toward the close of the session.

After the first observation-conference, any parent who has been negligent in responding to a teacher's suggestions regarding home activities usually becomes a hardworking member of the educational team, reinforcing at home the efforts made in the classroom. Parents are kept informed, through notes sent in children's tote bags, of the kinds of reinforcement needed.

Many parents keep in touch with the teachers for many years after the child has left the Child Developmental Center. Often these parents bring or send a report card to show the child's advancement.

PARENT-SPEECH THERAPIST CONFERENCES

All parent-speech therapist conferences are set up by appointment, and contacts are continued by means of notes to the parent, the child's speech notebook, telephone calls and person-to-person discussion at the Parents Club meetings. Speech therapists have the task of working as members of the educational team, focusing on language development, speech usage and other aspects of communication. Within the classroom setting, language development is an important phase of the total program. The speech therapist works with the teacher and support staff to bring about the development of communication skills in each activity. Individual therapy time is given to those children who need extra help. Parents are involved in helping a child develop speech sounds, vocabulary and other aspects of the language program by means of guided home activities.

PARENT-TO-PARENT

Parents need, and are eager to develop, friendships with parents who have similar problems, and such relationships are encouraged by the agency staff. Parents find it difficult to accept the handicapping conditions of their children. Through the support of other parents and the leadership of the social worker they manage to break through a time of denial of the handicap to a period of blaming someone else, followed by a time of talking about the disability with other parents and with each other. When parents reach the point where they can discuss a disability with the child himself, there is every hope for a child's future and for the development of community groups which will eventually bring about changes in public attitudes, in laws and in educational and job opportunities.

Parent-to-parent is as important in the building of such parent strength as yeast is to certain kinds of bread dough. For example, as a parent is able to discuss the child's disability with him, the parent can become able to discuss the child's feelings about his disability with him. Parents can learn how to say to an angry child, "I know you are angry because you can't run in the ball game like Jimmie does, but you can make a picture out of those big nails and that soft wall board in your room." In time these parents can avoid some of the problems illustrated in the following example.

A neurologically-impaired adult declared once in a national meeting that he knew he had made life hard for his parents. He did this because they pretended he was like other children and he knew he was not. He knew he had not caused his condition so he had to look around for something or someone on which to place the blame, usually his parents. He found it difficult to control his behavior; an inner force drove him to move almost constantly. He showed his anger through this hostile, agressive behavior, and usually his parents were his victims. He could not express his feelings in words, and no one else tried to express them for him: hence, his undesirable behavior.

PARENTS AS RESOURCES

The resource potential of parents is frequently overlooked by professional persons. Parents can be speakers and special workshop teachers. They can do TV programs and arts and crafts. CDC parents, with some of the teaching staff, wrote a book with illustrations, *Innovative, Inexpensive, Instructional Materials* (18), which is now being used by many agencies.

Parents serve on the Board of Directors of United Cerebral Palsy of the Blue Grass. They are on local citizens' committees and on state committees. They have been active in policy consideration, legislative changes and interpretation of agency achievements to clubs and other influential groups. They have recruited volunteers, referred children to CDC and continue to serve the agency in a thousand ways.

Any positive working relationship requires trust. A parent-professional team must recognize the differences in roles and training of parents and professionals, but each must respect and trust the other. Thus, children, parents and professionals are best served.

FOLLOW ALONG SERVICES

The Follow Along Service of CDC was the first of its kind in Kentucky. Through the Developmental Disability Services Act, seed money was obtained from state funds to develop the program. The primary purpose of the Follow Along Service is to provide problem solving help to the family of any child who attended CDC or to the child himself as long as he is in the state of Kentucky. Children who have largely overcome their handicaps but who may have a problem now and then as they adjust to the mainstream of community activities can receive help or be referred to the appropriate resource by calling the CDC office.

An example of this type of prevention of problems through timely intervention occurred when a mother reported that her daughter who had adjusted well in regular public school classes for three years was now failing, did not wish to go to school, and pretended to be sick. The CDC worker obtained more information from the mother in an interview, visited the school and talked with the principal and teacher. In the meantime the child was referred to the medical center for a physical examination. The parameters of the problem came to light — the child, who was in good physical health, felt rejected by the parents, both of whom worked, and was overwhelmed with feelings of jealousy toward an older sister. With the help of the CDC social worker, the teacher, the parents and another agency that took responsibility for counseling the sister, the child's behavior changed. Her grades improved as did her school attendance and her personality.

Another illustrative case is that of a little boy who became very distractible and disruptive after a few wonderful weeks during which he was a star pupil in first grade. The mother asked for help. The agency worker arranged for a conference with the teacher, who confided that when she learned the child had been in a preschool program for handicapped children she felt sorry for him and was not requiring much of him. After discussion about the fact that the term *cerebral dysfunction* does not necessarily mean a child is mentally retarded, the agency worker reviewed for the teacher the history of the child's gradual progress. The worker showed the teacher that the child was reading at the five-year level. The teacher decided she had been treating the child as if he could not learn and that consequently he was bored in school. She changed both her attitude and the program for the boy. Before another month had passed the child was no longer hyperactive or destructive. The teacher was doing a good job of letting the boy progress at his pace rather than hers. Without the time and effort given by the CDC worker, the child might have been dropped from that class. Without the Follow Along program, the mother would not have asked for help from the agency since her child had already left the CDC program.

Families with handicapped children have many problems over and beyond those in families of normal children, and these problems will increase without community help. Many families will return for help to a known agency but will not go to an untried resource. To prevent small budding problems from blooming into full-grown difficulties, the Follow Along Service was created. It has been immensely successful in the prevention of problems and the crystallization of progress made by the handicapped child.

CONCLUSION

It is universally conceded that many parents, perhaps most parents, would like to understand their children. To be effective, parents need to understand not only their children's needs and motivations at each stage of growth, but also themselves as parents. They need to understand their own feelings, attitudes and expectations and the influence of these on the child. They need to understand their total relationship with the child. Parents of handicapped children cope with the problems that other parents have in parent-child relations, but because of the child's handicap, these problems are magnified. McDonald (25) claims that it is a common observation that the home with a handicapped child is a handicapped home.

Parents have varying degrees of knowledge regarding both the stages of child growth and development and the physical and psychological needs of a human being, and varying degrees of recognition of some common parent-child relationship problems. However, we must reckon with the fact that such knowledge does not carry with it a natural capacity to function successfully and satisfyingly as a parent. Parents can learn, regardless of age. Under leadership, they can exchange information, acquire additional information, and relate this material to their own lives, all of which results in a new perspective that will be used as a basis for new behavior.

Not only can parents learn, they *want* to learn, as may be shown through their active participation in group discussion. However, in order to learn, parents must be free of pressure from the group leader. Parents must be allowed to move into a discussion in their own fashion. They must be allowed to learn in their own way.

Although many parent organizations try to meet parental needs through the presentation of new knowledge by experts, many agency leaders believe parents learn best when they learn from each other. In the latter case parents' interest is great. This is consistent with the contention that interest is greatest when the material to be learned is related directly to the specific interest and experience of the learner (6). Parents learn best when they share in the development of the content of discussions and shape their educational experience to their own needs and wishes.

Expression of emotions frequently causes anxiety on the part of group members, particularly if the emotions expressed are those of hostility, conflict or ambivalance. However, these negative feelings can be explored along with positive ones as participants realize that all feelings are part of normal human living.

Parents learn from one another because sometimes they can recognize ideas in another which they had not been able to recognize in themselves. The bulk of experiences discussed in parents groups increases the factual information and broadens the knowledge and experience of each member.

Discussions based on experiences with children can encourage parents to test their own ideas and convictions until they gradually take a position for themselves. The group leader can facilitate this process by giving due respect to each comment and by encouraging, but not pressuring, those who may not talk freely at first.

One of the most important aspects of parent group discussions is the encouragement each parent is given through the leader's attempt to create a climate of trust and safety. In such a climate, participants may examine any situation without fear of reprisal, learn concepts that are applicable to them, and generalize these concepts to situations that have not been discussed in the group.

Recognizing the fact that parent group education is an emotional as well as intellectual experience, the leader can help to bring about an understanding of the dynamics behind behavior. Expression of feelings in relation to substance of parent-to-child relationships and to family living are important. The leader must be alert so as to maintain a balance between outer reality and parents' emotional responses to situations.

Over television and radio and in printed materials people are urged to avoid stress and live longer. Parents of exceptional children *cannot* avoid stress, but they can learn to master it and to use it. Project COPE helps parents to recognize that stress can be bad;

stress can also have potential good. For stress to be productive a parent must feel he is successful in handling the stressful situation. The parent must find the strength from within to match the strategies of problem solving which can be supplied by resources from without. Through child observation, parent education can be obtained with appropriate help, and stressful situations can become a challenge which leads to conquering the external forces that overstrain the inner self.

The ultimate goal of professional service is to help the child overcome his developmental lag, learn to compensate for his handicap, and successfully enter the mainstream of living in our complex society. Intervention programs involving parents now are an accepted facet of many agency service programs. The question of how to involve parents in the education of their children is eliciting many innovative efforts. Time has demonstrated that parents are the most important teachers of the young. To change their patterns of teaching, parents need to learn how to handle their own emotions and feelings of inadequacy; they need to learn how to use and enjoy their children's tools for learning. To help handicapped children, a parent education curriculum must focus on the child's problem with specific emphasis on language and perceptual development, problem solving in personal-social and cognitive areas, motor development and emotional maturation. A parent cannot be a good teacher, however, until he or she has learned to master stress and crisis situations. Through many types of parent activities, such as those undertaken in Project COPE, parents can learn to expect much from themselves and their children.

It is well to recall a truth flawlessly recorded by Locke, "The faculties of the mind are improved by exercise, yet they must not be put to a stress beyond their strength" (23).

REFERENCES

1. Becker, W.C.: *Parents are Teachers.* Champaign, Res Press, 1971.
2. Birch, H.G. (Ed.): *Brain Damage in Children.* Williams & Wilkins, 1964.
3. Bucker B., and Lovaas, O.I.: *Miami Symposium on the Prediction of Behavior: Aversive Stimulation.* Coral Gables, U of Miami Pr, 1967.
4. *Children Today.* Available from Children's Bureau, Office of Child

Development.

5. Cohen, D.H.: *The Learning Child.* New York, Random House, 1972.

6. Dodson, F.: *How to Parent.* New York, New American Library, 1970.

7. Duvall, E.: *Building Your Marriage.* Public Affairs Pamphlet, Washington, U.S. Government Printing Office, 1965.

8. *Exceptional Children.* Available from Council for Exceptional Children.

9. *Exceptional Parent.* Available from Psy-Ed. Corp., Boston.

10. Gesell, A.: *The First Five Years of Life.* New York, Har-Row, 1940.

11. Gesell, A.: *Child Behavior.* New York, Dell, 1955.

12. Goldstein, J., Freud, A., and Solmit, A.: *Beyond the Best Interests of Children.* New York, Free Pr, 1973.

13. Grothe, J.: Source unknown.

14. Haring, N.G. (Ed): *Behavior of Exceptional Children,* Columbus, Merrill, 1974.

15. *Heaven's Special Child.* Author unknown.

16. Holt, J.: *How Children Learn.* New York, Dell, 1970.

17. Holt, J.: *Freedom & Beyond.* New York, Dutton, 1972.

18. *Innovative, Inexpensive Instructional Materials.* Lexington, UCPB, 1974.

19. Irwin, J.V., Ward, M.N., Deen, C., and Greis, A.: *Lexington Developmental Scale,* Lexington. UCPB, 1973.

20. Irwin, J.V., and Marge, M. (Eds.): *Principles of Childhood Language Disabilities.* New York, Appleton, 1971.

21. *Journal of Learning Disabilities.* Available from the Professional Press, Chicago.

22. Kaiser, B.: *New Light of Hope.* New Canaan, Keats, 1974.

23. Locke, J.: Essay. In Hargorth, F. G. (Ed.): *The Conduct of Understanding.* New York, Teachers College, 1966, p. 90.

24. Mare, D.R.: *What Makes a Marriage Happy?* Public Affairs Pamphlet 290, 1965.

25. McDonald, E.T.: *Understand Those Feelings.* Pittsburgh, Stanwix, 1962.

26. Mussen, P., Conger, R.J., and Kagan, J.: *Child Development and Personality.* New York, Har-Row, 1969.

27. Reik, T. (Ed.): *What Shall I Tell My Child?* New York, University, 1970.

Chapter 7

INTERDISCIPLINARY COUNSELING
IN A MEDICAL SETTING

Mary Todd and Marvin I. Gottlieb

INTRODUCTION

PARENTS of *exceptional,* or chronically-handi-capped, children are in particular need of counseling and guidance; professional-parent communication may be required over extended periods of time. Frequently pediatricians render these services as part of the comprehensive management of the child. A successful counseling program reflects the physician's expertise and philosophy. Unfortunately, however, didactic and clinical experiences necessary to develop skills in family counseling may be neglected in basic medical training. As a result, physicians may feel unprepared and uncomfortable when called upon to provide these services. The Leigh Buring Memorial Clinic for Exceptional Children (CEC), dedicated to training physicians in developmental disabilities, offers numerous opportunities for counseling experiences with a variety of allied health specialists who offer professional supervision.

The CEC functions as a service and teaching division of the Ambulatory Pediatric Service of the University of Tennessee Center for the Health Sciences. The active outpatient department logs over 35,000 annual clinic visits and a multitude of diagnostic challenges. The CEC receives referrals from the ambulatory services as well as from a variety of community agencies — board of education, speech and hearing center, public health department, Head Start Program, mental health centers and many others. In addition, the CEC assists practicing physicians and private schools in evaluating selected children referred for suspected developmental disorders. As shown in Table 7-I, a myriad of problems are encountered — academic underachievement, learning disorders, mental retardation, isolated developmental delays, multiple organic handicaps, disorders of communication, socio-economic deprivation, emotional problems and behavior disorders. The clinic functions in a medically-oriented environment but is interdisciplinary in its philosophy and operation. The CEC staff includes medical students, pediatricians, social workers, pediatric nurse associates, speech pathologists, audiologists, psychologists, pedodontists and other professionals. The emphasis is on training medical students and pediatric house staff, but students of all disciplines are welcomed. For most of the students this is their first opportunity to work with exceptional children and to participate in family counseling under the supervision of experienced professionals. Clinic participation is a mandatory training requirement for all medical students at the University of Tennessee Center for the Health Sciences as part of the pediatric program. Clinical experiences are augmented by a series of didactic seminars and lectures. Training emphasizes the role of physicians as necessary members of the interdisciplinary team. The clinic experience helps enhance the student's expertise in developmental disabilities, broadens his concepts of comprehensive medical care, and augments his appreciation for interdisciplinary interaction.

Developmental jeopardy comprises social, emotional and educational functioning as well as physical growth and maturation. Physicians-in-training can readily appreciate developmental disabilities as they affect the child, his family and his community. Medical responsibility involves enriching a child's potentials in all parameters of psychosocial and physical development. The family, teachers and other professionals often look to the physician for coordination and long-term management of the child with a chronic handicapping condition. Family counseling is an integral part of the rehabilitation program. In order to assist the child, family cooperation and participation are essential.

As a rule, exceptional children have exceptional families. Physicians are familiarized with the range of parental reactions to having a handicapped child. At the CEC, parent-professional communication is stressed within the teaching and service programs. Medical students, interns and pediatric house staff are

TABLE 7-I

DIFFERENTIAL DIAGNOSIS OF DISTURBED EDUCATIONAL DEVELOPMENT

| CAUSE | CHARACTERISTICS OFTEN REPORTED BY: | | |
	PARENT	TEACHER	PSYCHOLOGICAL EVALUATION
SPECIFIC LEARNING DISABILITY	Usually no problems except for school difficulty. Plays well with friends.	Puzzling, child may perform well in some academic and social areas. May have superimposed behavior problem.	Some normal performance and some areas are depressed.
MENTAL RETARDA- TION	Usually no family disrup- tion. Plays with younger children.	Child unable to compete at grade level or with children of same age.	Usually depressed in all areas.
ORGANIC HANDICAP (e.g. hearing loss).	Functions well in uninvolved areas.	Functions well academically in uninvolved areas. Peer rapport good.	Depressed in area affecting modality.
SOMATIC ILLNESS	No difficulty except for illness.	Change in per- formance related to onset of illness.	May be depressed as a result of illness.
PSYCHOSIS	Disturbed parent relationship; affects relation- ships with sibs., peers (social relationships — poor).	Bizarre responses. May be withdrawn and unresponsive.	Bizarre responses, possibly with islands of normal functioning.
BEHAVIORAL DISORDERS	Better 1:1. Occasionally disturbed parent- child relation- ship.	Attention seeking behaviors. May annoy classmates. Acting out behaviors.	Good results if child cooperates.

SOCIO-ECONOMIC DEPRIVATION	Functions well in own cultural environment. Friends with similar circumstances.	May be characterized as poorly motivated.	Generally depressed; can reflect cultural bias of test items.

In part adapted from J. L. Schulman, Management of Emotional Disorders in Pediatric Practice (Chicago, Year Book Medical Publishers, 1969).

assisted by experienced social workers, psychologists and other professionals in developing an understanding of the needs of families with exceptional children. In some situations the family needs are unique, challenging and extensive. For most, professional guidance is basically designed to provide parents with opportunities for (1) understanding the nature of their child's handicapping condition, (2) expressing and resolving parental anxieties, and (3) initiating long-range therapeutic planning for the child. Effective parent-professional communication is essential to insure success of a comprehensive remedial program for the youngster with a chronic handicapping condition. Parental interest and cooperation may be enhanced or depleted, depending upon the quality of the professional intervention.

Family involvement is a necessary adjunct, and the clinic provides parents a resource to which they can turn for continued advice and support. The training of physicians within this framework is an effort to augment the quality of comprehensive pediatric care for the chronically-disabled child.

ESTABLISHING RAPPORT:
THE INITIAL COUNSELING SERVICE

Many families are referred to the CEC by teachers, physicians, counselors, welfare workers and others. Frequently parents reveal little insight into the nature of their child's handicap. Although sincerely concerned, they are often uninformed or misinformed. The recommendations to seek an evaluation may come as a shock to the parents. The initial counseling interview serves the dual function of exploring concerns of the parents and of assessing their understanding and reactions to the problem. For many parents, the initial counseling session is a catharsis; often parents have been harboring fears, apprehensions and misconceptions for which they had no resource for communication or interpretation.

Initial interviews are usually conducted by members of the medical and social work staff. Contact is first established in the outpatient department by a member of the pediatric house staff. Medical, educational and social problems are reviewed with a physician. Frequently children with chronic handicaps are referred to the CEC by members of the outpatient staff for an in-depth interview by a member of the social work division. Special attention is focused on determining the parents' awareness of their child's problem, their concept of levels of functioning, and parental expectations. Initial contacts are considered to be critical and should convey a sincere interest in parental attitudes and concerns. At this time parents are familiarized with the clinic, its diagnostic services and its programs.

The first parent-professional encounters are usually relatively brief interviews in which parents are encouraged to express their views. Parents are offered opportunities for professional intervention but are not pressured into making final decisions. Parents may be apprehensive about the evaluation process and several counseling sessions may be required before their acceptance of the child's need for evaluation. Involvement begins with a free communication between the parent and a member of the professional staff. The following case histories illustrate types of parental reactions encountered during initial contacts:

Mrs. R. brought her nine-year-old son to the clinic at the school's request, but she was unable to specifically define the child's problems. No physical complaints or behavior problems had been noticed by the mother, and she seemed confused by the school's referral for medical evaluation of the child. The mother was willing to cooperate with both school and clinic, but further explanation of the need for medical intervention was necessary to clarify the child's situation and to involve the parent. Mrs. R. was unable to conceive of her child having a learning problem that could not be handled by the teacher.

. . . .

Mrs. K.'s five-year-old son was referred for evaluation by his kindergarten teacher, but the mother reported no "serious" problems and talked only of the progress her son had made during the year. Although both the teacher and school counselor had discussed the child's lack of school readiness skills with the mother, she continued to deny the child's difficulty. Attempts to involve the parent in considering alternatives to first grade placement had been unsuccessful. However, further exploration of the communication between parent and referring agency helped in understanding the parent's lack of acceptance and awareness of the child's difficulty. Denial of the child's problem was caused by underlying feelings of guilt and hostility.

PARENTAL REACTIONS

Families referred to the CEC present differing backgrounds, socially and economically. Family psychodynamics involve a spectrum of relationships which profoundly influence the planning for an exceptional child. Table 7-II summarizes possible family relationships and psychodynamics. Families of children with handicapping conditions are vulnerable to a host of extrinsic and intrinsic stresses. The child may disrupt family continuity or may exaggerate previously-disturbed relationships. The following case history is an example of this reaction:

D.P., a four-year-old girl, had been diagnosed as having a severe hearing loss at nine months of age. The parents, a young couple, had recently moved to the city and had no relatives or close friends. The parents readily admitted that D. was "the center of their lives." Mrs. P. reluctantly left the child at a special preschool each day and usually arrived to take her home an hour before dismissal. Neither parent pursued former interests or new friendships, saying that "most people did not understand how to relate to a deaf child and they would rather avoid problems." While some of the withdrawal was attributed to an initial adjustment reaction and to the loss of familiar and supportive surroundings, the family's social isolation persisted. It became apparent that the parents' overinvolvement with the handicapped child enabled them to avoid social situations that would have unmasked marital problems. Counseling revealed that the precarious marital relationship, while being

TABLE 7-II

FAMILY RELATIONSHIPS AND PSYCHODYNAMICS

TYPE OF RELATIONSHIP	PARENTAL REACTIONS	EFFECTS ON CHILD
CONFUSED	Concerned but unsure of how to cope with child's difficulty. Usually has tried un-successfully to work with child; frustrated. Sense of failure, guilt. Ambivalence may interfere with seeking pro-fessional intervention.	Child appears anxious; always testing limits. Child's self-concept reflects parents's confu-sion, frustration.
INCONSISTENT	Parent uses varying to control child, no pattern. Parents transmit two opposite messages at same time.	Child confused. Child may withdraw. Child may become anxious and rebel.
DENIAL	Minimizes or does not admit to child's difficulty. Parents' goals, expectan-cies, dreams for child have been thwarted. Parent usually first reacts by feeling child will outgrow problem.	Child confused and frus-trated because of dichotomy between reality and parents' denial, This confusion may bring withdrawal or acting out. Feeling of insecurity may occur. Self-confidence is shaky.
VICARIOUS	Parent lives through the child. Child is to realize aspirations parents could not achieve. Child's handicap destroys the parents' dreams for the child.	Child may be pressured to achieve despite handicap. Child may be pushed to overcome handicap. Child may have poor self-concept.

TYPE OF RELATIONSHIP	PARENTAL REACTIONS	EFFECTS ON CHILD
SYMBIOTIC	Abnormally close tie between one parent and child. Parent begins to devote his/her life to this child. May reflect deep-seated emotional problems in the parent.	Child does not develop an independent personality. Lack of independence, infantile reactions, fear of separation.
OVERPROTECTIVE	Parents try to shield child from ordinary hazards of life, exaggerated with a child with a handicap. Parents' concerns are limitless. Parents may reflect guilt feelings.	Child may become fearful; self-confidence and esteem are low Handicap becomes exaggerated and out of proportion to reality.
OVERPERMISSIVE	Parents permit a wider range of behavior than normal. Parents cannot set limits. Parents may be ineffectual. Parents may be responding to guilt feelings.	Child with handicap may be given free rein because of misconceptions, pity, etc. Child may not conform socially. Child may become overly dependent.
RIGID	Parents set very high standards. Parents may be perfectionists. Parents are organizers, compulsive at times. Applies these standards and rules for child; expectations higher than child's capability.	May be disappointment to parents because of handicap. Child may also strive for perfection. Child may rebel actively or passively. Child may withdraw and regress.
DISINTERESTED	Often seen in multiproblem or disorganized households. Child's problems secondary to more pressing problems/conflicts family faces each day.	Child usually withdrawn or passive; loner. Later, child is likely to act out; run away, delinquent. More likely not to conform socially.

TYPE OF RELATIONSHIP	PARENTAL REACTIONS	EFFECTS ON CHILD
NEGLECTFUL	Parent exhibits lack of responsibility for child. Child's handicap may create negative feelings in parent. Parent has ambivalent feelings toward child.	Range of neglect, including physical and emotional needs of child. Child feels unwanted and unloved. Child may focus on handicap as cause.
FRAGMENTED	Parental discord of pathological degree. Parental separation usual result.	Child may see handicap as cause of parental problems. Feelings of insecurity and rejection.
REJECTING	Parents may actually reject child; may be precipitated by handicap. Something about child may cause negative feeling.	Child feels unwanted or unloved. May blame handicap for feeling of rejection. Causes poor self-concept; apprehensive about all peers and adults.

In part adapted from J. L. Schulman, Management of Emotional Disorders in Pediatric Practice (Chicago Year Book Medical Publishers, 1969).

held together by the child, was also jeopardized by the parents' unexpressed feelings of blame, guilt and resentment about the child's organic impairment.

The child with a chronic handicapping condition generally precipitates unique and prolonged stresses for the family constellation. Professional assistance is required to overcome the early difficulties families have encountered in handling the child's problem. The exceptional child is often unable to fulfill many parental expectations; generating feelings of guilt, frustration, disappointment, anger and resentment. Parents may feel helpless in the ability to cope with the social, emotional, physical and educational needs of their child. Family members who are unable to express their feelings and confusions are usually unrealistic in their expectations. Frequently parents have apprehensions about the child's future.

Each parent seeks a diagnostic evaluation with his own unique expectations. Often, denial of the problem or unwarranted apprehensions create delays in securing professional assistance. Parents may even fear that they have mismanaged or created the child's problem, particularly if the child has a learning disability. These children, who exhibit no overt organicity, are often inconsistent in academic performances and exhibit behavior problems which add to parental confusion. The following case history illustrates parental denial:

J.L., a seven-year-old girl, was referred for evaluation by her teacher because of poor academic performances. She was retained in the first grade. The mother reported no evidences of difficulty until the child began school and was "shocked" by the child's school failure. During the course of the evaluation, Mrs. L. admitted that she "drilled the child every night" and would become upset if homework was not assigned each night. The diagnostic screening revealed a generalized delay in development and an obvious lack of readiness skills for a successful first grade experience. Psychological examination confirmed suspicions of intellectual and educational delays. The child had become increasingly withdrawn at home and especially at school. Parental pressures and repeated school failures had adversely affected the child's self-concept and confidence. Even in a supportive learning setting the child would initiate new tasks reluctantly, saying, "I can't do this." The teacher reported that J.L. always appeared "on the verge of tears." Extensive counseling was required to familiarize the parents with the nature of J.L.'s handicap. Recommendations for special education placement were initially dismissed as unwarranted by the parents. After several counseling sessions with a social worker and physician, the mother became more realistic about J.L.'s present level of functioning. Eventually recommendations were accepted as "best for the child." Counseling involved a cooperative effort between the school, the clinic and the family. Counseling goals for the parents included acceptance of the child and her handicaps, expression of latent feelings of guilt and anxiety, and involvement in planning the child's educational program.

The following case history is typical of parents who seek an evaluation for their child with a suspected learning disability:

R.B., a ten-year-old boy, was evaluated at CEC because of a learning difficulty since beginning school. In obtaining the history, the mother expressed many of her personal reactions to the child's learning difficulty. She confided a fear that the youngster's poor school performance was related to social immaturity as he was the youngest child in the family and had been pampered. The following school year she felt his problem was simply laziness because the child had above-average abilities in some learning areas. Mrs. B. expected above-average work in *all* areas. As the academic program continued to be more and more difficult for R.B., she rationalized that she had not given his school work enough attention. Mrs. B. set aside time each evening to tutor, to drill and prepare R. for tests. The frustrations she encountered with homework tended to reinforce her feelings of inadequcy, hostility and disappointment. At the time of the evaluation, the family felt responsible for the child's difficulties. Traditional approaches in helping their other children had been of little value with R.B.; the parents interpreted this as their ineffectiveness. Subsequent evaluation revealed that R.B. had a severe learning disorder. The family was encouraged and relieved when informed that R.B.'s learning disability would require specialized instruction available at his school.

THE EVALUATION PROCESS:
A MEANS OF ENCOURAGING PARENTAL INVOLVEMENT

The format of the CEC diagnostic evaluation is designed to engender an atmosphere that is conducive to parent counseling. Following the initial screening interviews, the parents are advised of their specific clinic appointments. The parents meet with a member of the medical staff (medical student, intern or pediatric resident) in order to complete a comprehensive data-gathering interview. The history delineates a profile of the child as perceived by the parents. The data base is a panoramic view of the youngster from conception to the present, reviewing present complaint, developmental milestones, past medical history, educational progress and behavioral characteristics. Table 7-III summarizes the information obtained. The interview is conducted in a private, quiet and unhurried setting. The child is not present in the room during this session. The meeting is designed not only to gather data but to enhance rapport between historian and recorder.

The historical profile in part describes the child's strengths and weaknesses. The assessment may be modified by emotions, expectations, personal feelings and personalities of the parents. The contact at this time provides ample opportunity for exploration and interpretation of developmental norms, comparisons of abilities with siblings, and parental views of functional levels. In addition, the interview serves as an entree for additional comprehensive family counseling programs. The rapport established between clinic, patient and patient's family greatly influences future efforts to obtain medical and community services for the child.

At the time of the interdisciplinary diagnostic screening, the parents are briefly informed about the clinical impressions formulated. Where there is a need for additional diagnostic procedures this need is explained and appointments are scheduled. The parents are advised that more comprehensive discussions with them will follow the interdisciplinary staff conference. Appointments are scheduled to inform the family of the findings and recommendations of the staff.

AFFECTING PARENT-PROFESSIONAL COMMUNICATION

Upon completion of the diagnostic process and the tentative design of a therapeutic program, parent-professional interaction is provided to share findings with the family. The basic objectives of follow-up counseling are to (1) provide the parents with a working knowledge of the child's handicap as uncovered by the diagnostic screening, (2) insure parental understanding and cooperation in securing and maintaining appropriate rehabilitative services, (3) establish realistic parental expectations, (4) provide the family with a base for professional communication, and (5) offer appropriate follow-up services. To achieve these goals, various approaches are utilized inasmuch as no two families have exactly the same problems.

TABLE 7-III

CASE HISTORY INFORMATION OBTAINED

1. Chief Complaint
2. Course of Presenting Problem
3. Obstetrical History
   Number of Pregnancies
   Number of Living Children
   Number of Miscarriages (cause if known)
   Birth Order
   High Risk Factors

Infections	Trauma
Toxemia	Excessive Nausea and Vomiting
Diabetes	Other
Bleeding	

   Weight gain (or loss) during pregnancy
   Excessive use of tobacco, alcohol or drugs
   Exposure to toxins or x-radiation
   Length of gestation
   Mother's age at conception
   Father's age at conception
   Mother's past medical history
   Father's past medical history
   Prenatal care (by)
   Hospital for delivery
4. Perinatal History
   Labor
   Induced or spontaneous
   Duration
   Complications
   Delivery
   Presentation
   Preceps
   Complications
   Condition at birth
   Apgar score
   Onset of cry and respirations
   Birth weight
   Discharge weight
   Head, chest circ., length
   Sleepy, irritable, lazy
   Jaundice
   Cyanosis
   Convulsions
   Tremors
   Vomiting
   Feeding difficulties
   Other problems

Attending physician
Breast or bottle fed
Number of days in nursery
Discharged with mother
5. Developmental History
Smiled
Followed objects
Laughed
Held head up
Rolled over
First tooth
Sat alone
Pulled up
Crawled
Walked
Ran
Talked, words
Talked, sentences
Toilet-trained
Age at which bed-wetting ceased
Rode tricycle
Rode bicycle
Comparison with siblings
6. Past Medical History
Estimate of general rate of growth (compared with sibs)
Serious illnesses
Serious injuries
Hospitalizations & operations
High fevers
Convulsions or neurological problems
Staring spells or blackout spells
Head trauma with loss of consciousness
Anorexia, vomiting, diarrhea causing dehydration
Medications taken at this time and dosage
Childhood diseases or vaccines (ages and complications)

Measles	Pertussis
German measles	Scarlet fever
Mumps	Roseola
Chickenpox	

Immunizations and severe reactions
Estimate of general health
Attending physicians
7. Review of Systems
General health
Allergies
Head
Eyes
Nose
Throat
Lungs

      Heart

      GI

      GU

      Skin

      Lymph nodes

      Bones and joints

      Muscular

8. CNS Review

      Parents' appraisal of intellectual status

      Eye blinking or strabismus

      Dysphagia or drooling

      Spasticity or hypotonia

      Coordination problems

      Ataxia

      Speech problems

9. Educational History

      Nursery (age started, performance)

      Kindergarten (age started, performance)

      List of schools attended

      Current grade and school

      Teacher

      Problems reported by teacher

      Grades completed

      Grades repeated

      Previous psychological testing

      Results of achievement test

      Tutoring (by whom)

      Parent's observations of

       Word or letter reversals

       Reading approximations

       Handwriting difficulties

       Difficulty following multiple directions

      Child's school attitude

10. Social History

      Household members

      Father's occupation

      Mother's occupation

      Marital history

      Discipline

       By whom

       Type

       Frequency

       Response

      Relationship with siblings

      Problems with siblings

      Passive or aggressive with other children

      Sleep away from home

      Close friends

      Living quarters

11. Family History (construct family tree)

       Mental retardation
       Neurological problems
       Emotional disorders
       Learning disabilities
       Diabetes
       Cancer
       Cardiovascular
       Renal

12. Behavioral History
       Evaluation of motor activity
       Attention span
       Distractibility
       Temper tantrums
       Impulsiveness
       Destructiveness
       Emotional lability (mood swings)
       Reactions when frustrated
       Cruelty to animals
       Cruelty to children
       Hobbies
       Favorite TV programs
       Favorite school subjects
       Worst school subject
       Favorite sports
       Participates in sports
       Additional organized activities (Boy Scouts, etc.)
       Plays with younger or older children
       Sleep habits
         Hours/24 hours
         Nite lite
         Security objects
         Bedroom shared
         Nightmares
         Bizarre night habits
         Enuresis
       Particular fears
       Nervous habits
       Tics
       Ritualistic activities
       Parents' description of child's worst habit
       Behavior at home compared to behavior at school
       Evidences of poor self-concept

13. Nutritional History
       Evaluation of diet
       Food likes and dislikes
       Pica (e.g. wall plaster, dirt)
       Food allergies

Individual Counseling

Following the diagnostic evaluation, the parents return for an informing interview conducted by the staff social worker. Counseling sessions are designed to meet particular needs of the families involved, including the meaning of the child's handicap, and ways of coping with behavioral reactions for counseling. The following case study illustrates some of these problems:

S.M., a five-year-old boy, was referred by his kindergarten teacher shortly after enrollment because of poor peer relationships. The teacher was concerned about the child's limited group participation and requested evaluation of the child's visual acuity, perceptual skills and behavioral patterns. In school the child did not appear to see and often stumbled over classmates. During group activities such as exercises S.M. would stay close to his cousin and appeared to mimic her body movements rather than attend to the teacher at the front of the room. The child was unable to complete work involving use of paper, crayons, puzzles and scissors, and was poor at other manual skills. The initial interview revealed that the parents had been advised by an ophthalmologist of possible severely decreased visual acuity and that a more definitive diagnosis could be made as the child matured and could be conditioned to testing procedures. The family's denial of the child's handicap was evidenced in their expectations for the child at home. No allowances were made regarding his safety; similarly, the mother had enrolled the child in a regular class without an explanation of the child's possible limitations. Evaluation revealed a youngster who indeed was visually impaired. The child was referred to an ophthalmology clinic for therapy. Subsequent counseling with the parents focused on their becoming more realistic about S.M., recognizing that many of his bad behaviors were attributed to his limited eyesight. In addition, counseling provided the mother an opportunity for expression of fears that she had created the handicap as a result of a faulty pregnancy.

Multiple interviews may be necessary to fully clarify the problems involved. The following case history illustrates the benefits of additional counseling sessions in assessing the family's understanding of the child and of the remedial process:

M.B., a four-year-old boy with a severe communication disorder, was referred to the clinic by a neighbor who had previous experience as a student in CEC. The patient lived with grandparents, and, while they had recognized the child's delayed speech development, they had no knowledge of the nature of the problem. They were confused as to how the child's delayed language development was jeopardizing other areas of functioning, especially his social and emotional adaptation. Following extensive diagnostic screening, including complete physical and neurological examination, developmental screening, audiometric evaluation (including impedance audiometry), speech and language assessment, and appropriate laboratory investigation, a therapy plan was recommended. M.B. was referred to a community resource for language therapy and to a preschool center. Referral to community services for proper therapy was explained to the grandparents during the informing process. The grandparents were counseled in child management techniques and developmental needs. During the informing sessions, expression of their feelings, fears and sense of responsibility for the child's problems emerged, and supportive counseling continued over a period of six months.

Group Counseling

Parent group interaction has been a meaningful method of providing counseling services for families of children with developmental problems. Frequently parents are concerned about the unique demands placed on them by exceptional children. Problems regarding discipline, educational needs, social interactions and behavioral problems need to be discussed. Group services require appropriate professional leadership; psychologists, social workers, speech therapists, teachers and physicians can serve as leaders. The specific group program is flexible and tailored to meet the parents' needs. Group sessions have unique supportive and preventive qualities. Parents are encouraged to participate in group programs provided through CEC, community agencies and other organizations.

A group for parents of preschool children diagnosed as developmentally delayed was organized within the framework of the clinic. It was designed to work with several parental concerns regarding the evaluation process and diagnosis, principles of discipline and planning for the education of their handicapped child. Leadership was provided by professionals — a pediatrician, social worker and special educator. Although the group format was primarily educational, each group meeting included discussion of experiences and apprehensions. A second group program was created for parents of preschool children diagnosed as having severe communication disorders. The group sessions were designed to encourage a positive approach in coping with the child's language delay. Programmed materials, observation and home assignments were used to facilitate parent involvement. The parents met with the social work staff while the children simultaneously participated in a language therapy group under the direction of a speech pathologist. In the group discussions the parents were able to share their feelings, child rearing problems and experiences related to their child's disability.

Several parent groups organized through the clinic have focused on methods of behavior management. Prior evaluation at the clinic was a prerequisite for group participation. Professional leadership for behavior training groups has been shared by psychologists and social workers. Contracting with parents regarding program, time, responsibilities, etc., has been an effective means of insuring parent involvement. For one group an enrollment fee was charged and the parents were partially reimbursed for each session attended. In working with low income families, materials such as household items have been provided as incentives and rewards for group attendance and completion of assignments.

Through group participation, parents have the opportunity to share their experiences, successes and failures; their particular problems no longer seem to place them in isolation. The mutual sharing, or the supportive component of group work, makes this approach most meaningful. Stimulating an interest in educational programs, recreational facilities and parent associations is more readily accomplished when parents can discuss these services with one another.

Community Services

Total patient care for the child with a chronic handicapping condition requires a continual process of monitoring, coordination and follow-up services. Re-evaluation and reassessment must be performed periodically to determine effectiveness of therapeutic programs. Ongoing communication with rehabilitative agencies is a necessary adjunct of the follow-up process. The patient remains on the active clinic roster until recommended services have been thoroughly explored and/or secured.

Interagency communication, a form of professional counseling, is essential in providing comprehensive care for children with chronic handicapping conditions. Consultation is extended to professionals with other agencies related to the diagnostic findings, suggestions for therapy and familiarization with the results of parent counseling sessions. In turn, agencies that assist the youngster provide progress reports for the CEC. Frequently, professionals from various contributing agencies meet to coordinate their efforts. Agencies providing foster care services are a frequent source of referral to the clinic. Disturbed family relationships tend to compound problems of the handicapped child. Child placement agencies often assume many of the responsibilities and roles formerly ascribed to parents.

K.P., a five-year-old girl, was the product of an unwanted pregnancy. The mother was unprepared for the responsibilities of parenthood and, as a result, the child suffered years of emotional and physical deprivation. K.P. had been removed from her home and taken into the protective custody of the juvenile court before being placed with relatives. Evaluation was completed two months after the foster home placement and in that short time the effects of a loving and caring environment were evident; K.P. was no longer withdrawn or nonverbal. Developmental delays were noted, and the therapeutic program included continued foster home placement, a developmental preschool program and periodic medical care to monitor her growth and development. The evaluation and follow-up services involved the cooperation and coordination of several community agencies providing legal, social, medical and educational services.

A child's behavior may vary dramatically from one setting to another, especially between home and school, causing a disruption in communication between the parents and school personnel. The clinic, by offering an independent assessment of the child's total functioning, often re-establishes the needed communication between the school and parents. The following case study illustrates how the evaluation process can assist both the school and the family in reassessing the child's problem:

S.T., a seven-year-old boy referred for evaluation of behavior problems at school, was reportedly destructive, active and aggressive in the classroom. His parents reported no behavior problems at home and were upset by the school's attempts to deal with the behaviors, e.g. there were frequent phone calls, conferences and suspensions, all of which had been futile. The parents believed the school was ineffectual and lax in its handling of the child and felt little responsibility as the behavior problems were school-related. School personnel interpreted the parents' attitude as disinterested, resulting in an impasse between the family and school. Psychological evaluation by the school and medical examination both indicated subtle neurological and motor deficits associated with learning disabilities and central nervous system dysfunctioning. Interpretation to both the parents and school helped to re-establish communication necessary for planning and coordination of educational and medical intervention.

MEDICAL PARTICIPATION IN COUNSELING

Medical students and pediatric house staff are usually included as members of the counseling team. Parents appreciate the opportunity to share questions of a medical nature with physicians. Frequently, interpretations must be conveyed to parents regarding etiology, diagnosis, medical management and prognosis. Involvement of medical personnel in individual or group counseling is essential when dealing with exceptional children. In a program for developmentally-delayed preschool children, a physician and a social worker served as group leaders. The parents were anxious to discuss problems regarding their child's development, preschool training and discipline. Perhaps for the first time many parents had an opportunity to talk informally with a pediatrician away from the office. The group setting provided a comfortable mechanism for interchange between parents and physicians and resolved many areas of parental confusion.

Physicians participate in informing interviews because diagnostic findings and recommendations may be of a specific medical nature. Parents are generally receptive and cooperative when a physician is available to discuss the need for additional laboratory tests, psychological evaluation, special remedial programs and periodic medical re-evaluations. It is important that parents fully understand their child's functional abilities and potentials before staff recommend specific rehabilitation programs. A child's physical and medical limitations can best be conveyed by the examining physician, as the following case illustrates:

A two-year-old boy was referred for evaluation because of a suspected hearing deficit and delayed motor development. The mother reported that the child was not talking or imitating sounds and that he was clumsy. On physical and neurological examination mild psychomotor delay was noted and further hearing evaluation substantiated a moderate to severe hearing deficit. In the informing interview the parents had many questions regarding the organic nature of the child's disabilities and his development. In talking with the parents it became apparent that they needed the physician's reassurance and authority to assist them in planning for the child.

Basic objectives of the medical training program at CEC are to enhance the philosophy that (1) parent counseling is essential in the comprehensive care of the child with a chronic handicapping condition, (2) counseling is a medical responsibility regardless of the child's handicap, and (3) if limitations of time or expertise prevent direct medical intervention, then appropriate allied health professionals must be selected to perform this function. It has been the experience of the faculty that students of medicine appreciate opportunities to counsel parents when trained professionals are available to assist.

Home management suggestions

1. **Be firm.** Establish clear ground rules when the child is young and keep these rules (with whatever needed amendments) on into adolescence. As the child improves in judgment, give him more leeway.

2. **Do not flood the child with petty time-consuming decisions;** for example, what dress to wear, what shirt, etc. If he dawdles and shows indecision, then make these decisions for him.

3. **Whenever possible, do consider his opinion in some larger matters;** for example, to go or not to go to Jimmy's birthday party, to go fishing with a friend, etc. If there is no real reason to deny the child, then allow him the option of "yes" or "no." However, many MBD youngsters will need time to picture the situation and think it through before deciding.

4. **Do not haggle or negotiate or wheedle about small things:** an extra TV program; whether or not a helping of a new food is accepted; etc. A decision, even if it's in error, is better than haggling. Have faith in yourself.

5. **Give the child chores by all means:** setting the table for supper; helping serve at table; clearing the dishes; making the bed; etc. Boys as well as girls should do these chores. Parents must share their duties and chores with their MBD child for the child's good. Such activities build self-discipline and a sense of responsibility. Select one or two chores and be prepared for the fact that it will take your time, effort, goodwill and many *calm* reminders to get these chores done. Withholding a desired privilege for a short time *may* be necessary if the child fails to do the chore assigned.

6. **Be prepared to accept the absentmindedness of most MBD children.** These youngsters need to be reminded again and again but without the irritating "I've told you a million times." Try to avoid the normal and usual escalation of irritation when directions or reminders need to be given over and over. When you have to repeat a direction say it each time as though it were the first time. These children are not being willful and stubborn when they can't remember; at this point in time, they just can't keep the many things we expect them to remember at the forefront of consciousness.

7. **Be alert to the MBD youngster's absentmindedness in regard to care of tools and other implements, toys, etc.** Note where you see him lay the kitchen shears, saw, hammer, etc. Check later and if the object is still there, give a calm reminder to put it away properly.

8. **Short lists of tasks are excellent to help a child remember.** A list is impersonal and reduces irritations; the child will gain satisfaction as he checks off tasks completed.

9. **Many MBD youngsters seem to "never hear" or to ignore parents' directions and commands.** Often these children do not process multiple requests quickly or accurately. Therefore, it helps if parents first make sure they have the child's attention before making a request. After they've stated their wish in simple, clear, one-concept commands, the child should be asked to repeat what was said. Speaking at a slower rate of speed to the child often is helpful too.

10. **Since many children with MBD are disorganized, they may sometimes have difficulty relating an event in proper sequence.** Family members often need to quietly ask "who, what, where, and when" questions to get the necessary information. Again, a calm, uncritical and non-irritable manner should be the rule.

11. **A common characteristic of many MBD children is their difficulty in waiting their turn** e.g., in playing a game or when participating in a conversation. Some interruptions when adults are talking may be allowed, for the youngster is impulsive. However, having permitted some infractions of good manners, par-

ents should correct the child sharply if he persists in interrupting; send him from the table or discipline him in a similar fashion if he should continue with this behavior.

12. Do not permit the MBD child to be unduly loud and noisy in a public place. Do something about it quickly, then and there, even if it is embarrassing for all concerned. Saying, "Just wait till I get you home" will not help the child and will only make parents feel frustrated.

13. Routines are helpful for all children and seem to be particularly needed by the MBD child: a regular time for meals, homework, TV, getting up and going to bed. Each family should find the schedule that suits it best.

14. In the majority of instances, parents should not try to tutor their own child. It is helpful to a youngster who has problems in reading to have someone in the family read material aloud for content purposes. But to "teach" a child spelling or reading words, or to drill him on the concepts of mathematics, is usually unsuccessful. More is lost because of the strained relationships which often result than is gained in improved skills.

15. Punishment should be:
a. Designed to fit the child and to vary with the offense. The cardinal rule is to "punish *behavior* and not the child."
Generally, physical punishment should be avoided because other forms of discipline (short periods of isolation or withholding privileged activities) focus more on the behavior of the child and less on the child's self-concept.
Realistically, however, some physical punishment is likely, and care should be taken to be sure that it is not too severe or prolonged.

b. Punishment should follow immediately after the offense so that the association between the undesirable behavior and the punishment which follows such action will be strengthened.
c. Punishment should be of *short duration*. It must clear the air; the parent should not continue to accuse and grumble, but the child may be allowed to grumble a bit.

16. Help other members of the family recognize and understand the MBD youngster's differences. This child can't help being impulsive, loud, forgetful, clumsy, etc. The siblings' patience with their brother or sister who has these problems will be of great assistance to him.

17. Parents themselves need to come to terms with their child's deficits and strengths. The child with MBD has a handicap with which he will often need help for many years. Goals should be those that challenge but do not extend beyond his capabilities. If parents can accept their child's assets and liabilities, the child can then begin to accept himself.

Figure 1
(Copyright 1973 by John E. Peters, M.D., Joanna S. Davis, M.S., Cleo M. Goolsby, M.S.W., Sam D. Clements, Ph.D.)

READING MATERIALS

The distribution of selected reading materials is a valuable adjunct to parent counseling. Parents appreciate the opportunity to privately review pamphlets and simple books which are related to their child's problems. Excellent problem-oriented materials have been compiled by pharmaceutical companies, educational institutions and other public agencies. The physician may prepare his own brochure for distribution to selected parents. Often these monographs answer questions that parents failed to ask or have not thought to ask their physicians. Literature should be frank, honest and in a language that can be readily understood by nonprofessionals. A parent handbook is being developed by the staff of the CEC that will include developmental information, materials on children's behavior and a list of community facilities that provide assistance.

Parents of children who are experiencing school and social adjustment difficulties are often confused about their roles. Occasionally, well-prepared pamphlets or handouts can help support a counseling interview. Parents frequently need time to review and digest information in order to help them understand their child, his problems, behavioral reactions and possible therapeutic programs. An example of a typical kind of reading resource is the pamphlet published by Ciba, "Minimal Brain Dysfunction: The Child with a Learning Problem." This pamphlet is presented as Figure 7-1.

Under no circumstance should a pamphlet, brochure or a book be a substitute for parent-physician interaction. These materials are adjuncts for, but not substitutes for, professional contacts. Indeed, reading materials may be a way of initiating parent and professional communication. Parents must never be made to feel that reading materials are offered as replacements for professional interest.

SUMMARY

All professionals recognize that parent counseling is an essential component of the comprehensive management of exceptional children. Participation by the physician in either individual or group counseling sessions is to be encouraged. The CEC training program attempts to enhance medical expertise in the art of counseling by providing opportunities for supervised counseling. Skills, insights and confidences are enhanced by clinical experiences.

The CEC provides opportunities for various parent-professional contacts, meeting both patient service needs and student educational needs. Communication between members of the professional staff and parents is an ongoing process. Similarly, interagency communication is essential in comprehensive patient care. Physicians-in-training are provided numerous opportunities for interaction with other members of the health team and with community agencies.

Counseling the parents of children with chronic handicapping conditions is essential in providing quality care. Medical responsibility involves participation with other professionals in rendering this service.

Chapter 8

COMMUNICATING WITH THE PARENTS
OF EXCEPTIONAL CHILDREN

NORMAN E. BISSELL

THE phenomenologist assumes that we behave in accordance with our perception of what is real. Our perspective or frame-of-reference provides the only possible context for making the best decisions. For each human being the world is as he sees it — a world created from the sum of his experiences, past and present, sensory and psychological.

What do we believe to be *real* about the parents of exceptional children? It doesn't take a massive search of the literature (3, 4, 5) or more than a five-minute conversation with a group of special educators to discover that (1) parents are frequently viewed from a pathological perspective in terms of maladaptive adjustments to their handicapped children; (2) parents are seldom viewed as desirable or competent full-fledged members of the interdisciplinary team; and (3) parents are dehumanized by categorical references and generalizations about the parents of the mentally retarded, learning disabled, deaf, etc. We act as though we believe there are two discrete groups of parents — those with normal children and those with exceptional children. This is a remarkable observation, particularly at a time when we are endorsing prescriptive, individualized, noncategorical approaches to the education of exceptional children.

Because the author does not believe there are two discreet groups of parents, this chapter will explore a *normalized* approach for counseling and communicating with the parents of exceptional children. This approach has been developed during approximately thirteen years of experience in special education as a speech pathologist, administrator of a preschool for multiply-handicapped children and a professor of special education committed to the exploration and the implementation of parent input into teacher education. The approach requires a perception of all parents as individuals capable of positive contributions as active members of the team.

THE TEAM

Special educators who are interested in normalizing parent-professional communications must begin analyzing the term *team approach.* Team approach is an appealing concept with longevity in the terminology of special education, medicine, psychology, social work and other disciplines. Professionals associated with the habilitation or rehabilitation of exceptional persons know that a single expert or discipline cannot have all of the answers. The team approach is a positively-oriented term. However, it is commonly implemented in so-called team conferences or staffings where individuals (patients or clients) are fragmented into their speech behavior, academic achievement, ambulation, intelligence, motivation and social adjustment by the various disciplines. Decisions about etiology, diagnosis, prognosis and plans for treatment and education require a wide base of expertise and information. Does this base of expertise and information require the active participation of parents?

As early as 1957, Kanner (5) and other professionals expanded the team concept to include parents as members with equal standing. Letha Patterson, the parent of a retarded child, wrote an article in 1956 which was reported in Wolfensberger (7); it included specific suggestions for professionals and referred to parents as "partners." These writers clearly viewed parent-professional communications as reciprocal and not one-way. Professionals were not to be the exclusive givers of advice. Few professional reference books and textbooks on counseling the parents of exceptional children fail to include excerpts from Kanner's and Patterson's suggestions. The apparent endorsement of the total team concept which actively includes parents is admirable, but there is still a gap between what we say and what we do in special education. A dramatic example of this credibility gap is the fourteen-year time lag between Kanner's inclusion of parents as team members and the Landmark Court Decision in

Pennsylvania in 1971, mandating educating for all exceptional children in that state. Special education legislation in Pennsylvania includes a *requirement* for parent participation and approval. The necessity for including this requirement demonstrates the fact that many professionals never really meant or understood the implications of *full team membership* for parents. The team they conceptualized was captained or coached by the professional. Parents were generally on the line, on the bench or, in many instances, in the bleachers.

PARENTS WITH PATHOLOGIES

The writer's first experience with parents of exceptional children occurred as a novice speech clinician. He diligently attempted to practice what he had learned in courses and textbooks about the parents of children with speech disorders. He knew many things about parents. He knew parents must cooperate with the clinician in order for the youngster to achieve maximally in his communication. He knew that *these* parents often denied the child's problem, were not accepting, and frequently were critical of clinicians. He had learned that parents of exceptional children were more anxious than other parents and that they ran a greater risk of marital disintegration, and they needed support, information, therapy and other special services. He had learned that the parents of exceptional children could be described by a *pathological profile* of their special needs, problems and other negative aspects of their affective and cognitive functioning and potential.

The writer was awed with the special needs of these parents and felt remarkably inadequate in the shadow of their burdens and unique problems. His initial high levels of anxiety related to a perception of these parents as pathological and this did not enhance the probability of establishing a climate of positive mutual regard and effective communication. Only through experience was he able to learn that each parent is a unique developing individual, and his helping efforts were maximized as he became able to discard negative perceptions. The clichés and myths about exceptional parents and techniques for *handling* them were minimized by real experiences with parents as persons.

THE COMMUNICATIVE ROLE: SOME STRATEGIES

Communication is a general term encompassing specialized functions such as counseling. Until all special education personnel have the benefit of training in the techniques of counseling, most will have to be sensitive to the limits of their abilities and aware of professional counseling resources in the community and school. Even with the rapid increase in university courses and field experiences in parent counseling, many special education teachers will not be prepared for counseling in the specialized sense of the term. Most special education teachers will not meet state requirements for certification or licensure as counselors. However, any special education teacher can become a more effective communicator with parents.

Textbooks for the preparation of early childhood personnel provide an excellent resource for learning about parent conferences, home visits, parent observation and group meetings. The rationale for this comprehensive concern with parent contacts and communications is based upon the fact that the young child is still very dependent upon his home and his relationship with his parents. In order to have a smooth transition toward increased independence as a result of the preschool experience, teachers and parents must share similar goals; they must communicate well. This early childhood point of view is analogous to special education.

The developmental tasks leading to self-sufficiency for a child with a handicap are more arduous, and their attainment is sometimes reached in almost imperceptible increments. Some tasks are never possible. The parents, teacher, physicians, social workers and other persons engaged in helping the exceptional child must coordinate and concentrate their efforts and observations in order to efficiently effect desirable changes in the child, leading toward maximal independence. Not a single wasted idea or conflicting action can be afforded. Communication is the key to understanding among all those concerned with the child. It takes practice for parents and teachers to become effective communicators.

Special educators cannot establish rapport with parents if they only see one or both of them once or twice a year, have never been in the home, and have had only fifteen or thirty minutes scheduled for annual parent conferences at school. Tightly-scheduled routine conferences may assume the form of impromptu interviews with the teacher on one side of the desk and the parent perched precariously in a small chair on the other side of the desk. The teacher may hand the parent examples of school work, say the child is doing well, and thank them for coming for the conference. The parent might get a chance to ask one small question such as "When will school be dismissed this year?" Administrative structuring of parent conferences can impose severe limitations on the special education teacher as a communicator, but it does not eliminate the teacher's responsibility for attempting to establish a continuum of communicative experiences with parents throughout the year.

The suggestions for effective parent-professional communications in this chapter are based upon the assumption that the parents of exceptional children are, first of all, *parents*. They share the same desires and expectations regarding the teacher and the school as all parents. An early publication by Stout and Langdon (6) described characteristics shared by all parents:

1. Parents want their child's teacher to be a person who likes children and commands respect of both children and adults.
2. Parents want to feel assured that the classroom teacher will let them know if anything is not going well with their child.
3. Parents want the teachers to be honest.
4. Most parents want to know what goes on in school, but hesitate to ask.
5. There are suggestions and objections parents would like to make, but they doubt if they would be welcomed.
6. Parents are usually pleased when the classroom teacher asks their help in carrying on the classroom activities.
7. Parents want the teacher to know their child as an individual, to like him and to accept him.
8. Parents expect great things of the school.
9. Many parents think parent-teacher relationships can gradually taper off as the student grows older.

Viewed in the context of exceptional children and special

education, the preceding list of parent characteristics provides a justification for the development of reciprocal communications and parent involvement.

Parent-professional relations will be enhanced and effective involvement facilitated if communications with parents (1) build a parent-teacher partnership team to directly serve the child, (2) provide growth experiences for the parents themselves, and (3) provide opportunities for the establishment of friendly relations and mutual understanding. These communicative goals cannot be achieved unless the teacher is able to unconditionally accept the parents. This acceptance will be difficult without frequent effective contacts. Mutual participation in a system of communication will bind parents and teachers together more closely regardless of the content or structure of the communication. To a great extent, the following generalization made by Kagan (2) makes a lot of sense: "A teacher, doctor, or parent who cares about what he is doing can do almost anything and win . . . " Teachers must care about parents as well as children.

The vehicles or instruments of communication available to the special education teacher are infinite. It is true that the imagination of many special educators may not go beyond the minimal traditional communications such as progress reports, annual parent conferences and occasional notes sent home with the child. Unfortunately, when parent counseling or parent-school relationships are discussed it is likely that the teacher's stereotyped concepts of the functions close her mind to innovation or experimentation. There can be no formula for successful parent-professional communications. All one can hope to do is to dislodge traditional special educators from the apathetic position of wishing that the parents would be more interested to an active position of aggressively searching for the best strategies for developing a participatory relationship with parents. Contrary to an opinion that is frequently voiced, the responsibility for establishing a good parent-professional relationship *does not* rest with the parent. This relationship is an integral part of the responsibilities of the special educator. The special education teacher must actively structure communicative experiences with the parents in accordance with the educational goals for each of the students. Parent contact must not be left to chance or the minimal requirements of school policy.

Interviews, written messages, verbal messages and formal reports are common channels of communication between teachers and parents. The effectiveness of each of these channels depends upon careful planning, the establishment of rapport and a focus on specific goals to be accomplished. It is interesting to note that special educators frequently use the type of communication most convenient to them. This sometimes means sending a note home instead of scheduling a personal interview. Normalized communication requires a parent-centered approach. In other words, teachers should not ask themselves, "What is the easiest way to communicate with these parents?" Instead, they should ask themselves, "What is the most effective way to communicate with these parents?" Using the communication channel which seems easiest may be, in the long run, a hindrance to further open communication.

Parent conferences or interviews can be effective ways of communicating, but the parent must be willing and able to travel to the school for the conference. The effectiveness of parent conferences in the school will be enhanced if educators can tear down the old concept that parent conferences are only held when the child or parents are at fault in some manner. Many parents have negative perceptions of schools and conferences which may inhibit or prevent quality communication. The image of the school, the principal and the teacher may be formidable and negative in the eyes of parents. However, even if the parents are solidly opposed to the school, they can learn to appreciate a teacher as an individual separate from the institution if the teacher makes an honest effort to communicate, to welcome the parents to the school, and if he shows an interest in and appreciation for the child and his family. In some situations, conferences may be scheduled or meetings arranged in a neutral nonschool setting.

Parent conferences will be more effective if the teacher projects a feeling that the meeting was arranged so that the teacher and parents can learn from each other. (The teacher must believe that he/she can learn from parents or his/her efforts to project the feeling of mutual learning will fall flat.) Honest reports of the child's growth and development should be included. The more frequently conferences are held, the easier it will be to establish rapport and to feel a mutual involvement in helping the child. The establishment of certain days and times throughout the school year when parents may make appointments for interviews may encourage frequent conferences if the parents are made aware of the schedule and feel welcome.

The parents should not leave a conference empty-handed. A brief written resumé of the child's accomplishments, copies of some of his school work, examples of what he's been doing in crafts, or a snapshot of the child during a school activity are concrete examples for the parent attesting to the value of their trip to the school. Verbal exchanges with teachers, doctors, social workers or other professionals can seem quite remote when a parent returns home unless he brings with him a concrete reminder of the occasion. Tangible evidence of the worth of a conference increases the probability of attendance at future conferences.

Written communications are generally not as effective as personal contact, but in some instances are appropriate. Letters are more dependable and attention-getting than student-carried notes. Letters should be businesslike rather than personal, and a copy should be retained in the child's file. Sometimes it is an excellent learning experience resulting in a more thoroughly-read letter if the student helps write it.

Progress reports have historically been described as poor instruments of communication. However, if the development of these reporting systems can be shared by parents and teachers, it may encourage an ongoing dialogue and result in the development of effective communications regarding the child's progress. Progress reports should not be merely the traditional mechanism for reporting grades. This is especially true in special education where qualitative data is essential. *Describe* a student's progress toward specific goals and parents may be able to help in the attainment of those goals.

Most teachers of special education have met parents who were more expert in a certain area of professional knowledge than the teacher. Some parents know more about learning disabilities, behavioral disorders or mental retardation than the special educator charged with the responsibility of teaching the child and communicating with the parent. The teacher who can avoid the pitfalls of feeling threatened and inadequate because of this abundance of parental knowledge can benefit from the information. Parents and teachers can work toward feeling comfortable in exchanging information regarding current developments in areas of special education, medicine, child rearing, etc.This exchange can be a valuable mutual resource. There's nothing demeaning about learning from parents.

The special education teacher should avoid assuming the role of one who prescribes the reading of certain books or articles in order to straighten out the parent's thinking. Where reading is desirable, a mutual parent-teacher search for current information which will help them in working and living with the child is preferable to prescriptive bibliotherapy for the parents. Conflicting points of view encountered in various publications, popular as well as professional, will encourage an open-minded attitude of inquiry by both teacher and parents.

Telephone calls should be reserved for making appointments and reporting emergency situations. A phone call is a poor substitute for an interview. There is no way of insuring that the time of the call will be appropriate and facilitate the thoughtful participation of the parent. The call might arrive at a time when the baby is crying for his bottle, food is boiling over on the stove, and the door bell is ringing. This would not be an ideal way to discuss a child's academic or behavioral situation. When telephone calls are necessary, they should be brief and to the point. The teacher should avoid prolonged, chatty social calls.

Although educators are sometimes afraid of the power of parents and do not want them meddling in school affairs, parent groups are frequently formed as adjuncts to the school program. These may range from PTA meetings to group psychotherapy. Ginott (1) outlined the main advantages of parent education groups in child guidance clinics, and these advantages may be generalized to other types of parent group meetings in special education.

1. The parents become aware of a world of feeling in them and their children.

2. For the first time they take time to think about the right to have negative as well as positive attitudes; they are free to feel.
3. They learn new methods of relating to their children.
4. They acquire a large body of information on child behavior.
5. They learn to be more objective; they have less guilt.
6. They learn new methods of dealing more effectively with specific problems of children.
7. Groups enable a minimally-staffed agency to render extensive service to the community.

Most special educators will have had experience with at least one or two of the following models of parent groups:

1. PTA with parents and teachers of *normal* and exceptional children combined
2. A miniature PTA for parents and teachers of exceptional children enrolled in a special class or school
3. Meetings of local chapters of national organizations such as the National Association for Retarded Citizens, Inc. and the Association for Children with Learning Disabilities
4. A limited series of child rearing meetings with speakers or films and group discussions
5. Group therapy with a qualified clinician
6. A formal or informal association of parents of children enrolled in a special education program — this type of group is intended to be in contrast with teacher or administrator-dominated groups. The social and/or educational functions of this group are determined according to the needs perceived by the group.

A group with autonomy and flexibility such as the last-mentioned is uniquely suited to meet the needs of a majority of parents of exceptional children. The appropriate role for the special educator in this parent group is as a facilitator for the group and/or a member of the group with equal standing. His particular contributions may be in terms of securing speakers, films for special programs or engaging in other facilitating efforts which may be possible for him because of his professional interests, contacts and status, but he must resist the lure of telling the group what it should do and what its programs should be. It may be that the group does not even want programs. The special educator should be an enabler rather than an authority in helping parents develop effective groups.

The meeting place for parent groups may also be crucial to the success or failure of a group. It may never be possible for many parents to overcome their feelings that the school building is a formidable and disapproving environment. A parent's negative experiences as a child may prevent him from ever feeling totally open or comfortable in a group meeting in a school. The possibility of meeting in more comfortable and relaxed environments should be explored. The strategy of planning a nonmeeting has been an effective way of increasing parent attendance.

Professionals (and parents) planning nonmeetings for groups of parents will consciously avoid the stereotyped mixed bags of objectives, ritualized program formats and conventional settings. Few parents will be excited at the prospect of (1) assembling in a school lunchroom; (2) being welcomed by the director of special education; (3) listening to a discussion of psychological testing and classification by the school psychologist; (4) hearing each teacher describe the goals for his class; and, perhaps, (5) climaxing the event with a business meeting including minutes, treasurer's report and a condemnation of those parents not caring enough to attend. We know how to turn people off. We can also turn people on if we care enough to try. The concept of a nonmeeting may provide a new perspective or framework for planning.

For an initial nonmeeting the planners should shelve all grandiose arrangements and expectations. A gathering of parents and special education personnel might be held in a community meeting room where citizens frequently attend enjoyable social events. Simple objectives, such as socialization while watching a slide presentation of the children in various activities, are better than covert attempts to modify parent attitudes or obtain instant parental cooperation. Adherence to reasonable time limits is essential. It is a pleasant surprise when a program ends on time or earlier than expected, and it increases the probability of good attendance in the future. Nonmeetings will also encourage spontaneous and informal communications which enhance the building of warm and respectful continuing relationships.

Special educators should work toward the creation of a *community* of parents and professionals.

If parents seldom come to the school, the teacher should go to them. The home visit can provide the teacher with a more comprehensive understanding of the child and an appreciation of his parents. Even when the parents do participate in school conferences or activities, there will be gaps in information which the teacher can fill in if she visits the home. In a home visit, as in an interview or a parent group, the teacher should not play the role of an expert primed to tell the family what to do, but as one who has a sincere interest in the child and the family, is eager to help if possible, and is hopeful for new ideas. If the teacher can establish a cooperative relationship, the chances are much greater of helping the exceptional child.

Communicative structures which bring the parents into the school and permit them to see their child engaging in academic and social learning experiences make a valuable contribution toward the development of more realistic parental attitudes. Parents who observe the child in the school milieu will have a better understanding of his limitations and assets. The teacher's demonstration of acceptance and objectivity can provide an excellent model of behavior for the parents to emulate. They will discover that a class for exceptional children is many things, but it is not a sad, pitiful, soul-wrenching haven for hopelessly-impaired children. The teacher's emphasis will be on the children and not on the gloomy adjectives which some parents might feel would permeate the air of a special classroom. Parents will probably be surprised that the situation is hopeful, happy, constructive and often amusing.

POSTSCRIPT TO PROFESSORS

Those who prepare special educators are urged to consider adopting a positive and participatory view of parents. If university professors can experience the exhilaration of quality nonpathologic interactions with the parents of exceptional children, they will be effective models for their students. Positive models who cherish parent participation and abhor educating the parents will teach far more significant lessons than textbooks dwelling upon the lexicon of unconscious motivations and categorizations of disordered personality characteristics demonstrated by maladaptive parents of exceptional children.

Consider the value of direct input from parents in teacher-preparation programs. This input can be through videotape recordings or in-person interviews. Be courageous enough to ask parents to share experiences and even give advice to special educators in training. Establish a teacher education advisory group of *parents* who volunteer to help prepare special educators for effective communications with parents. Why role play and read professional journals when real life preparation experiences are possible for the asking?

REFERENCES

1. Ginott, H.G.: Parent education groups in a child guidance clinic. In McDaniel, H.B. *et al.* (Eds.): *Readings in Guidance.* New York, Holt, 1959.
2. Kagan, J.: Letter to the editor. *Harpers,* March, 1967.
3. Noland, R.L.: *Counseling Parents of the Ill and Handicapped.* Springfield, Thomas, 1971.
4. Noland, R.L.: *Counseling Parents of the Emotionally Disturbed Child.* Springfield, Thomas, 1972.
5. Noland, R.L.: *Counseling Parents of the Mentally Retarded Child.* Springfield, Thomas, 1972.
6. Stout, I.W., and Langdon, G.: Parent-teacher relationships. *What Research Says to the Teacher.* No. 16, 1958.
7. Wolfensberger, W., and Kurtz, R.A.: *Management of the Family of the Mentally Retarded.* Chicago, Follett, 1969.

Chapter 9

ISSUES IN PLANNING
FUTURE PROGRAMS FOR PARENTS
OF HANDICAPPED CHILDREN

Vilma T. Falck

ASSUMPTIONS CONCERNING THE NEEDS
OF PARENT POPULATIONS

Every family must deal repeatedly with experiences that temporarily disturb equanimity. Many families can deal with these periodic disruptions without disintegration, particularly if the disruption can be resolved quickly. The family with a handicapped child is more often required to have an infinite capacity to adapt to stress. These parents have a lingering responsibility for coping with the handicapping condition and must deal with the constant potential threat to financial resources, time available for siblings, emotional stability and other dilemmas, all of which would interfere with a full and happy life.

For some families, despite an environment with continued stress, adaptive capacity allows them to cope, to meet all conditions without serious interruption in the lives of any family member. Other families are more susceptible to stress; their resources and adaptive mechanisms do not allow them to focus with optimism on the likelihood of resolution of problems. Nonadaptive families are in serious need of help from society. Even the most adapting families, however, benefit from programs which help alleviate environmental and mental stress.

One of the more important primary functions of an organized and civilized society is to provide for each of its members. However, each person, although a distinct creature, cannot be considered complete without his personal history — his *self* as influenced by the past and, from moment to moment, by the continually-dynamic forces that change him over a period of time. Each person becomes what he becomes because of a wide variety of physical, psychological and sociological external events. These external events coexist with internal experiences derived from countless numbers of interactions with others which allow that self to develop an assumption of his own personality and character.

Interactions among all members of a family are important influences on the *assumptive world* of each of them. Frank (20) uses the term *assumptive world* as a shorthand expression for the complex interacting set of values, expectations and images of one's self and others. As a member of the family unit, the child with the problem develops a feeling of self and a concept of worth. He develops an expectation for his own security and success from family interactions which can ultimately make the difference in his problem becoming a handicap or remaining a disability to which he will continue to adapt throughout life.

Thus, any rehabilitative or therapeutic program aiming to provide comprehensive attention to the problems of children which does not give serious consideration to the family unit fails to take advantage of the total environment. Such a program cannot be considered adequate.

This philosophy that families are an integral part of therapeutic programs has led to certain specific assumptions about the needs of handicapped children and their families.

1. The family should be considered the primary resource and source of help for the handicapped child. It has continued responsibility for him and is the most significant potential change agent for behaviors and attitudes.

2. For handicapped children, early detection and appropriate educational programming are critical in order to allow for appropriate intervention to interrupt progression from a disability to a handicap.

3. Parents have the need and the right to play a part in the decisions made concerning their children.

4. Profoundly multihandicapped children are almost automatically identified and do not require elaborate screening; to subject parents to repeated diagnostic sessions with the

objective of identifying the disabling characteristics is often cruel. Elaborate identification plans that do not lead directly to remediation are wasteful and perhaps harmful.

5. Identification of handicapped children must not focus exclusively on test information; it must also consider the tasks required and environmental variables which affect the child's performance in the home.

6. In establishing priorities, greater time and effort should be given to educational programming for the handicapped child than to identifying, screening and testing.

7. Greater emphasis should be given to diagnoses that lead to teaching strategies and rehabilitation within school and home and community environments than to data collection.

8. There is no one acceptable regime for family education, nor is there only one acceptable educational intervention strategy for handicapped children. Therefore, different solutions for solving the identified problems and meeting the specified objectives are possible.

9. In order to provide for comprehensive educational services which include the family, multidisciplinary coordination and cooperation are necessary. Such coordination will require teamwork on many levels.

10. It is necessary for a team to learn to work together before it can most effectively perform the work for which it was formed. This learning to perform as a cohesive unit is necessary in order to avoid presenting fractionated or dysynchronous services to the family.

11. An adequate parent or family education program for the handicapped child, in addition to educational services, includes consideration of a full health program with psychological, nutritional, dental and medical services. This approach with parents of handicapped children is conceived to encompass educational, health, social and parent involvement components.

Based on these assumptions, the needs of parents of handicapped children could be met by overcoming existing barriers to comprehensive educational and health programs. These barriers, unfortunately, represent serious obstacles as they are reflections of the present social and economic state of development in society. Some of the barriers to be overcome are the following: inadequate distribution of services, insufficient numbers of competent professional personnel, the limited number of comprehensive programs, inadequate coordination between existing health/educational services within communities, a restricted number of instructional materials organized into units for meaningful use by parents, inadequate provision for the continuing education of parents, incompetent paraprofessionals and professionals who may be involved with the problems of the handicapped child, inadequate mechanisms to provide information to families who seek help in order to overcome specific problems related to their handicapped child, and financial barriers. There are also those cultural characteristics such as misinformation, prejudice, superstition and habit patterns which prove to be obstacles for even the most well-motivated families of handicapped children. However, it is the zeitgeist, the spirit of the times, to confront these barriers.

CONFIRMATION OF ASSUMPTIONS CONCERNING THE NEEDS OF PARENTS OF HANDICAPPED CHILDREN

The validity of the assumptions made about the worlds of parents has been confirmed by a series of studies conducted in Texas by this author in 1974. These studies utilized (a) personal interviews with individuals and with small groups of parents, (b) written responses to a questionnaire mailed to representatives of parent organizations for the handicapped, and (c) documents prepared at a statewide conference for leaders of organizations for the parents of handicapped children. Each of these sources of information will be discussed.

Personal Interviews with Parents

Parents of twenty-five handicapped children were interviewed and asked to discuss the following: initial problems (when they were first advised of the existing disability), their active ongoing problems (e.g. difficulties with management), their anticipated problems (fear of future, etc.), their special situational problems (e.g. convulsions) encountered. The statements made by parents in response to these items were influenced by a number of variables, e.g. the current age level of their child, their socioeconomic status, the size and sophistication of the home community, and their educational background. The twenty most frequently-occurring problems cited by parents interviewed are the following:

1. Becoming cognizant of the need and responsibility to help their handicapped child develop skills and abilities

2. Lack of knowledge regarding the availability of programs, services and vocational training in the community

3. Difficulty in getting help during the early period of childhood (1 month to 3 years)

4. Difficulty in getting a handicapped child accepted into a day care program

5. Lack of availability of legal services and counseling

6. Lack of, or difficulty arranging, transportation to schools, workshops and programs

7. Problems with trying to insure equal education for the child with a handicap

8. Lack of physician awareness of the child's total health care needs

9. Scarcity of socialization programs for the handicapped adult

10. Lack of police awareness of retardates and their special needs; there also is need for availability of attorneys who understand retardation

11. Concern for parents who do not know about possibilities for help or do not have the means to seek help (most of the parents with whom professionals have contact are concerned and active)

12. High cost of needed materials, i.e. braille writers, educational toys and various tools

13. Need for mobility training to begin at an early age

14. Inadequate education of the community regarding the needs of the handicapped, e.g. poor architectural design of buildings, need for ramps, barriers, etc.

15. Need for parking regulations which provide for children and adults who use wheel chairs

16. Problems in employment of handicapped for monetary gain or recreation

17. Concern for the need to develop competence and confidence in those whose physical capabilities have been reduced

18. Problems in obtaining help for psychological problems

19. Ineffective (and insufficient number of) sheltered workshops

20. Difficulty obtaining help for the handicapped older child and young adult

Responses to Questionnaire

The following summary lists topics in order from highest to lowest priority obtained from returned questionnaires which had been mailed to representatives (usually the president of the organization). As previously discussed (19), questionnaires were completed by representatives of the following organizations: Texas Association for Children with Learning Disabilities, Texas Association for Retarded Children, National Society for Autistic Children, United Cerebral Palsy, Parents Association for the Deaf, Parents of Mongoloids. Representatives of the following groups were also included: blind, orthopedically-handicapped, emotionally-handicapped, multihandicapped, auditorily-impaired, deaf-blind, muscular dystrophy and cleft palate. The questionnaire asked parents to rate a list of suggested topics relative to their importance as items on an agenda to be discussed during a formal conference. The ratings on the questionnaire items from 1 (highest) to 14 (lowest) are summarized as follows:

1. Getting special help from public schools

2. Communicating with legislative representatives so that they will understand the needs of handicapped children

3. Educating the community as to the problem

4. Knowing where to turn if an emergency comes up in handling the child

5. Getting help with activities of daily living

6. Educating peers as to the problems of the handicapped child

7. Getting financial help for special services and needs
8. Getting special materials so parents can help their children at home
9. Getting needed medical help
10. Being able to talk freely with teachers
11. Getting needed dental help
12. Being able to talk freely with doctors
13. Managing behavior within the family unit
14. Dealing with sibling problems

Findings From Conference for Leaders of Parents' Organizations

A statewide conference for leaders of organizations for parents of the handicapped met for two days at the Thompson Conference Center on the campus of the University of Texas at Austin in June, 1974. The activities of this conference have been documented via an audio cassette-slide series and a documentary 16-mm film. The variety of provocative questions raised during this conference confirmed assumptions which have been made regarding the needs of parent populations.

The expressed concerns and needs have been categorized into the following areas: Providing Direct Sources for Parents/Families, Management Problems, The Rights of Children, and Specific Problems.

Providing Direct Sources for Parents/Families

At this conference, leaders of parent organizations recognized the need for continuing support of parents and families of handicapped children. They also recognized parental needs for involvement in their child's program. Their concerns are reflected in the questions they listed — What can and should be done to provide counseling for parents and/or children? How best can parents be involved in the educational programs of their handicapped child? How can needed support services be provided if families are incompetent? How best can groups of parents be organized to help other parents? How best can we provide respite care for families who cannot share the responsibility of raising their handicapped child with others? What barriers can be overcome in order to provide useful and meaningful instructional materials for parents to use in their homes? Is a home learning resource center a viable plan?

Management Problems

Conference participants recognized that parents have continuing problems as well as lingering responsibilities in the management of their handicapped child. Even though problems are often individualistic and personal to each family, there was willing recognition of the advantages to be gained by management via coordinated action with others who have similar problems. Possible obstacles to effective organization and group support on a state or regional level were reflected in the questions raised by the participants — Should parents have lingering responsibilities for adult children? How can communities be helped to understand the special aspects of handicapping conditions at this time of mainstreaming the handicapped into society? What are the common problems among all types of disabling or handicapping conditions? How best can groups of parents identified by the specific handicaps of their children continue to work for alleviation of the unique problems without losing their identity, but at the same time work in a coalition for the common good of all? What are the advantages of a coalition of all organizations for the handicapped?

The Rights of Children

The mechanics of legislative action were of intense interest to participants as reflected in the following questions: How and when is lobbying done for maximum results? What does due process mean? How can appeals be made which will be useful and successful? What should be done about data banks? How much information about children should be computerized and by whom should it be retrieved? How best can a central clearing house be implemented to help all parents know how and where to get specific help? How can a legal advocate of the handicapped be funded?

Other Problems Outlined by Parents

Questions not specific to the above categories included those such as: How best can parents of the handicapped child (as individuals or in groups) communicate with the physician, the teacher or the legislature in order to get good cooperation and encourage coordination between them? Do parents of drug addicts or juvenile delinquents have problems similar or identical to parents of *exceptional* children? What are the problems common among all children? What could/should the handicapped be trained for in today's market? These questions reflect the breadth and depth of parental concern and desire for personal involvement in solutions to problems.

Conclusions Regarding Identified Needs

A needs assessment was conducted to support the philosophy which mandates involvement of parents in programs which provide service for disabled or handicapped children. This assessment included tabulation of concerns expressed in personal interviews, analysis and rank ordering of written responses on a questionnaire distributed to parents with proven leadership qualities, and evaluation of the most pressing problems encountered by families of handicapped children as summarized by parents during an intensive two-day meeting in Texas for parent representatives of organizations for the parents of handicapped.

The results of this assessment and the identified areas of need are serving as guidelines in projects which seek to provide education, assistance and training to families. These projects were planned to increase the adaptive capacity of the entire family as well as the disabled child in meeting experiences which may disturb equanimity and cohesiveness, and thus interfere with a full and happy life. The results of the assessment are serving also as guidelines for training professionals who plan programs for parents and families of the handicapped.

RATIONALE FOR PROCEDURES USED WITH PARENTS

The most cogent reason behind the need to involve parents and families in the educational and therapeutic process is that they already are a part of it; they always have been. Parental involvement has not always been recognized, and in certain instances their involvement has not been constructive.

An analysis of the assumptive world of parents can often reveal why certain homes present antitherapeutic environments. In these homes, even routinely helpful procedures may not prove beneficial. There are many well known examples of parents who *know* their child cannot walk, talk or cooperate. Children with such *knowledgeable* parents too often become therapeutic failures despite the best efforts of professional teams. Self-fulfilling prophecies from parents and teachers are now well documented by such authors as Rosenthal and Jacobson (30) and Frank (20).

The role and impact of parent involvement programs cannot be underestimated; therefore the advantage of educating parents as well as children is efficient as well as highly productive. For example, it has been estimated that 20 percent of the incidence of Down's Syndrome could be prevented if all pregnant women over the age of forty were referred for genetic study. One might consider this the responsibility of the physician, but others could also help educate future mothers; one cannot deny the fact that mothers have a right to complete understanding and knowledge of technological advances which are applicable to their personal lives.

The rationale behind parent involvement programs is based on parents' need to know and their right to know. In order to insure knowledge acquisition on the part of individual parents and parent groups, communication of information is necessary on the part of the professional. The professional must be able to influence parental attitudes and behaviors in constructive ways. Also, the professional must reinforce the parents' feeling of confidence and parents' increasing ability to manage their handicapped child. As all of this is done, it is equally necessary to convey sympathy and respect for the parents' side of the management problem.

Ability to convey necessary information must be accompanied by the ability to communicate in understandable terms. Written reports as well as oral discussions and conferences are necessary for parents. Professional competency is mandatory as specific advice and help is required; unfortunately there are far too many instances of professionals who do not develop two-way communication with parents, professionals who do not dare to listen as listening may imply they do not already know everything.

Parents need to be considered primary partners and kept informed at frequent intervals as to whether their child is progressing. Behavioral and performance objectives for the child should be set for small increments so that small successes do not get overlooked in the total growth and development of the child who has a disabling condition. When one evaluates the child within the family constellation, it is easier to help the family as well as the child to recognize progress in cognitive, affective or motor areas. A broader range of possibilities for effective growth then exists.

Professionals must help parents find solutions for everyday problems of management. Procedures unique to solving problems in the home and in the community for health, education and employment must be found. The solution may be limited to parents' knowing a source of help. For example, over the long term, parental awareness of available federal, state and local resources may be as vital a part of an educational program for any one parent-child unit as is the availability of a specific therapeutic regime within a legitimate geographical range. Of course parents and children must have access to given therapeutic programs within their locales as well.

Finally, the rationale for providing help for parents of handicapped children includes recognition of the need for coordination of services. Presently in the United States a multiplicity of service agencies, institutions and activities exists. Although there are many service agencies, there are still inadequacies. In the face of inadequacies and limitations, confusion, inefficiency, duplications and voids in service often occur. A study in Cameron County, Texas (11), for example, demonstrated that seven different kinds of personnel were visiting homes with little or no coordination of effort. These home visitors included the following: public health nurse, family planning aide, nutritional aide, immunization aide, health council outreach worker, multiservice outreach worker, and the Planned Parenthood worker. This author has learned of nineteen separate professional or paraprofessional groups receiving training to enable them to visit homes and provide help to families. It is not inconceivable that, in certain communities, all of these separate workers could visit high-risk families and children during the same week. Coordination and cooperation among professional workers are mandatory if homes are not to be disrupted and families confused by being overloaded with professionals.

In one approach to parents of the handicapped child presently underway in Texas, an effort is being made to develop a family/community educational specialist as the key or pivot figure. All service is funneled to the home through this one individual who will work most often on a one-to-one basis with the family. This specialist most often serves in a three-fold capacity; her responsibility is to interface with the family of the handicapped child to get help, support and services needed to overcome those basic deficiencies and social incompetencies which are correctible. The specialist's awareness of problems which are likely to be encountered by given families facilitates communication and interaction and, thus, encourages family cooperation for the resolution of areas of difficulty.

FORMATS FOR DELIVERY OF SERVICES
FOR PARENT POPULATIONS

With the above considerations in mind, professionals can develop a number of ways to deliver services to parents and children. The following formats illustrate several possibilities.

Delivery of Services Via Family/Community
Educational Specialists

The role and responsibility of the family/community

educational specialist is to serve as a link and liaison between the child and his family and the total community including school, health and other agencies. This specialist also provides counseling for children and parents, individually and in groups, concerning problems arising out of the child's handicapping condition. The family/community educational specialist may also assist in the collection and analysis of appraisal data pertaining to educational and sociological variables.

Such a specialist may be identified by a variety of other labels or titles, e.g. visiting teacher or home counselor. The essential feature which does not change, despite the variation in titles, is that he or she serves as the liaison between the child in his family and the community at large. Working within this environment forces interfacing between the parents, the schools, health professionals and all other community resources. The family/community educational specialist must be competent to relate to all facets of the community, to help plan for and evaluate success, to state useful objectives, to communicate for compliance, to provide or find solutions for families, and to coordinate activities with objectives on the basis of a full understanding of available and perhaps even unavailable resources.

The family/community educational specialist initiates evaluation of each child and family identified for comprehensive programming. Evaluation will be done via a problem-oriented system (25) which allows for careful, systematic and orderly display of acute and ongoing problems, intervention strategies to overcome the problem, and coordinated activities and record-keeping to allow charting of progress.

Delivery of Services Via Home Learning Resource Centers

Continuing education for parents can be offered in a variety of formats — meetings, conferences, institutes and via television and radio programming with loaned or given instructional materials which can be used by professionals with parents or can be used by parents alone. Toy and book-lending libraries are widely available. In addition, an innovative possibility is a home learning resource center (31, 19). Several programs are now underway to explore the value of establishing relatively structured home learning resource center (31, 19). The purpose of such a home center should be to help train and inform parents so as to maximize the effectiveness of time spent in the home by increasing the likelihood that help will be provided when needed, often and early. Another advantage to the presence of a home learning resource center is the potential involvement of the entire family; each member has access to materials and equipment for his own personal use.

Many questions exist regarding the effectiveness of a learning resource center in the home. The center itself can range from a single but consistent location within the home utilizing a cardboard box which holds toys, games, books, readers, etc., to the relatively sophisticated desk with built-in equipment reported by Smith (33). Among the anticipated questions involved with this concept are those regarding how material and equipment can be provided on a rotating basis; the cost and selection of suitable materials and programs; supervision of the center in a home; and availability of materials from federal, state and local agencies. Questions will also arise regarding maintenance, accessibility, effective use, parent attitudes and limitations and cost/benefit ratio of home learning resource centers.

A project which will seek to evaluate the potential for learning resource center in the home of multihandicapped children representing various socioeconomic levels is planned. It will follow completion of a pilot evaluation project which has been initiated in Texas and will seek to answer some of the above questions.

At the 1974 summer conference, described previously, representatives of parent organizations for the handicapped were asked to consider desirable characteristics for a home resource center. Specifically, this group of parents was asked who would or should use a learning resource center in the home, why they might need a center, and what questions arise in association with the plan to help parents develop a personalized learning resource center. The following summarizes the points of view of the representatives who responded.

The home learning resource center was thought to be usable and helpful for all of the following persons who would have contact with the child: parents, siblings, relatives, teachers, close friends of the family, other persons coming into the home to help the child (such as professional assistants or baby-sitters, neighbors and the children of neighbors.) Respondents also considered the center to be extremely useful to the handicapped child. Such centers were thought to be needed in order to

1. Stimulate parents' ideas, and train and inform parents who can provide continuing education for others
2. Relieve parents' frustrations, allowing them to cope better and improve parents' self image by allowing them to contribute
3. Provide early help and utilize resources at hand in the home so as to help the child by maximizing the learning potential of time spent at home
4. Involve the whole family with the child's growth
5. Improve the parent-child relationship
6. Supplement educational programs and assist teachers
8. Educate persons outside the home

Questions that were raised by parents about using a learning resource center included the following:

1. How extensive is this concept?
2. Where would the learning resource material come from; who pays the cost of such a center; how will materials be selected and by whom; how will materials be kept up-to-date; who plans the program and supervises it; and how are material exchanged and maintained?
3. Who would use a learning resource center; who would train the parents to use the center?
4. Is it applicable to early childhood programs, young adults, parents?
5. Is it versatile enough to use materials from various agencies and professional consultants (regional resource centers, health agencies, doctors, librarians etc.), and does it relate to other local services?
6. Is such a center permanent or temporary; how will it be integrated into daily family life?
8. How are results evaluated?

Conference participants visualized certain problems with home learning resource centers. They pointed out that for home centers to be effective, up-to-date materials must be selected and available, must be in good condition, and must not be prohibitive in cost. Parents who need this service must be trained to utilize materials effectively to integrate them into family living and must be supported in their efforts. In short, there are complications inherent in the concept of home centers which will need to be studied further. Questions stated by conference participants and issues they raised will assist in such study.

Delivery of Services Via Parent Groups and Parent Coalitions

Parents of handicapped children can be helped to help themselves. There are many effective self-help groups. Historically, such groups have provided mental and moral as well as material assistance for their members. Often, they have acted as pressure groups to change attitudes and legislation within society. There is a trend for separatist influences to be minimized as specific interest groups merge for common good into coalition groups which can explore mutual interests for the purpose of maximizing productivity while minimizing costs and expended energy.

More and better services can be delivered to individual parents as well as parent groups by the formation of voluntary coalitions of parent groups. Not only can public education and public relations improve, but it is also easier to develop educational programs and special social services (e.g. case work) to help parents. Utilization of medical, education and other facilities can be improved with coordination and cooperation. Parent institutes which offer specific in-service programs regarding legal rights, child management, use of instructional materials and group counseling can be organized by and for organized coalitions of parents at less cost and more efficiency.

PROCEDURES USED TO APPROACH PARENTS

Even as there are many possible formats for involving parents of handicapped children, there are also many procedures that can be used by specialists to improve their work with parents.

Approaching Parents Via Family/Community Educational Specialist

After assessment of needs and careful study has been made of available resources and facilities within the local community, a central resource facility should be available with responsibility for the continuing education of the family/community educational specialist. Continuing education of the specialist will provide not only education but also moral support. It will insure that he or she will know how best to help the parent-handicapped child unit. A state educational agency, institution of higher education, local educational agency or professional association could provide continuing education opportunities. Ideally, however, a specific central resource institution will be given responsibility for the program within each state in order to insure personalization and individualization in developing a continuing education program for the specialist.

In addition to continuing in-service opportunities, a variety of instructional materials must be available. They can be organized to provide a library-type resource for use by the family/community educational specialist in parent involvement programs. In a recently-instituted program in Texas materials have been organized into five content areas and placed in instructional kits which can be easily transported. Instructional material can be taken from, for example, a regional educational service center or school to the home. When it is not possible to visit all homes, parents can meet in a church, hospital or community center for work in small groups to learn how best to work with materials and with their children.

The five content areas in which materials have been organized are cognition; health education; mobility and coordination; socialization and self care; speech, language and communication. A family/community educational specialist gives each parent a brief description of the content area in which parent involvement is needed. This description is given in both oral and written form with suggestions for materials appropriate to development in each area. Instructional kits are organized in each content area in association with sequentialized lesson plans for use by the parents or by the family/community educational specialist in her work with parents. The description of each content area given to parents is as follows:

COGNITION. Experience with people, objects and events contributes to the child's understanding. Every child has the need to know, to think, to learn about his community in all ways. Although the environment exerts an important influence on a child even when he is passive, it is necessary for him to have opportunity to be active in that environment, to discover the world around him. In this way a child develops understanding; he learns to solve problems, to remember what he has learned, to become creative and to know in what ways he is part of his world.

HEALTH EDUCATION. Professionals in the health fields are trying to teach us all that the important thing is to maintain our healthy bodies, to try to prevent and discourage disease and illness. Prevention of heart disease, for example, begins in early childhood. Most parents are well aware of the need to try to provide a proper balance of nutrition, rest, exercise and cleanliness to avoid disease. At the same time, many parents do not know how best to take advantage of facilities, agencies, organizations and health professionals to insure the health and happiness of their children. Being sure children have immunizations, knowing when and how often booster shots are necessary, protecting against vision and hearing difficulties through health measures, and knowing the importance of dental services for the protection of teeth that should last a lifetime are all important areas.

All members of the family need to be alert to the importance of remaining healthy, remedying any existing medical or dental defects, and improving the health of the total community in which they live.

MOBILITY AND COORDINATION. Through activities such as rolling over, sitting up, crawling, walking, reaching and grasping a child learns to become independent; he learns to move around, and in this way controls his environment. Coordination of eyes and hands allows him to develop skill in the activities of daily living such as eating, writing, using tools, etc. These activities are all part of a normal life pattern and contribute to a sense of independence and an awareness of the strength of the entire body. Physical well-being through exercise and all forms of recreation contribute to his self-concept and to his self-control.

SOCIALIZATION AND SELF CARE. As a child interacts socially with his parents and other members of his family, he learns about himself. Everyone must learn to be a part of human society, to play and to work and to love and to be loved. Social interaction and cooperation with others helps children learn to become responsible, to take care of themselves, and to care for others. The child who cannot or does not take care of himself may have difficulty being sensitive to the needs of others.

Parents must help their children develop a feeling of self-confidence, a concept of self which is strong and independent. Encouraging family interaction with specific activities can become the base for social interaction which will last throughout a lifetime.

SPEECH, LANGUAGE AND COMMUNICATION. Communication skill allows us to think with precision, to talk with and understand the ideas of other people, and to express our own feelings and ideas.

Children who do not develop well in this area are severely handicapped in their relationship to other people. It is helpful for parents to encourage their child to talk, to use speech creatively. This will help the child learn how to make decisions and solve problems. It is helpful to parents to listen to their child, thus setting an example so their child will listen to others. Parents can help their child learn ideas and concepts as he develops language proficiency, and encourage feelings of security and love which grow as a result of verbal understanding.

In addition to giving parents a verbal and written description of the content area in which help is being provided for the child, the family/community educational specialist may leave an instructional kit containing toys, games or other materials which can be used by the parents to help the child develop in the particular area of need. The kit and its materials circulate among many families.

New materials replace the previously-used materials at the time of the next visit of the parent and specialist. As much as possible the materials are inexpensive and can be replaced easily or, preferably, duplicated by the parents. Also, as appropriate, lesson plans are left with the parents, in written or verbal form, following demonstration.

The family/community education specialist fulfills a role as the link between the school and the home by improving the interfacing between the two environments. Instructional lessons, materials and goals will be reinforced through good communication when all adults interacting with the child are working together with common purposes and objectives.

Approaching Parents Via Other Parents

Convening with parents with the purpose of alerting them to the advantages to be gained from working together has excellent effects. Their sharing of ideas, problems and solutions is conducive to the development of programs which help. At parent meetings a variety of conference techniques can be used. These include large and small group discussions, professional speakers who speak informally on key issues, and participation by parents in assessing the previously-mentioned instructional materials suggested for use by parents. Parents can be involved in decision-making at the time of the conference through procedures such as individual report-writing responsibilities. It also is possible to organize parent task forces which will take responsibility for planning activities to improve programs for parents of all handicapped children.

As a result of the 1974 Texas conference for parents of handicapped children (19), responsibilities for writing a *rights* brochure and defining educational opportunities needed for parents will be managed by task forces of parents. The parents plan to use a language style which is fully comprehensible and will include in the rights brochure suggestions such as enforcing present laws and becoming knowledgeable about laws, visiting legislators, providing useful information to allow legislators to approach their tasks with authority, discussing such rights as those of the individual and those of the child and rights to privacy and to education. They will also deal with admission and commitment restrictions, dealing with professional conflicts including those with disagreeable school personnel and legislators who are not helpful, and cost considerations. Parents will have been educated through group meetings so they will know how best to approach legislation, write to school boards and get documentation for everything that occurs in order to be prepared to take legal action if necessary.

Parents organizations are becoming well-organized; they have become able, via continuing educational opportunities, to defend the point of view that every child has the right to a full life, that every parent have the right to supportive diagnostic and remedial services which meet their needs and to reject those which do not. For example, whereas a state or federal organization is seldom in the position of blacklisting a clinic or center, parents have no such compulsions or restrictions. Parents may, by word of mouth, bring about greater change in professional performance and standards by asking for reports, suggestions and results than could ever be accomplished through bureaucracies and self-serving or private interests.

The parents of all newly-identified disabled children soon may not have to go through each of the stages of decision making hampered by inadequate or faulty information, becoming frustrated by indecision, lack of support and inadequate services within their community. With the help of other parents, they will come closer to being able to approach the resolution of their own problems.

EXPECTED OUTCOMES OF THIS APPROACH WITH PARENTS

It is thought that expansion of organized task forces of parents who plan (via state and local programs) to initiate and expand self-help programs, as well as to combine strength, will increase parental influence and resources. There also is every reason to expect continued development by professionals to initiate or improve services provided directly to parents. In the areas of child management, considerable effort is now underway by a wide variety of professional and paraprofessional groups to help parents know how best to help their child learn, interact with others and function within society. Improved family interaction which will result in personal self-confidence, and independence can be encouraged through the use of referral to resources often available through educational and social services in the local community. Parent effectiveness training programs and family counseling groups now exist in many communities in the United States. The use of such materials as those developed by Gordon (23) and by Dreikurs and his associates (14, 15, 16, 17) identify two of the better-known family education programs in the United States today. These group movements which stress responsibility for self and others are of great potential benefit for families of handicapped children.

More useful and meaningful instructional materials to help children learn earlier and more effectively can be expected as a result of improved coordination, cooperation and communication between the school and home communities. Hopefully, instructional resource centers in the future can respond to the need for instructional materials in the home by providing materials associated with specific plans for their use, accompanied by personalized and individualized instruction for the person who is assisting the child or parent, be that person a teacher, parent or other worker. The family/community educational specialist, by working with the family, should help parents become more recognized and responsible members of the teaching community.

Parent-teacher workshops in the future can be expected to provide opportunity for preparation of instructional materials as well as to serve as information-sharing sessions. Both parents and teachers, with full recognition of respective competencies, can be expected to understand the necessity of improving their interfacing in support of one another in order to focus attention and reap full benefit from work with the handicapped child.

Parents who attended the Texas Conference for Parents of Handicapped Children in 1974 have recommended the development of a legal or child advocate in all states and, in time, in local communities. Despite present funding patterns which preclude budgeting for this position, awareness of the need for advocacy in the schools, in the courts, in industry and business, and in health information and treatment may ultimately result in ombudsmen or advocates for child and parent. What is more likely in the immediate future is further development and distribution of community guides, directories or central telephone number hotlines to provide needed information regarding services and resources for parents.

Finally, as stated by Smith (32), although all parents go through certain relatively-prescribed stages after learning of the potentially-handicapping condition of their disabled child, these normal reactions can be eased by effective programs of help. Awareness of the child's problem is first associated with disbelief, then flight for the miracle solution or action to find a cure. Parents feel guilt, but, ultimately, should become mobilized to take positive steps to achieve specific goals. At this final stage more parents are ready to consider action needed to help all children, not only their own. We are just beginning to learn how necessary parents are to the ultimate outcome and life-style of the disabled child.

REFERENCES

1. Ayrault, E.W.: *You Can Raise Your Handicapped Child.* New York, Putnam, 1964.
2. Baroff, G.S.: Some parent-teacher problems in mental retardation. *Training School Bull,* 1963.
3. Barsch, R.H.: *The Parent-Teacher Partnership.* Reston, Council for Exc. Children, 1969.
4. Barsch, R.H.: *The Parent of the Handicapped Child.* Springfield, Thomas, 1968.
5. Becker, W.: *Parents Are Teachers.* Champaign, Res Press, 1971.
6. Beecher, M., and Beecher, W.: *Parents on the Run.* New York, G & D, 1967.
7. Bice, H.V.: Parent counseling and parent education. In Cruickshank, W. (Ed.): *Cerebral Palsy: Its Individual and Community Problems.* Rev. Ed. Syracuse, Syracuse U Pr, 1966, pp. 541-559.
8. Bower, T.G.R.: *Development in Infancy.* San Francisco, W. H. Freeman, 1974.
9. Bradley, R.C.: *Parent-Teacher Interviews: A Modern Concept in Oral Reporting.* Wolfe City, Univ Pr, 1971.
10. Brutten, M., Richardson, S.O., and Mangel, C.: *Something's Wrong With My Child.* New York, HarBrace J, 1973.
11. Catalogue of Health Services in Cameron County. Cameron County, Texas, Board of Health, 1973.
12. Carter, R.: *Help! These Kids are Driving Me Crazy.* Champaign Res Press,

1972.

13. Dodson, F.: *How to Parent.* New York, Signet, 1970.
14. Dreikurs, R.: *The Challenge of Parenthood.* New York, Merideth, 1948.
15. Dreikurs, R., and Soltz, V.: *Children the Challenge.* New York, Hawthorn, 1964.
16. Dreikurs, R., and Cassel, P.: *Discipline Without Tears.* New York, Hawthorn, 1972.
17. Dreikurs, R., and Grey, L.: *Logical Consequences.* New York, Merideth, 1968.
18. Engelmann, S., and Englemann, T.: *Give Your Child a Superior Mind.* New York, S & S, 1966.
19. Falck, V.: *Report of Family Education, Assistance, and Training Project.* Dec. 8, 1973, June 30, 1974.
20. Frank, J.O.: *Persuasion and Healing,* Schocken Ed. New York, Johns Hopkins, 1963.
21. Ginott, H.G.: *Between Parent and Child.* New York, Macmillan, 1965.
22. Ginsburg, H.: *The Myth of the Deprived Child.* New Jersey, P-H, 1972.
23. Gordon, T.: *Parent Effectiveness Training: The No Lose Program for Raising Responsible Children.* New York, Wyden, 1970.
24. Gregg, E.M.: *What To Do When There's Nothing To Do.* New York, Delacorte, 1967.
25. Hurst, J.W., and Walker, A.W.: *The Problem — Oriented System.* New York, Medcom, 1972.
26. Katz, A.H.: *Parents of the Handicapped: Self Organized Parents and Relatives Groups for Treatment of Ill and Handicapped Children.* Springfield, Thomas, 1961.
27. Muller, P.: *The Tasks of Childhood.* New York, World Univ Pr, 1969.
28. Patterson, G.R.: *Families.* Champaign, Res Press, 1971.
29. Patterson, G.R., and Gullian, M.E.: *Living With Children.* Champaign, Res Press, 1968.
30. Rosenthal, R., and Jacobson, L.: Teachers' expectancies: Determinants of pupils' I.Q. gains. *Psychol Rep, 19:* 115-118, 1966.
31. Simpson, E.: *Personal Communication,* July 12, 1974.
32. Smith, B.K.: The Good of Parenthood. Address to Conference for Parents of Handicapped Children. Austin, Texas, June 22, 1974.
33. Smith, E.: A learning resource center for home or office. *Tex Med,* 1973, pp. 56-58.
34. Solomon, G.: What do you tell the parents of a retarded child? *Clin Pediatr,* 4(4): 227-232, 1965.
35. Wolf, J.M., and Anderson, R.M., (Eds): The *Multiply Handicapped Child.* Springfield, Thomas, 1969.

Chapter 10

EDITOR'S SUMMARY

ELIZABETH J. WEBSTER

THE purpose of this brief discussion is to highlight some of the similarities and some of the differences in the thinking of the authors whose chapters have been presented.

There are a number of similar themes running through these chapters. All authors express their sincere wishes to include parents in programs for handicapped children. They all reflect compassion for these parents as well as respect. There is among them an awareness that in the past parents have been scapegoats and the desire that this situation should no longer exist. Further, there is the theme of awareness that it is not just parents who can grow and develop in the relationship with a parent counselor; the counselor also can participate in the growth process. Authors seem to agree that work with parents of handicapped children offers constant challenges and continuing opportunities for mutual growth and development. Parent counseling gives professionals continuing opportunities to learn because, obviously, even as no two children are alike, no two parents are alike, and there are unique differences between each family. In their interaction with these families, professionals can continue to reassess their own attitudes and values and test their hypotheses.

These authors agree that professionals should work with parents of handicapped children and should be trained for this work. The authors also seem to agree that the professional serves the following four functions:

1. To convey information that parents need to have in order to cope with and help the handicapped child, themselves and the family
2. To obtain information from parents so as to better help the handicapped child and all those concerned with the child
3. To help parents clarify their attitudes, ideas and understand-

ings of themselves, the child and the information they are given
4. To help parents experiment with ways of changing their behaviors

There are also differences in authors' approaches and continuing questions raised by them. For example, there is a difference of opinion about the use of bibliotherapy; some authors advocate this and others do not. There is a question of how best to use parents to train and support other parents; some authors contend that parents can be used as paraprofessionals to train other parents while other authors do not support this contention. There is also the lingering question about whether to bring parents to a central location for help, or whether professional persons should go to parents' homes. Some authors advocate that parents should be brought to a central location for training and treatment while others advocate home visitation.

Certainly, within the context of the basic similarities in these approaches to parents, these questions will be discussed for some time to come. However, the fact that there are differences of opinion is a very healthy sign; each person who works with parents is a unique individual, making operational what he or she values and thinks best. This individual creative expression avoids the kind of sterility that would accrue if all practicing professionals followed the same format.

The reader's task is to select those ideas which most closely fit his or her own value system. Having made such selections, the parent counselor can then articulate and elaborate on his own operational philosophy.

AUTHOR INDEX

257

SUBJECT INDEX

A

Abuse
  child, 148
  parent, 148
Acquired handicap, 31
Adult education classes, 55
Agencies, referral to, 58, 59
Aggressive behavior, 135
Aggressive parent, 31
Aha phenomenon, 85
American Association on Mental Deficiency's definition of retardation, 85
Aphasic, 22
Arcanum Arcanorum, 20
Articulation, defective,
  in the absence of hearing or neurological impairment, 131-134
  treatment for, 134-136
Assimilating information, infant's capability for, 94
Assumptive world, 234
Attitudes, parental, 118
Attitudes of professional people toward parents of handicapped children, changes of, 116
Audiologic clinic, 106
Audiologic evaluation, 104
Audiologic guidance, 106
Audiologists, 106
Audiogram, 107
Auditory channel, 132
Auditory discrimination, 133
Auditory sensitivity, 106
Autism, 8
  etiology of, 65
  psychopharmacological intervention, 67
Autism and developmental levels, 85
Autism and mental retardation, 83-85
Autism and normal development, 83
Autism and variability, 87

Autistic aloneness, extreme, 65
Autistic children, 116
  aberrations of behavior in, 69
  behavior characteristics of, 67-69
  giving information to parents, 83-87
  guiding parents of, 87-90
  inducing insight in parents, 82, 83
  language development of, 68, 69
  professional's realm of interaction, 79-81
  parent education program for, 70, 71
  program setting for, 69, 70
  psychoanalysis in, 65
  psychoeducational treatment for parents of, 65-91
  restoring parents self-esteem, 73-79
  social development of, 68
  specifics of work with parents of, 71-87
  treatment program for, 124

B

Behavior
  aberrations of in autistic children, 69
  aggressive, 135
  obsessive-compulsive, 44
Behavior modification, 29
Behavior modification approach used with paraprofessionals, 119-122
Behavior modification procedures, xii
Behavior modifiers, 120
Behavior therapists, siblings as, 122
Behavior therapy, application of, 120
Behavioral clues, 28
Behaviorists, 41
Beliefs, fixed, 21, 22
Bewilderment reaction of parents to handicapped children, 96-97
Bibliotherapy, 50-52
Binaural listening, 107
Biological factors in the child, 118
Body sculpture, 19

261